"Rich captures how digital currency can spin the flywheel for China's new digital trade platforms. He shows how trade partners not only gain access to digital currency, but likewise to new digital services. This book stakes out how digital currency will change our world."

— Federico Torreti, Head of Products, Amazon

"There are no other books covering China's digital currencies on the market. The book's narration is smooth and delivers tons of important information on China's payment systems and how they relate to the West. Plenty of facts with no political overtones."

— Albert Borowiecki, Senior Analyst at Contemporary China Studies Institute

CASHLESS:

CHINA'S DIGITAL CURRENCY REVOLUTION

RICHARD TURRIN

CASHLESS:
China's Digital Currency Revolution
by Richard Turrin
1. BUS114000 2. BUS045000 3. BUS004000
ISBN (hardback): 978-1-949642-74-2
ISBN (paperback): 978-1-949642-72-8
EBOOK: 978-1-949642-73-5

Cover design by LEWIS AGRELL

Printed in the United States of America

Authority Publishing
11230 Gold Express Dr. #310-413
Gold River, CA 95670
800-877-1097
www.AuthorityPublishing.com

DEDICATION

This book is dedicated to my mother, Doris Johanna Andreotta Turrin, who passed away just before this book went to press. Mom loved to read and shared her love of reading with me from a young age. She showed me that books could help you travel to faraway places from the comfort of your room. What mom couldn't predict was that reading would not be enough to sate my curiosity and that my love of reading would lead to a life abroad.

TABLE OF CONTENTS

PART 1
VERSION 1.0 DIGITAL PAYMENT SYSTEMS

PART 2
VERSION 2.0 DIGITAL PAYMENT
CENTRAL BANK DIGITAL CURRENCIES
(CBDCs)

PART 3
CHANGING RELATIONS

ACKNOWLEDGMENTS

The non-stop changes in China, the pandemic, and a personal loss made the year-long voyage of writing this book incredibly challenging. No sooner was a chapter written and edited than a breaking news item would change something I wrote just days before. Getting the book through final edits represented an arduous task of not only correcting grammar but updating key facts and figures to match China's evolving digital payment landscape. On top of this, the coronavirus presented lifestyle changes that hindered productivity for us all.

No book is a singular effort. At a time when social media has become a flashpoint for bans and blocks among conspiracy theorists and radicals, I am proud that this book represents the potential good that social media can do. I am privileged to have many supporters on LinkedIn who have contributed immeasurably to this book. The frequent debates we have about China's digital payment technology have helped shape and sharpen this book's narrative. I am very grateful to them all for their contributions and support throughout the writing process. I also want to call attention to the positive impact that social media can have when used responsibly by a group of people bound together by a shared interest even when they disagree.

I am grateful to everyone who shared with me on LinkedIn and Twitter who helped contribute to this book, but I would like to give special thanks to a few individuals who helped shape and polish the book's content. I have never had the privilege of meeting Max Senden in person, but I look forward to it because his contributions to this book were so great. Max helped me sharpen each chapter's message as he read through a pre-publication copy. His knowledge of the topic, patience, and eye for detail contributed to making the book, including its cover, a success. I would like to thank Max for his dedication in refining my book and the numerous discussions we had online discussing content that helped shape my thoughts.

Dr. Lauren Johnston graciously contributed the foreword to this book and helped me better understand how my book fits within the existing research. As both an author and a scholar of China's economy, she gave me confidence that this book fills a previously unexplored niche. She and Albert Borowiecki, another China researcher and steadfast contributor, helped me confirm that what I feared most was true: Digital currencies were so new that they were challenging for many without cross-disciplinary expertise to understand, and as a result were often either misunderstood or, worse, ignored. I am grateful to both Lauren and Albert for their generous support and advice from within the research community.

I was also grateful to receive regular comments and advice from Guy Vancollie, Cecile Gratien, Vincent Freund, Richard Goerwitz, Colin Bennett, Sean O'Neill, Joseph Wang, Simon Fox and Walter Sepp Aigner. They all gave me regular feedback and advice that shaped the arc of many chapters. Without their contributions, this project would have been limited and would have lacked the perspective they provided.

This second book was far more ambitious than my first, "Innovation Lab Excellence," and was put at risk several times due to its scope. Still, I was never alone on this project. I am fortunate to have an old friend who is an acclaimed author and editor to help shepherd this book to completion. Christa Weil Menegas has been a friend for what seems an inconceivable thirty years. Having her guidance throughout this project helped me immeasurably. I am not exaggerating when I say that this book would not have been completed without her encouragement. Her ability to shape my tortured prose into the smooth and accessible passages you will soon read speaks to her professional skills. It cannot show the patience and care she put into each line—the dedication that only an old and dear friend would be able to muster.

Finally, I am forever indebted to my wife Sharon, who put up with me throughout the writing process. Locking myself away in self-imposed exile for long periods of researching and writing only to emerge cranky and unapproachable wasn't easy on her. No matter how many hours I had been at the computer before emerging, she always lived up to her nickname "Sunshine" by radiating warmth and joy. Her constant love, encouragement, and support made this book possible.

FOREWORD

In October 2020, I couldn't believe my luck. I had feared my quest to find someone who understood China's digital currency plans would run dry. But instead, I found Richard Turrin's profile on LinkedIn. To learn he was writing this book was truly both exciting and a tremendous relief.

The background to my search is that I have been a scholar of the Chinese economy and language since the mid-1990s. I first moved to Beijing in 1997 and spent a total of a decade in the city. I earned a Ph.D. in Economics from Peking University. Despite that level of connectivity, and as COVID-19 fast-forwarded the world's digital trajectory, I rued my lack of a contact or knowledge of an expert whom I thought had all the necessary pieces of expertise to help me understand the full picture of China's digital currency plans.

I know specialists with amazing expertise in China's economy, including monetary issues. I know many experts on China's domestic and international political economy strategy and history. There are many around the world with deep knowledge of fintech and digital finance ecosystems. But I did not know anyone who had a level of expertise in all three areas, and who had also spent some time living in China so as to appreciate the full scale of China's extraordinary digital payments ecosystem. Hence, I feared not being able to assemble the pieces—especially in a period of tremendous global transition. I feared also for other China scholars and analysts who might miss the monetary paradigm shift emerging under our noses.

I wrote to Richard after finding his profile online. How could I connect? How could I partake of his expertise? Was there something I could read or watch to help me bring the pieces together and help others do the same? He wrote back with a friendly warmth, grateful for my outreach. He invited me to work as part of a team of early readers as he evolved his upcoming book on China's digital currency. I couldn't believe my luck, and I was so relieved. Someone had the right experience at the right time on an issue of tremendous importance to the world economy. And he was willing to share his knowledge by writing this book.

Whether you are a distant observer of world affairs, a banker, a China scholar, an investor, or just curious about what happened to Jack Ma's Ant Financial IPO plans late in 2020, Richard's book is truly for you. It is easy to read, despite covering very complex issues comprehensively. It draws the everyday reality of China's digital ecosystem together with the operational mechanics and global geo-economic implications of China's emerging digital currency. It is the best and only introduction to China's digital payments and currency world—which will affect us all over the coming decades.

This book is a truly compelling read—and, I would argue, essential for anyone interested in the 21st century world order.

Dr. Lauren A. Johnston,
Research Associate, SOAS China Institute, London, and Founder of New South Economics

PREFACE

The coming launch of China's new Central Bank Digital Currency (CBDC) will be a historic milestone in how we use money. As the first major economy to launch a CBDC, China is heralding a shared digital currency future for us all. Living in Shanghai, I've been fortunate to experience this transition firsthand, and as a career banker and technologist, I know that it's an important story to tell. The reason is simple: China's story of going "cashless" foretells the West's digital future.

CBDCs and digital payment presage a shared future because the pandemic dramatically changed our perception of cash. It's gone from a basic necessity to a potential source of contagion. Central banks that once viewed digital currencies as a nicety for a distant future are moving with a newfound urgency to bring forward digital currency research and trials. Motivated in equal parts by the pandemic, China's CBDC, the global boom in cryptocurrencies, and streamlining relief payments, your own central bank likely has a CBDC project underway. What was once far-off now seems imminent, ushering in a new urgency to learn what our "cashless" future will involve.

Going cashless won't be unique to China, nor will the changes it brings to our relationship with money. Despite the differences in culture, regulations, and government, the essentials of what digital currency wrought in China will be largely mirrored in the West. The systems and technology will undoubtedly be different, but the broad strokes of our own cashless future will likely follow China's. Thus, familiarity with China's transition is essential for anyone who wants to understand the digital payment future being thrust upon us.

I understand that China is a mystery to many. The idea of learning from that country feels unusual or even unsettling. News accounts are often contradictory, and it can be difficult to process the impact of their many digital advances. Trade wars and the pandemic have conspired to make China an even greater enigma. Still, many are aware that something big has happened in that country regarding digital payments. My goal is to demystify their digital revolution and show how these advances are relevant to the West. Sharing the story of China's digital currency achievements with a worldwide audience will help everyone make better sense of our shared future.

China's CBDC is also in the news for its potential threat to the US dollar's hegemony. Fear that China will have a "first mover" advantage with CBDCs is stoking fear that the current financial system, in place since the end of the Second World War, may be headed for an abrupt change. The dollar's recent weakness coupled with the explosion in cryptocurrency prices have contributed to a sense of urgency. Central banks transitioning to CBDCs, once considered a benign natural evolution, is now becoming an important geopolitical and strategic concern. Being left behind isn't an option. In leading the charge, China is instilling the fear of missing out by putting the world on notice that its CBDC will help achieve the country's goal of reducing its dependence on the dollar.

Whether China's CBDC will enable this strategic goal remains to be seen. However, given that China is the world's largest exporter, even small gains in RMB use through its CBDC can be significant to global currency markets. The new CBDC is a tool, positioned as a means of promoting and differentiating its currency from others in international markets. The goal is to bring the convenience of cheaper and immediate digital cash transfer to its trading partners—just as its citizens currently enjoy. Meanwhile, in domestic markets, the CBDC is a means of advancing China's agenda of broad-based societal digitization. For the rest of the world, it is a wake-up call.

As in my bestseller *Innovation Lab Excellence: Digital Transformation from Within*, I present topics I care about passionately because they bear directly upon my career. Much of my career has been invested in bringing technology innovation to life in banks with international trading floors. I have been told "it can't be done" so many different ways that writing a book on how to shepherd innovation through "the system" came naturally.

The same passion drives this book. A technological innovation is about to change the nature of money, and many are saying "it can't be done." This is a case where the siloing of knowledge is counterproductive. Technologists are writing about the CBDC's technological components with disregard for banking. At the same time, bankers argue the RMB's remote odds of assaulting the dollar's hegemony with no regard for changing technology.

Neither group seems to fully appreciate the combustible mixture of technology, finance, and government policy that is about to explode out of China and change our world forever. From my perspective in Shanghai, where I use these systems daily and understand their linkage to the financial system, their capability for disruption is a foregone conclusion. To me, the disruptive power of digital currencies is real and tangible. I'm committed to sharing my experiences with others so that they can better understand and navigate the disruption that digital currencies will inflict on the West.

INTRODUCTION

For many, China's CBDC will appear to have come out of nowhere, an isolated invention designed to disrupt domestic payment providers and international currency markets. Nothing could be further from the truth. China's CBDC is the result of years of planning and has been built on the shoulders of giants—i.e., China's first-generation digital payment systems. China's CBDC is a direct evolutionary descendant of these "Version 1.0" systems, which helped make the country virtually cashless during the past ten years that I've lived in Shanghai. The story of China's CBDC is inextricably linked to how digital payment evolved and transformed the financial system.

To bring this story to life and make it accessible to the widest possible audience, I have divided this book into three distinct parts to illustrate digital currency's adoption and development, giving the reader a thorough background to understand China's digital currency. First, the book maps out China's current digital payment and how it developed. Second, it decodes CBDCs generally, and China's specific new offering. Critically, this includes a rigorous analysis of its market potential in both domestic and international use. Finally, in the third part, we analyze how digital payment transformed the Chinese people's relationship with money, and how CBDCs will build on this trend. To lend context and perspective, I include discussion of and comparisons to the West's systems.

Part 1: Version 1.0 Digital Payment
• Why China matters and is relevant • Digital payment technology • Regulatory changes that allowed disruption • Analysis of a fintech disaster

Part 2: Version 2.0 CBDCs
• What are CBDCs? • Design considerations • China's version • China's CBDC in domestic and international use

Part 3: Changing Relations
• What changed in China with digital payment? • Relating China's experience to the West. • Ant and regulators • Challenges with CBDCs

PART ONE:
VERSION 1.0 DIGITAL PAYMENTS

The first section highlights the design and construction of China's Version 1.0 digital payment systems: Alipay and WeChat Pay. This includes an overview of their technology, the regulatory space, and why they were so quickly adopted in the marketplace. China's CBDC is an evolution of these systems, and it is impossible to understand China's CBDC without the context these systems provide. They are the world's first national payment systems to achieve country-wide adoption, resulting in a nearly cashless society.

PART TWO:
CENTRAL BANK DIGITAL CURRENCIES

The second section is designed to provide the reader who has no pre-existing knowledge of CBDCs a detailed guide to help them understand the digital currency's construction. Next comes an in-depth discussion of why China adopted these specific design choices. All countries will have to undertake a similar design process to arrive at the combination of features that meets their unique needs. Understanding China's choices can help you anticipate and understand the design choices your central bank has to make, and also how China's CBDC will impact your business.

Part Two also contains a lengthy discussion of how China's CBDC will be used in their domestic and international markets, with estimates of likely market sizes. International use of China's CBDC is currently capturing global attention due to its potential ability to reduce US dollar dominance. This section provides a detailed assessment of the potential international market size, and how China will incentivize trading partners to use its new digital RMB. The use of China's CBDC in cross-border trades heralds much more than just choosing to use China's RMB currency. It is an entry token to a new digital logistics system the likes of which the world has never seen.

PART THREE:
CHANGING RELATIONSHIPS AND
DIGITAL CURRENCY

The third and final section shows how digital currencies have changed China's banks and financial services, just as these changes will come when CBDCs arrive in your country. China's adoption of Version 1.0 payment systems had a profound impact on the country's financial services, which will only be accentuated with the launch of a national digital currency. The changes in China with the broad adoption of digital payment will not be unique or restricted to China. CBDCs launched elsewhere in the world will manifest similar changes to those in China, even though technical aspects of the systems differ. What is critical is how digital payment changes people's relationship to money, and the new paradigm for services that results from digitizing payment. China is providing a blueprint or road map to our digital currency future.

HOW TO READ THIS BOOK

This book was written to tell how China became the first country to go "cashless." Some readers may be well versed in China's digital payment systems, but for most this story will be a revelation. My goal was to write a book that speaks to a diversity of readers. To assist each of these groups, let me suggest reading plans catered to differing knowledge bases.

ALL READERS

All readers, regardless of their level of understanding of China's payment systems, should read Chapters 2, 7, and 8 in Part 1. These chapters explain why China's experience is relevant to the West, and will help you appreciate the regulatory tumult that China is currently experiencing. Regulators' concerns over anti-trust and credit creation are not new, even though many Western media outlets portray them as such. China is home to the world's first and likely largest fintech disaster with its Peer-to-Peer loan market collapse. The regulator's response to the Ant IPO and subsequent regulatory demands on China's Big Tech all spring from that transformational event.

READERS WITH LITTLE KNOWLEDGE OF CHINA'S PAYMENT SYSTEMS

Readers with little knowledge of China fintech or CBDCs should read Part 1 in full as background for the following two parts. This part clarifies how China became the world leader in digital payment. I strived to make the text accessible and kept the use of jargon to a minimum. It gives the reader a thorough knowledge of China's payment systems and how they led to the development of China's CBDC. China's digital currency revolution didn't start with its CBDC; it began years earlier when China's Big Tech companies were allowed to become payment companies. It's a story with direct relevance to Western markets where Big Tech is inching ever closer to providing financial services.

SOLID KNOWLEDGE OF CHINA'S PAYMENT COMPANIES

For readers with solid knowledge of China's digital payment systems, I recommend focusing on Chapters 6 through 8 in Part 1 and the entirety of Parts 2 and 3, which introduce the new CBDC. Even if you have a good knowledge of China's digital payment companies, I believe that the impact of technology, regulators, and fintech failure laid out in Chapters 6-8 represents a different perspective than is commonly held. It will complete your understanding of China's fintech and give you an insider's perspective compared to what has been written by those living outside the country.

DIFFERENCES BETWEEN CHINA AND THE WEST

Even if you're only flipping through the book, be sure to read the chapter headings, which start with noteworthy quotations from business leaders in China and the West. Both amusing and instructional, they are designed to highlight the considerable differences in how the West and China view digital currencies, technology, and regulation. Their insights offer a fascinating window into each society.

TERMS AND SYMBOLS FOR CHINA'S CURRENCY

The official name of the currency introduced by the People's Republic of China at its founding in 1949 is "renminbi," which means "the people's currency." The yuan is the name of the unit of measure, or denomination, for renminbi (RMB) transactions. The term yuan is the basis of the international abbreviation for China's currency CNY with the symbol (¥). A one hundred yuan banknote refers to the number of units of renminbi the note conveys. When making payment in China, I can say either yuan or renminbi as the two terms are interchangeable. This is slightly more complicated than in the US and UK, where the official currency name contains the name for the unit of denomination. The official name for the US and UK currencies are the "United States dollar" and the "pound sterling," which are denominated in dollars and pounds.

The terminology for China's new central bank digital currency (CBDC) has not yet been fully standardized. The variations in the name for China's new CBDC follow the terms RMB and yuan for its paper currency. The term e-CNY is the official name for bank and retail displays and more recent central bank publications. All of the following are acceptable and are found in the literature:

digital RMB, eRMB, e-RMB

digital Yuan, eYuan, e-Yuan, e-CNY

The People's Bank of China, generally though not exclusively, refers to its new CBDC in its English language printed materials as DC/EP, which stands for digital currency/electronic payment.

For practical purposes, the terms CBDC and DC/EP are interchangeable, as are e-CNY and DC/EP.

Above are the two symbols for China's new digital currency. The PBOC uses the symbol on the left, while banks, shops, and vending machines have adopted the symbol on the right. The right-hand image, a shop sign stating: "Welcome to use the digital renminbi," also displays e-CNY.

ABBREVIATIONS

ABS	asset-backed securities
ASEAN	Association of Southeast Asian Nations
BIS	Bank for International Settlements
BRI	belt and road initiative
BSN	blockchain service network
CBDC	central bank digital currency
DC/EP	Digital Currency/Electronic Payment, China's term for central bank digital currency
Digital RMB	China's central bank digital currency
DLT	distributed ledger technology
eRMB	electronic RMB, China's central bank digital currency
GAFA	Google, Amazon, Facebook, Apple
GDP	gross domestic product
IMF	International Monetary Fund
IP	intellectual property
IPO	initial public offering
KYC	know your customer
M0	M-Zero, a measure of money supply that includes only the most liquid form of money, cash, central banknotes, and coins.

M1	M-One a measure of money supply including M0 constituents plus checking accounts, traveler's checks, demand deposits.
M2	M-Two, a measure of money supply including M1 constituents plus savings deposits, money market securities, mutual funds, and other time deposits.
NFC	near field communications
P2P	peer-to-peer lending
POS	point of sale
PBOC	People's Bank of China, China's central bank
QR	quick response code (example on book cover)
RMB	China's currency: the renminbi
SEC	US Securities and Exchange Commission
SME	Small- and medium-size enterprises
SWIFT	Society for Worldwide Interbank Financial Telecommunication
UTXO	unspent transaction output
WTO	World Trade Organization
Yuan	China's currency: the renminbi (RMB)

PART 1

VERSION 1.0 DIGITAL PAYMENT SYSTEMS

1

"WUHAN WILL STARVE"

China on the Digital Revolution:

> "I believe it's not the technology that changes the world. It's the dreams behind the technology that change the world."
> Jack Ma, Cofounder and former Executive Chairman of Alibaba Group.

The West on the Digital Revolution:

> "In today's era of volatility, there is no other way but to re-invent. the only sustainable advantage you can have over others is agility, that's it. Because nothing else is sustainable, everything else you create, somebody else will replicate."
> Jeff Bezos, Founder of Amazon

Upon hearing the news on January 23, 2020 that the city of Wuhan and its eleven million inhabitants were in lockdown, a clutch of journalists avowed "Wuhan will starve." I knew instantly that these journalists had never lived in, or even visited, China. Anyone who has lived here in the past few years certainly understood that mobile apps and digital payment could carry Wuhan through lockdown. I've been in China for over a decade now. When I read these headlines, I just smiled. Yes, some reporters may have heard of Alibaba, JD.com, or Meituan, but they didn't fully grasp these firms' capabilities.

In a way, I don't blame the reporters for misunderstanding China's capabilities. The digital revolution that thrives in this country has received only limited press coverage in the West. Yes, we all know that China's use of AI is fantastic. We know that it blocks Facebook, causing some people to cross China off their travel itinerary. The problem is, we see these reports of China's digital life in isolation, without understanding the bigger picture. When Wuhan went into lockdown, most outsiders didn't comprehend that no one would starve, and that digital shopping and delivery, with government assistance, could provide for an entire city.

China's financial technology (fintech) is a more specific case of the same kind of blind spot. Only a few in the fintech or mobile payment space have been following China's advances in digital payment. For most of the rest, China's use of mobile payment is nothing more than a local quirk, rather than evidence of digital transformation at a national level. China boasts an impressive ecosystem of products based on first-generation digital payment technology. A second-generation digital Chinese currency (RMB) will soon launch, but its potential impact has been widely under-estimated. I don't blame you if you haven't been following China's fintech scene; out of the press, out of sight and out of mind, what happens there has little impact on the West and your life. But we're coming to a point where that knowledge gap impairs your ability to envision our shared cashless future, and more importantly, make strategic decisions to adapt to it.

A lack of knowledge about China's advances falls into the comfortable category of "you don't know what you don't know." You aren't expected to, and won't worry about it until not knowing becomes a problem. Unfortunately, this philosophy is flawed. We would all benefit from the clearest possible view of our digital future—none more so than those working in financial services. After the coronavirus, no one would dare argue that the use of cash payment in the West is on the decline. That said, most of us don't know how a society that relies wholly on digital payment would look. China provides that answer. Examining how can help us make better decisions as our own world evolves into digital payments as a way of life.

As the first major country to launch a digital currency, China is sending shock waves throughout the Western financial world. The digital RMB is a loud and clear signal for you to shift this subject into "things you don't know about, but need to." Why? Because China's efforts are poised to leave national confines and migrate Westward. China's first generation of digital payment transformed it into a mostly cashless society, but for the most part it remained limited to China and duty-free shops. The digital RMB, however, could bypass traditional banking networks and create an entirely new way to pay – one that some believe threatens the US dollar's dominant role. That, above all, is what is making the West sit up and take notice.

Death of the dollar? Certainly, this is a provocative catch-phrase, but the real question is, can a combination of the digital ecosystem and digital payment truly threaten the dollar, and lead to a long-term decline in its use? The US dollar has seen its share of competition in international currency markets. The euro launched in 1997, presenting a similar inflection point. Importantly, it was a new competitor but not a new way to pay, because it relied on traditional banking networks. These two currencies live in harmony in part because they use the same financial system. The banks that serve their respective users are united by a common framework of money transfer, know-your-customer (KYC) regulations, and international sanction enforcement.

The digital RMB is dramatically different. It relies on a new and separate system of money transfer, independent of the Western financial network and its rules and regulations. It offers a different network, a new type of currency, and, most importantly, new possibilities unhampered by entrenched regulation. If that isn't a revolution, what is? The "death of the dollar" is in no way assured, but for the first time, it may meet a worthy foe, which challenges it both as a store of value, and as a passkey into a new digital ecosystem with unique benefits to its users.

China's digital RMB didn't just miraculously materialize out of nowhere. And despite what some have claimed, it was most certainly not a response to Facebook's attempt with Libra (since renamed Diem) to build a corporate-backed global digital currency. My goal is to explain not only what China's digital currency means for the West, but where it came from and why this fintech scene is without parallel.

Despite its seeming novelty, China's new digital currency and other advances result from thirteen years of painstaking innovation, featuring both colossal failures and successes. Critical to understanding the significance of the digital RMB is understanding the story of fintech in that country. This book hopes to close that gap so the reader sees the digital RMB as a culmination, rather than as a sudden development.

AN INSIDE VIEW

A decade in Shanghai is like a lifetime anywhere else, due to the blindingly fast pace of change. My decade in Shanghai started with one of the largest "coming out" parties ever thrown: the Shanghai Expo in 2010. An expo that is memorable not just for being big, but for having heralded Shanghai's ambitions to recapture its title as an international city on par with New York, London, Paris, or its cousin, Hong Kong.

When I arrived in Shanghai in 2010, there was no digital payment. Cash was king, and debit cards were used at the ATM or for payment at large or mid-sized stores with point-of-sale card readers. Smaller stores were cash-only. I distinctly remember that my weekly routine in Shanghai included ensuring that my front pocket contained a relatively large wad of 100 RMB ($US 14) banknotes, the largest denomination, to meet life's needs.

I arrived in Shanghai after the financial crisis had rudely interrupted my career in banking. I had passed the booming 1990s and more tentative 2000s innovating new financial products on the trading floors of several international banks. The banks changed over the years, but the work was a constant: assemble a small team of mathematicians, coders, and structurers to use technology to innovate new ways to manage institutional clients' risk. I didn't know it at the time, but my work was a harbinger of the changes coming to the retail sector, where technology and finance would intersect under the moniker "fintech." When I arrived in Shanghai in 2010, I was unaware that I had come to the very part of the world that was going to redefine not just how we use money, but the nature of currency and how we relate to it.

CHINA JOURNEY

Expatriates in China like to talk about their "China journey" because of the speed and fortuitous nature of life here. My journey had both of these qualities. Following a few years teaching MBA students, I eventually landed right back where I started, using technology to make the financial system work more smoothly with leading banks. Now firmly planted at IBM and on the tech side of the business, I was taking part in China's explosive and groundbreaking fintech scene, using the best that new technology had to offer in support of finance and banking. Unlike my time in New York, where I brought technology to a limited few, the focus of my work in China was bringing risk management and trading technology to China's massive retail market. Armed with even bigger technology like cloud, AI, and "big data," the scale of the innovation I could conceive had no limits, and China's financial players were receptive to any digital advantage they could find.

Immediately apparent to me was that the objectives of my clients in China were different from those of the banks I knew and had worked for in New York a few short years earlier. Everything in China was about modernizing the banking experience and going digital to keep up with the equally stunning advances seen on the internet. Some of this might have been considered "catching up" with their Western counterparts, but certainly not all of it. The zeitgeist was different: China was going digital, and if banks didn't do it, there was the sense that big tech would, a fundamental difference from their Western counterparts. Banks in the West were still licking their wounds from the financial crisis, yet felt so secure in their "too big to fail" status that digital technology was not considered a threat despite the explosion of digital services like Airbnb and Uber.

Following a few modest contributions to China's fintech scene, I eventually transferred with IBM to Singapore, where I headed their fintech efforts at inhouse "cognitive studios"—a smooth and enjoyable corporate segue, given my focus on innovation. It exposed me to Singapore's explosive fintech market and eventually became the fodder for my book "Innovation Lab Excellence: Digital Transformation from Within." This book was dedicated to helping innovators everywhere, but particularly those in banks where I already had many years of intimate familiarity with the myriad ways bankers can say "no" to innovation.

SHANGHAI GOES CASHLESS

When I returned to Shanghai in 2018, I immediately noticed something new: QR codes were everywhere—high tech served up in a low-tech way, glued to tables as plastic tags at restaurants, haphazardly taped to walls on a dirty piece of paper at my hardware store, laminated to a plastic card passed to me by a taxi driver. It was the most conspicuous sign that Shanghai had virtually gone cashless and that Alipay and WeChat Pay had taken over. Other than these signs, all was quiet. No one seemed particularly surprised by this switch to cashless, other than newbies or returnees like me.

I pride myself on some predictive prowess as to how fast new tech can be adopted. When I left Shanghai in the winter of 2016, Alipay was my payment method of choice when buying on the internet. I was swiping debit cards mostly for large-value payments. Most of my local shops had not yet converted to using the mobile payment system, and for incidentals I mainly used cash.

If you had asked me in 2016: "How likely is it that Shanghai, a city of almost thirty million, would go cashless in 2.5 years?" I'd have said you were crazy. Now, here I am back in Shanghai, and the 300 RMB I keep in my pocket, mostly out of habit, has been there for months. I'm living the dream of a cashless life. Cash is still used and accepted, but for practical purposes, most residents don't touch paper money and don't bother carrying any.

How did this happen so fast, and why so unceremoniously? These are big questions this book will explore, because the answers are key to understanding why China is embracing a fully digital RMB, and why their mobile payment systems will be a model for what will happen in your local market. Your local companies are obviously different, and the technology you use may differ as well, but the sea change in how we use money will be similar. Its seamless integration into that society is nothing short of jaw-dropping for those who see it at work for the first time, yet it is shrugged off as entirely normal by its native users.

THE PEOPLE'S FINTECH

Fintech is thriving in China. It is developing at a rate and with a sophistication that is incomparable with any in Western countries. By some estimates, including my own, it is about a decade ahead of the West. This isn't just in banking but in every part of the financial spectrum. Insurance giants Ping An and Zhong An invested heavily in digital technology to make taking out insurance as seamless and effortless as sending a mobile payment. Micro-insurance policies that feature widely in discussions for financial inclusion in Africa and India are alive and thriving here. Personal investing was also disrupted with Ant Financial's breakthrough money market fund, "Yu'e Bao," which briefly became the world's largest, based on investments as little as one RMB or fifteen cents.

Whether in banking, insurance, or investment, China's fintech has one constant and straightforward goal: bring financial inclusion to China's massive population, many of whom had long been passed over by traditional financial services. Fintech in China isn't an amenity or an optional add-on for China's financial institutions. Instead, it is a national instrument to increase productivity and raise the standard of living for all. China's forward-thinking attitude toward fintech is a serious business and has a social conscience.

CHINA'S FINTECH IS GOING GLOBAL

Given the success of China's fintech, it should come as no surprise that the firms responsible for this growth are going global. Moves by WeChat and Alibaba to join Western markets have not found an enthusiastic welcome. Alibaba's attempt to buy MoneyGram International met with skepticism by the US, and the Treasury Department blocked it. In the meantime, a much slower, more organic approach is also underway. China's fintechs are heading to Southeast Asia, most notably into Thailand, Malaysia, Indonesia, and Singapore.

China's fintech growth tightly follows the nation's vacationers, who want access to their China accounts abroad with the same convenience they have at home. Local banks set up the necessary connections to Alipay and WeChat Pay in their networks, and the tourist money flows into the local economy. Once established in tourist zones, these payment systems seep into the local economy because the local player's digital offerings have nowhere near the same convenience. While COVID-19 may have interrupted the travel market, the seeds planted across the globe are growing, particularly in Asia.

With digital banking licenses awarded to Chinese fintechs in Hong Kong, however, the stakes of the game are now extending beyond tourist spending. These licenses enable direct connection to the Western financial market, along with competition with Western banks on their home turf. With Hong Kong digital banking licenses in hand, China's fintechs just won new licenses in Singapore, with the hope of bringing their digital prowess ever westward.

In 2020, the Peoples Bank of China (PBOC) unleashed its fintech prowess with the first trials of a digital currency prior to full rollout. China is the first major country to fully digitize its national currency. Launching a digital currency for internal consumption is groundbreaking, but China also plans to use it in international trade. Despite China's careful planning for the project, and regular press releases following its development, the announcement sent shockwaves worldwide. The immediate result was that Facebook's Libra proclaimed itself as the West's rightful heir and competitor. Most Western governments disagreed.

What is clear is that China's fintech is making waves in international circles and isn't going to stay within the country's borders. Now with COVID-19, digital currencies are seen in a new light as fear of infection diminishes people's love affair with coins and cash. Governments are also suddenly receptive to digital currencies as they represent a potential leap forward in easing the distribution of stimulus funds.

COMING TO A BANK NEAR YOU

Much less apparent is how China's fintech is coming to a bank near you—or is already there. China's software developers are nothing short of miraculous, and you should not be surprised to find that many larger banks have a software development team in China. There are dozens of development teams here, and the next time you see your bank or insurer rolling out a new feature, it may have been designed and built in China.

When these coding teams work on solutions for use overseas, you can be sure that the way the coders think and approach a potential solution will, in no small degree, bear the influence of the fintech that they use every day. So Chinese fintech has already achieved global impact. "Made in China" is more than just your iPhone or computer; it may extend to the buttons you click on the next time you log on to your bank's internet site or mobile app.

ORGANIZATION OF THE BOOK

Living in China, I have a front seat on fintech development that will eventually change our world. My central thesis is that China's advances will, to some degree, be replicated in the West. I understand that the technology, companies, and how we access it will be different, but no doubt about it: digital payments are coming. Understanding how China, the world's second-largest economy, adopted digital payment and what it built with it will be a guide or template for the West.

This book is divided into three sections. The first will cover China's fintech development in what I call Version 1.0 digital payments. It provides the background for China's groundbreaking use of mobile payments, which led to a nearly cashless society. These provided the template used to develop Version 2.0 payment, a central bank digital currency (CBDC). The first section will also cover China's noteworthy fintech failure: peer-to-peer (P2P) loans. While China's fintech successes outweigh its failures, it is essential to understand how these failures helped advance fintech in China.

The second section focuses on CBDCs and takes the reader through the general development and use of these new financial instruments, before focusing on the known details of China's latest entrant, prior to its launch. While some details of China's CBDC, aka DC/EP, digital RMB or eRMB are state secrets, we can spell out the basic features, how it will be used, and what it means for China and the dollar. I hope the reader will have a better understanding of the design decisions China made in its CBDC, having reviewed the first generation of digital payment systems. These systems are intertwined; one springs from the other.

Many pundits report on China's CBDC in isolation, as though it stands independent of the preceding digital payment systems. It is essential to understand that China's CBDC didn't suddenly spring up out of nowhere. Years of work helped prepare the Chinese people to accept and adopt this new technology, via the world's most advanced mobile payment systems.

The book's third section will focus on how China's digital payment affected the populace's relationship with money, and how this will evolve even more quickly after the launch of the CBDC. Everything from how you bank, your access to credit, and the relationship with financial intermediaries all change with digitization. The benefits of digitization are not just for the upwardly mobile middle class, but also for the rural poor, who now enjoy higher levels of financial inclusion. Digital payment isn't just about how you pay, even though many tend to have this myopic view. Digital payment and the infrastructure built around it fundamentally change your relationship to money and how you use it.

The book focuses on the technology of the top players that led the revolution, rather than the individual companies that comprise the balance of the ecosystem. China's fintech companies are changing at a fantastic rate, so writing only about the companies themselves would make for a book that ages quickly. For example, Ant Financial's name change to Ant Group, dramatically "paused" IPO, and subsequent restructuring shows how fast company-specific chapters would need a rewrite. That said, the underlying technologies aren't going anywhere; they are the foundation of China's future developments. Most importantly, I hope to show the human side of how this technology allows people to change their relationship with money.

My front row seat is yours to share, and my goal is to help you better prepare yourself and your business for the arrival of this tech, no matter who brings them to your door. That said, China's fintechs are expanding westward, and knowing who these companies are and what they are capable of is essential if you want to work with them or compete against them.

If you think that this doesn't apply to you, think again. Have you noticed the symbol for Union Pay on any internet checkout pages? Or how about the Alipay logo at tourist sites and even drug stores? Chinese fintech is on the march despite talk of bans emanating from the US. Understanding this technology and the companies behind it will provide you with a decided strategic advantage as these technologies come to your markets.

2

PRECONCEPTIONS OF CHINA

China, on innovation:

> *"You should learn from your competitor, but never copy. Copy and you die."*
> Jack Ma, co-founder and former executive chairman of Alibaba Group

The West, on Chinese innovation:

> *The Chinese "don't innovate."*
> Carly Fiorina, Ex-HP CEO,
> Republican Presidential Candidate

Getting Westerners to take note of China's booming fintech scene hasn't been easy, and residual bitterness over the coronavirus has not helped. Only now, with China launching its central bank digital currency, and Ant Group's dramatically thwarted IPO, has the world become aware of China's fintech revolution. The rapid succession of groundbreaking AI, blockchain, and now digital currencies are getting global press and putting China on the fintech map.

I regularly discuss China's digital financial technology with people of all nationalities. Many are dismissive of China's capabilities, and happily live in ignorance. Until recently, the majority saw China's technology as merely an inferior copy of something that already existed elsewhere. Even worse, in many cases, China's fintech has been dismissed out of hand as an extension of the Chinese government, whose policies are viewed as suspect. It's an unfortunate way to view the world, but not without precedent—witness the US bans on WeChat and TikTok.

When it comes to China, it's hard to break through the preconceived notions of otherwise sophisticated and intelligent people. This problem is even worse now, in the post-coronavirus period. The problem with being dismissive of China's success with digital finance is that it far exceeds that of the West. The balance has shifted. Learning from more advanced users of any technology is a good thing. We should be eager to learn whatever China can teach us. I am not, of course, making a blanket statement for all sectors of technology, but in fintech and digital banking, China's gains are evident, and it's up to us to understand how, why, and what that means for our own future.

CHINA'S LEAD IN FINTECH

China's lead in fintech has been noted and documented by some expert analysts. The consultant EY graded countries by their level of fintech adoption by both consumers and small- and medium-size enterprises (SMEs). EY's "Global Fintech Adoption Index" shows a disturbing trend for the West. China's consumer adoption rate is tied with India for first place at 87%, while the US's score of 46% ranks 24th. Interestingly, developing countries take the top six spots, showing a trend for emerging markets to leapfrog developed ones in their adoption of new technology. Note that the top two European leaders are in 7th and 9th place. If these statistics tell us anything, it's that China and India's adoption of fintech have been nothing short of miraculous.

Rank	Country	%	Rank	Country	%
1	China	87	14	Argentina	67
2	India	87	15	Chile	66
3	South Africa	82	16	Switzerland	64
4	Russia	82	17	Sweden	64
5	Columbia	76	18	Germany	64
6	Peru	75	19	Brazil	64
7	Netherlands	73	20	Australia	58
8	Mexico	72	21	Spain	56
9	UK	71	22	Italy	51
10	Ireland	71	23	Canada	50
11	South Korea	67	24	USA	46
12	Singapore	67	25	Bel & Lux	42
13	Hong Kong, SAR of China	67	26	France	35
			27	Japan	34

Consumer fintech adoption across twenty-seven markets, rate in percent. China and India are global leaders in fintech adoption although China's mobile payment market is much broader and more mature.
Source: EY Global Fintech Adoption Index 2019

While India's fintech gains are impressive, they pale when compared to China's. India's total mobile payment volume was estimated to be roughly $200 billion in 2018, which is dwarfed by China's massive $42 trillion payment volume. To make plain the technology gap, US mobile payments for 2018 were a mere $120 billion.

THREE STRAWMAN ARGUMENTS OFTEN USED TO DOWNPLAY CHINA'S FINTECH

China's impressive figures for fintech adoption and mobile payment demonstrate how digital finance is transforming that country. But before we dive headlong into the subject, I want to address in detail the three most popular critiques leveled against China's tech scene. "Strawmen" are claims used to deflect or derail a discussion before it can even get going. In this case, their use betrays a desire to dismiss the technology rather than examine it based on its merits. I hear these platitudes raised in so many discussions that it would be better to deal with them up front than allow them to linger. They are:

A) China copies, and doesn't innovate.

B) It's different over there and not relevant to our experience in the West.

C) There's no internet privacy, so it can't be good.

A. CHINA COPIES

Taking these in order, let's deal with the perception that China simply copies from others and doesn't create in its own right. I will state unequivocally that during China's digital boom of the past twenty years, some Chinese companies copied foreign technology. It serves no purpose to debate how much and from whom, but it's clear that some Chinese companies played fast and loose with others' intellectual property (IP). This is a well-documented phenomenon, one that continues to be a headline item whenever you discuss China and technology.

The good news is that China's respect for IP is improving as China is increasingly an innovator and exporter of ideas rather than an importer (in 2019 China leapfrogged the US to become the world leader in patent applications). Even as IP remains a hot button issue, foreign companies working there acknowledge the improvement. According to the 2019 China Business Climate Survey, conducted by the American Chamber of Commerce in Beijing, 96% of respondents acknowledged China's efforts to improve the way IP laws are written and enforced.

In any case, China is not unique in its pursuit of foreign technology. Japan, during the 1980s, faced similar accusations of using US auto manufacturing technology to upend the US car market. Taiwan, Korea, India, Japan, and Russia, among others, are all on the US's infamous Office of US Trade Representative "Special 301 Report" for IP adequacy in 2019.

As for fintech specifically, it would be hard to argue that China was building off technology originating in the West. There are no cognates or equivalents for China's innovations in this sector. How can you check? Simply look in your wallet and on your phone. Unlike microchips or software, where the origin of the technology is difficult to assess without specialized knowledge, most fintech is out in the open, designed to be seen and used. Does your phone hold anything with a QR code related to payment? Not likely, unless you are in India or a few European countries.

This was far less the case in China in, say, 2010, when I arrived. Back then it was easy to see how Baidu copied Google, Alibaba copied eBay, Tencent's Weibo and Sina Weibo both copied Twitter, and Tencent's QQ and RenRen copied Facebook. The cognates were obvious. Most of China's services already existed in Western counterparts and were roughly comparable. For many, the China story ends here, and no subsequent advances matter.

Let's step back for a second to remember a critical point. Imitation is not necessarily a bad thing; in some cases it's the most efficient way forward. In the late 1980s, the basic functions or tools we use on the internet, like search or social networking, didn't exist in China. In order to build new systems in Mandarin, they decided against reinventing the wheel. Seeing what worked in the US, where internet development was miles ahead, simply made sense. I am now recommending that same pragmatic approach to you. Learn about China's digital financial technology because of China's advances. Imitate it, learn how to use it, and prepare yourself for when it, or something like it, eventually arrives.

Since my arrival in China almost a decade ago, what was once copycat technology has evolved so much so that it is now almost unrecognizable. Each one of the companies that once closely resembled US platforms morphed into something new, with different features and new business models that are uniquely Chinese. What happened in this decade? Simple: China's internet companies created new products and services to serve their market and gladly moved away from their origins. They became innovators with apps like TikTok, which are most definitely "Made in China" and now causing concern in the West.

If we were to believe that China still simply copies, I wouldn't be writing this book. Copying could not account for the development of financial services provided by China's internet companies. While not all have prospered, many have morphed far away from their original business model, and they've gone on to make new categories of business all for themselves.

Take Meituan-Dianping, China's largest restaurant delivery service, which sees more than 600,000 scooter delivery people in 2,500 cities serving 400 million customers, in conjunction with China's biggest restaurant rating platform. It's somewhat like Uber Eats, but the reality is that this company has morphed into something uniquely Chinese that has no parallel in the West. It's like an "Amazon for services," where people are dispatched to do short-distance delivery not just of food, but other retail products, earning an average of $US 0.75 per delivery with an average delivery time of 30 minutes. This explains why yellow-shirted delivery people are seen all over Shanghai, physically running to pick up or drop off after hopping off their scooters. It also explains why during the coronavirus shutdown, entire cities like Wuhan were well supplied.

Meanwhile, Meituan started with a "deal of the day" platform that somewhat resembled Groupon. Dianping bought it, and now the joint company has evolved into something completely new. If China were simply copying, that and many other companies would not exist. The level of innovation is so great that some liken Chinese internet companies to gladiators in a kill-or-be-killed digital arena.

I will argue that the creativity of China's internet firms is unparalleled. If you were to compare the basic functions of Twitter, Facebook, and Google with those available in 2010, have they evolved as much? Not really; most are still recognizable when compared to their earlier incarnations. This is our first clue as to why you need to go to China to study fintech and digital banking development. The major Western internet companies are massive and, having already achieved monopoly status, their thirst for evolution is limited.

B. IT'S DIFFERENT OVER THERE, AND NOT RELEVANT TO OUR EXPERIENCE IN THE WEST

There is not a day that goes by when I don't get this impression. Yes, China is different; that's a good thing, and why I love living here. The fact that it's different does not mean that its developments are irrelevant outside the country. Its very difference enabled China to birth a new digital financial world.

China's banks, internet companies, and government all faced a unique set of challenges, and saw digital finance as the solution. The government wanted to lift its poorer populace into the mainstream. Banks begrudgingly acknowledged that they needed a better way of reaching the rural poor, with services previously limited to the urban wealthy. Finally, internet companies wanted an easy way for people to buy things on the net. In the most basic sense, these are the conditions that gave birth to China's digital finance. Intriguingly, they are not unique to China. One could argue that India, the world's other fintech leader, as well as many other developing countries, share the same problems. But China got to the digital solution first. Why?

> *It doesn't matter if the cat is black or white*
> *as long as it catches mice.*
>
> *Deng Xiaoping*

I'll say it, because I know what you're thinking: it's because China is communist. When it comes up, many speak this word in a soft voice. Others, upon hearing the word, simply switch off. That China does not truly practice communism, but instead "socialism with Chinese characteristics" and has revamped its economy to encompass many free-market reforms, is a subtle point missed by many. But here's the truth, contrary to what many viewing China from afar may believe: what makes China different is not its political system, but its culture. When I wake up in the morning and say "China is different," it has nothing to do with the political reality of modern China, and everything to do with the 5000-year-old culture of China's people and how they relate to their world. Embedded in this ancient culture, or perhaps because of it, is a willingness to accept new technology, despite a reverence for age, tradition, and the tried-and-true. It is this characteristic that allowed China to make the transition to digital money in a heartbeat, without looking back or giving it a second thought.

Let me address the most critical role of government in fostering the fintech innovation that we've seen in China. The spark came in 2014 when the government allowed WeChat (Tencent) and Alibaba to open digital banking operations. To understand the significance of this, just imagine if banking licenses had been granted to Amazon and Google in the West in 2014—it would have been disruptive in the best sense of the word.

Now without question, the government worked in close conjunction with both companies before the launch of their payment services to ensure that they would not blow up the banking system. This was not, however, a Chinese government command-and-control program to digitize banking. The government let private sector internet companies, merchants, and the public figure it out for themselves; it did so at the expense of state-owned incumbent banks!

While the government closely monitored the success of digital banking, as they measured the success of myriad other digital programs that were underway throughout the economy, it is clear that they had a more laissez-faire attitude than that with which they are credited. Proof is evident in the disastrous P2P lending program—which collapsed as a direct result of the government's hands-off attitude toward digital lending.

So let's avoid any ambiguity. If you think that "China is different" because it designed, built, and forced digital banking on the populace and that this is the secret to its success, you're mistaken. The government's contributions were more nuanced, and your perception of the Chinese government as forcing this to succeed needs revision. That the government had a role is clear and praiseworthy. They had the forethought to allow tech companies to enter financial services at a time when there was broad government support for programs that digitized social systems throughout the country. Why wouldn't banking be included? The government also saw how incumbent banks were not serving large numbers of China's "unbanked" and that this represented a societal ill that incumbents wouldn't fix on their own.

C. THERE'S NO INTERNET PRIVACY, SO IT CAN'T BE GOOD

Although there is no internet privacy in China, there is no "right" or expectation of privacy by China's internet users. All internet activities are subject to government overview, and internet platforms all have a backdoor for government access to their data. So what is perceived as a "right" in the West does not exist in China.

What does this mean for users? In practical terms, it does not inhibit online financial activity one bit. Most assume, as do most in the West, that the government already knows where the majority of our funds come from; where the funds go is a lesser issue. So for practical purposes, there is little concern—a situation not unlike most who receive direct deposit paychecks in the West. What does, of course, change is that because everyone knows that the internet is a privilege and closely monitored, it is not the place to put harsh dissenting political opinions unless you are exceedingly brave. That said, discord is better tolerated than you might think. Dissenting or complaining is not itself a problem; China's internet sites are livelier than you've likely heard. What is critical is the nature, tone, and severity of dissent. China's internet users monitor government sensitivities closely and are careful to remain on the right side of a movable line.

I understand if this sounds like a place where you don't want to surf the web. For now, I will limit my comments to China's fintech and digital banking services, which operate unencumbered from government interference while definitely under surveillance. For China's more than one billion mobile payment users, their use of these systems is on an "as is" basis, and no one gives surveillance much thought as no one knows anything different. This is simply how it is, and always has been. I've dedicated part of chapter 19 to a more in-depth analysis of privacy expectations with digital payments, because I understand it's a hotly charged subject.

To be honest, the government does not care about the vast majority of your financial or internet life, and users use their cell phones and computers just like you do. Internet users do not sit at a café surfing the web in fear of state surveillance. It is of so little concern that it rarely comes up in conversation with either Chinese or expatriates except when the latter group laments Facebook's block in China. The use of digital payment and banking is without fear of government interference, and surveillance is both out of sight and out of mind to users and many government agencies.

The thought that all of China's government agencies are automatically connected to and viewing your data in real-time is another fallacy. Frankly, even with modern technology, the data requirements for real-time monitoring of an entire population's financial transactions exceed the limits of computing power. That said, should the government have reason to investigate you for tax evasion or other financial crime, there is no need to request access to your records, as they are open to the authorities. Compare this with the US where the Internal Revenue Service will ask permission to access your digital records if you're under investigation for tax evasion, and then take them directly from your financial institution if you refuse. In the end, in either China or the US, your digital accounts are an open book.

So here's the question: can financial systems built without the expectation of privacy be of value to us in the West? In my view, the answer is clearly yes, because even the most cursory review of China's fintech would show the uninitiated that they're doing something different there that works. Privacy is, for the most part, built into the back end of the system that controls where and to whom data flows, and is unique to the country of use. The front-end functionality, what the system does, is just as relevant in the West as it is in China.

So, imagine examining mobile payment systems from WeChat or Alipay. Would the front-end of these systems be of sufficient interest to examine the use of QR codes in creating such successful products? Of course, even if we acknowledge that the systems have privacy that is not up to our expectations, we can still study or even copy the functionality if it suits us. So China's unique privacy issues should not automatically disqualify China-based technology from a closer examination.

The next question is whether these privacy concerns disqualify China's technology from actual use. This is a very personal decision, but seeing how many are now using WeChat for messaging or TikTok for video makes me wonder if this may be less of an issue than it is made out to be. Or perhaps it's a devil's bargain where we trade privacy for convenience? It sounds a lot like what we do when we use Facebook and Google.

CHINA DISPROVES THE "BANKS ARE HISTORY" DEBATE

Examining China's digital financial revolution is more than an exercise in curiosity or voyeuristic view on China, its tech, and culture. It is a window onto our future, and this is why it's essential to see what's happening in China now. Even though the evolution of China's fintech products will undoubtedly be different from how they evolve in either US or European markets, many of the techniques and uses for fintech and banking technology that China pioneered will filter into our world. It's just a matter of time before they arrive. Understanding what happened in China will give you a head start in understanding what form they'll take and what they mean for your business. This is why learning about what is happening in China now is like having a crystal ball that allows you to see the evolution of payment, banking, and investing.

If China's fintech is a crystal ball, we've already had our first glimpse into the future and first revelation. Not a day goes by that I don't read an article about the pending entry of "GAFA" companies—Google, Amazon, Facebook, or Apple—into the financial services sector. Apple Card and Google's new checking accounts are the first steps for big tech into providing retail financial services. Many articles go as far as to proclaim that when GAFA companies go fully into retail financial services—buy a bank, for example—that the big banks will be "history."

> *The world needs banking,*
> *but it does not need banks*
>
> *Bill Gates*

That already happened in China, so we know the answer. WeChat and Alibaba, the very rough equivalents of Amazon and Facebook, entered the banking market. While they certainly did revolutionize how China pays for things and manages its money, the incumbent banks are still here and profitable. The services incumbents provide are changing to match their digitally savvy competitors, and they are quickly ramping up their digital presence, but they're still here, and there's no disaster.

Would it likely be the same in the US or Europe? Absolutely, because residents of developed Western countries are less likely than their Chinese counterparts to use technology companies as their banks, and are already showing some resistance to using new fully digital neobanks. So when one or more of the GAFA companies enter banking markets, they will undoubtedly transform many things about consumer banking, just like WeChat and Alipay did. Still, in the long term, they're not going to disrupt the incumbent banks.

Now, where this information is of critical importance is to the investors in the aforementioned digital neobanks like N26, Chime and Monzo. Investors in these banks have bought into the promise that these digital banks would "disrupt" incumbent banks and revolutionize banking. While they just might revolutionize banking by bringing new services to users, its already clear by studying China that major disruption is a stretch. For the record, I love neobanks, but I have to wonder if their unicorn valuations (exceeding $US 1 billion) represent value when disruption is taken off the table.

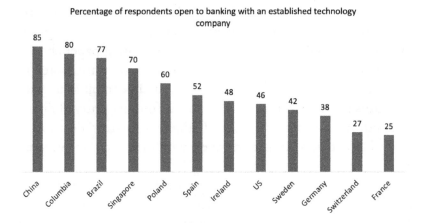

Percentage of respondents open to banking with an established technology company

Chinese customers are the most willing to try banking with
an established technology company, because many already are.
Source: Bain/Dynata Retail Banking NPS Survey, 2019

China's banking population rushed to use the new payment systems that Alipay and WeChat Pay provided, just as Western bank customers may flock to a new product or service offered by a GAFA bank. What is interesting is that Chinese banking customers were less inclined to close out the bank accounts they had held for ages in traditional banks. Trust in banking is hard-earned and long-lived, so while a newcomer's services may be appreciated, that doesn't translate to earning sufficient trust to move all of one's assets. Chinese customers also had another reason to stay put: opening a bank account in one of the incumbent non-digital banks is time-consuming, so closing the bank account you've had for a long time is a non-starter, especially if it's free to keep and you've had good relations.

This is an example of the insights that we can glean from following China's digital banking markets, and why a greater understanding of what is happening in China today is an excellent foundation to build on. It also has another side to it that is more disconcerting. As we look at China's advances, we have to ask why we don't have them in our own countries?

The United States, in particular, as a master of all things digital, is far behind China in the adoption of digital finance. Banks in the US still expect clients to wait three days for deposits to clear, as though we were still back in the days of paper checks. The reasons are difficult to untangle because they are rooted in resistance by incumbent banks to go digital, in combination with regulators that largely protect incumbents from the entry of digital competitors. By comparison, the Chinese regulators' decision to allow digital competitors to compete with their incumbents seem even more prescient and bold.

The US and Europe, excepting a few forward-minded countries like Sweden, have both fallen behind in digital banking. This was never more obvious than my last trip to Italy, where I was surprised to find something that felt strange or unusual in my front pocket. It was a large pile of change that had accumulated from all of the cash transactions that I had to make. That it felt unnatural or unusual was noteworthy because I'm used to a cashless world and frankly, I don't want to go back. The feeling of change in my pocket was quaint but unwelcome.

3

CHINA'S FINTECH IS ~~COMING~~ ALREADY HERE

China on Chinese innovation:

> *"China has come to the forefront of development. There is less and less room for taking the best from outside and improving on them."*
>
> Pony Ma, Founder and CEO of Tencent, parent company of WeChat

West on Chinese innovation:

> *Every time I see WeChat has a new feature that I like I send an email off to R&D.*
>
> Mark Zuckerberg, Chairman and CEO of Facebook, Inc.

As you may have noticed, China, or at the very least its fintech, is already here. The coronavirus crisis taught many lessons, one clear one being that China makes many contributions to the West that go unnoticed. It's easy to lament and potentially reduce the West's over-reliance on China's antibiotics or protective equipment. What may not be apparent is that China's fintech is crucial as well. This is not to strike fear in your heart, but rather to show how China's fintech is already making a productive contribution. In a time of coronavirus and trade wars, negative sentiments toward China abound. It's easy to get caught up in negativity that otherwise masks China's genuine contributions.

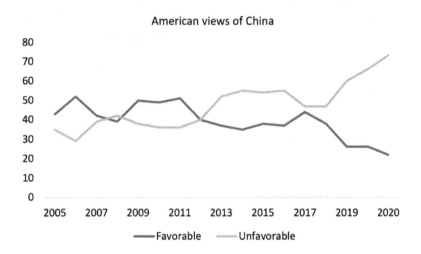

American views of China

Unfavorable views of China have peaked with the coronavirus, and conspire to mask China's genuine progress in fintech and digital banking.
Source: Survey of U.S. adults conducted June 16-July 14, 2020
Pew Research Center, Washington D.C.

CHINA'S DIGITAL PAYMENTS ARE ALREADY HERE

China's fintech is already having an impact on businesses on a global scale, but on a level not many outside that country have noticed. In less restricted times its middle class loved to travel. They brought their mobile phones with them, expecting the same convenience of cashless payment abroad as they have at home. According to China's Ministry of Culture and Tourism,

147 million Chinese tourists spent a total of $220 billion abroad in 2017.

To keep up with Chinese tourism, mobile payment operators Alipay and WeChat Pay began expanding into Chinese tourist hotspots globally, in the same way that Visa and Mastercard established franchises back in the 1970s. The newcomers' expansion into Southeast Asia came first, but mobile payment operators are seeking inroads worldwide to make it easier for Chinese to spend while abroad. The chart below, while no longer applicable in the age of COVID, gives an indication of the advance.

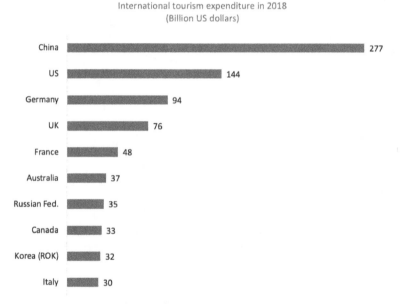

International tourism expenditure in 2018
(Billion US dollars)

China	277
US	144
Germany	94
UK	76
France	48
Australia	37
Russian Fed.	35
Canada	33
Korea (ROK)	32
Italy	30

China is the world's largest spender with one fifth of international tourist spending. Only around 10% of China's 1.4 billion inhabitants travel internationally.
Source: UN World Tourism, International Highlights, 2019

Likewise in pre-COVID times, airports all over the world, eager to access Chinese travelers' duty-free shopping power, rolled out Ali and WeChat Pay as a payment option. Thailand, for example, long a hotspot for Chinese travelers due to its visa-free travel policy for Chinese nationals, connected most of its banks to the WeChat and Alipay networks to better serve Chinese citizens throughout the country. Walk into one of Thailand's famous 7-11 stores, and you'll see both Alipay and WeChat logos on the register.

In the US, the national drugstore chain Walgreens has 7,000 stores connected to Alipay. At the same time, this company has a deal with the US's First Data to put its payment system on 35,000 other merchants. In the UK, Barclaycard and Alipay's partnership will bring Alipay to retailers in their network, which covers roughly half of the UK's credit and debit transactions. Finally, it should come as no surprise that airlines, including United, American, Delta, and KLM Airlines, now take Alipay at the checkout screen.

I have a challenge for you all. Next time you check out either online or at a significant retailer, look again to see if the WeChat and Alipay logos are present, though you may never have noticed. You might be in for a surprise.

Duty-free shops accept China's mobile wallets.
Chances are, so do some of your local retailers.

Western businesses accepting WeChat and Alipay are profiting from China's fintech ecosystem. Far from being a threat, it's a gateway to a new group of clients who may be more inclined to use your service or product if you meet them halfway, by showing them that you're sensitive to their payment needs. Remember, most Chinese travelers have ready access to traditional credit cards, but simply prefer the ease and convenience of using their home country's payment system.

By taking a step closer to China and its consumers, you're helping to organically spread these companies' networks and supporting their quest to gain recognition in Western markets. It's a fair trade for many, and part of a long-term organic growth strategy that shows how patient yet persistent Chinese companies can be.

YOU'RE ALREADY USING CHINA'S TECH

Many of you would be surprised to discover that you're already using China's technology online or at your local bank. Many global companies have significant computer programming operations in China. The cities of Chengdu and Xi'an are famous for their coding capabilities; a tour of their massive technology campuses reveals the logos of many Fortune 500 companies whose software, products, and websites you use daily. Xi'an software park boasts forty-five Fortune 500 companies, while Chengdu's high-tech zone features thirty-four.

This is to say nothing of other established tech development centers in Beijing, Shanghai, Shenzhen, and Hangzhou, which also build software and new products for foreign companies. Going to Google or Apple maps will show you a complete listing of tenants for any of these parks. If you look, you'll see the well-known names of banks in your home country, as well as the names of software producers like IBM, Oracle, and SAP, which build the software your bank uses.

Tianfu Software Park Chengdu, list of tenants.
Source: Tianfu Software Park

In some cases, the features of the latest edition of your banking app were derived from China's payment apps. One example can be found in a foreign bank's China-based innovation team. The team was quite surprised to find that the bank's payment app did not have a feature for splitting a restaurant bill among diners—something that is commonly found on payments apps in China. The team took it upon themselves to build similar functionality into their bank's payment app and it was quite a hit when launched. So while you'd never know it, the shiny new button on your bank app just might be "Made in China" and inspired by China's fintech.

To make the cycle complete, add to these achievements the work of a large number of prized Chinese nationals working in the West, designing and building digital solutions. China's emphasis on STEM (science, technology, engineering and mathematics) education and national push for all things digital means that young Chinese who excel frequently go to school in major Western universities and afterward find work in Western coding teams. The solution they build may be directly modeled on their experiences with digital services back home. So while you may not know it, China is already coming to you from more directions than you imagined.

YOU'VE ALREADY INVESTED IN CHINA

There's another area that gets little notice concerning China's fintech and tech industry, and it's personal. You may not know it but you've probably already invested in China's fintech and digital banks. The tech boom in China was comparable in scale to that in the US in recent years, making it enormously attractive to investors searching for yield. Add to this China's position as the world's number two economy, with a booming tech sector that rivals Silicon Valley, and you can understand why investors flocked to China.

China's tech boom was supported by venture capital and private equity firms in the US and Europe, which in turn took money from pension or retirement funds—perhaps of the company that employs you. In a recent study by NEPC investment consultants, 91% of US foundations and endowments had some exposure to China. Some of these investments have undoubtedly made it into China's vibrant fintech sector. At the time of writing, the trade and tech cold wars have cooled US investment in China's VC market by more than half of its 2018 peak. Nevertheless, the investments made in prior years helped propel China's fintechs and digital financial services companies to greater heights. The irony is that US investment helped enable a better digital banking ecosystem in China than exists in the US.

There are other ways that you may have invested in China's fintech and digital banking scene without knowing it. Private investors have flocked to exchange traded funds (ETFs) with the shift to passive investing strategies. If you own an ETF with a foreign return based on the MSCI Emerging Markets Index, you're invested heavily in China's fintech and banks. MSCI is the world's biggest index compiler, and its index for emerging markets is the most important within the sector.

As of January 2019, as much as $1.8 trillion in assets use the index as a benchmark. These passive investment dollars, some of which may originate with retail ETF products, flow into Chinese companies that are in the index. Interestingly, a look at the index's top ten constituents shows that the first and second constituents by weight are China's Alibaba, the corporate parent of Ant Financial (Alipay), and Tencent, the parent of WeChat. Further down the list are Ping An Insurance and China Construction Bank, two other heavily digital Chinese financial institutions. While this is an example of just one index, there are many others focused on emerging markets or China that have ETFs following them that will hold these stocks. So there's no escaping China's fintech and digital banking scene even if you don't think that you're part of it.

	Country	Float Adj Mkt Cap (USD Billions)	Index Wt. (%)	Sector
ALIBABA GROUP HLDG ADR	CN	552.28	8.67	Cons Discr
TENCENT HOLDINGS LI (CN)	CN	378.31	5.94	Comm Srvcs
TAIWAN SEMICONDUCTOR MFG	TW	368.29	5.78	Info Tech
SAMSUNG ELECTRONICS CO	KR	237.67	3.73	Info Tech
MEITUAN DIANPING B	CN	111.19	1.75	Cons Discr
RELIANCE INDUSTRIES	IN	86.39	1.36	Energy
NASPERS N	ZA	77.28	1.21	Cons Discr
JD.COM ADR	CN	66.07	1.04	Cons Discr
CHINA CONSTRUCTION BK H	CN	62.29	0.98	Financials
PING AN INSURANCE H	CN	61.12	0.96	Financials
Total		2,000.89	31.41	

MSCI Emerging Market Index Top 10 Constituents shows the importance of China's fintech companies.
Source: MSCI, September 30, 2020

NOT JUST THE WEST

While it did not receive much press in the West, Ant Group (Alipay) inked deals with the United Nations Economic Commission for Africa (UNECA) in cooperation with the International Financial Corporation (IFC) to bring its technology to bear on financial inclusion in Africa. WeChat and Alipay are forging similar deals with banks in South Africa, Kenya, and Nigeria, with the intent of building a network that extends throughout Africa. With the development of systems in Africa and with an already strong presence in India and Asia, these payment giants are most likely already the world's largest, by user count.

China's Belt and Road Initiative (BRI), the world's biggest and most expensive development program, did not directly promote either of these payment companies in Africa. While it is convenient to link the two programs together, it is not entirely accurate. Both WeChat and Alipay forged relationships with local partners on their own without government support. Still, some will see this push into Africa as evidence that all Chinese companies are under government control. Perhaps, but it would be hard to square this perspective with the companies' expansion efforts throughout Asia and Southeast Asia, which is independent of the BRI.

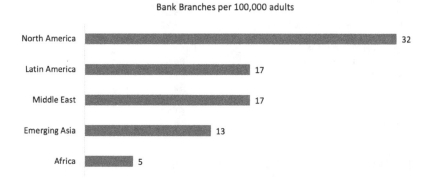

Low bank branch penetration in Africa and other emerging economies present an opportunity for China's digital payment companies.
Source: McKinsey & Co, Roaring to life, February 2018

China's fintechs are going global in a big way, and will be the top competitors to any efforts by Western-backed payment and banking initiatives. Bringing the same pragmatic systems tested in small villages in China, where many were unbanked, to a continent with the lowest bank branch penetration in the world and equivalent need for financial inclusion, is a good thing. Put another way, with their unique expertise in developing markets, who would logically be better able to do this than China?

COPYING CHINA'S FINTECH

As astounding as this may seem, China's fintech has another unexpected consequence: Western tech companies are copying Chinese fintech. Can it be a coincidence that Facebook, the social network most aligned with WeChat, is going down a similar path of combining payment from its Diem (Libra) coin project within its social network?

> *"At first I thought WeChat was a little over hyped. It's just WhatsApp for China, right? How good can a social network really be if it's not owned by us? Then I linked my bank card and I was like 'Wow!' now I get it."*
>
> *Mark Zuckerberg*

WeChat Pay was the first company to combine a social network with a digital payment system, and the result was such a smash hit in China that it certainly did not escape Facebook's attention. WeChat was also the inventor of "private groups" for online communication—another feature Facebook borrowed from WeChat. This raises the uncomfortable question, who is copying whom?

4

ALIPAY AND WECHAT PAY - DIGITAL PAYMENT 1.0

China fees for digital payment:

> *WeChat Pay and AliPay are free for most transactions.*
>
> *Fees of 0.1% start at withdrawals over 10,000 ($US 1,400) and 20,000 RMB respectively.*

The West fees for digital payment:

> *"Square's standard processing fee is 2.6% + 10¢ for card-present payment."*
>
> *"At PayPal, the flat-rate pricing structure is a base rate of 2.9% plus $0.30 per transaction."*

My days in Shanghai start and end with WeChat, as it does for the majority of China's population. WeChat isn't just the dominant social platform in the country;

it's the glue that holds much of my life here together. Whether it's my personal life, work, or banking, most of my world revolves around WeChat. It's hard to explain to someone who's never used it before how encompassing the WeChat ecosystem is. WeChat isn't just about buying coffee, ordering lunch, or paying bills; it connects you with the world in a more significant way. No, it's not like Facebook's WhatsApp, even if both send messages and are green. On the WeChat network, there are no limits, and you can go from chatting with friends to buying airline tickets to ordering coffee delivery without ever leaving the app. There is almost nothing that you can't do in the digital world on WeChat.

Calling it a "super-app" conveys some of the sweep that this app has in one's life, but it still makes it sound like just another app. WeChat is more like a separate version of the internet, with everything from messaging, gaming, banking, government services, healthcare, Zoom calls, and payment all in one. There is almost nothing it can't do, and that is why it has won the hearts of so many in China.

Calling WeChat the glue that holds China together is not an overstatement. Were WhatsApp to suddenly disappear, most in the West would be only slightly disrupted, and find a replacement within an hour. Were the same to happen to WeChat, China's economy and society would be crippled. Over a billion users, the majority in China, would suddenly find themselves without access to even the most basic of essential services. However unlikely, this scenario nicely illustrates WeChat's status within China and how different it is from WhatsApp. It is a marvel, and I can say without reservation that it greatly simplifies my life and has changed my relationship with money.

QR codes are an elegant and straightforward solution for payment.

While WeChat focuses on messaging and the digital world, Alipay (now a part of fintech giant Ant Group, an affiliate of Alibaba) concentrates on the physical world and all the things you need to do in it. While I mention Alibaba's Alipay after WeChat, it is in no way any less important to me. Precisely because they deal with the physical world, many of the creature comforts are brought to me from stores on Alibaba, and delivered by their couriers.

To say Alibaba is like Amazon is correct to a point, but the range of life services is much more expansive, including things like rubbish removal from your house, cloud computing services, banking, and investment. Alibaba brands itself as your life operating system (OS), and it has earned the right to use such an ambitious title. Imagine a company that provides storefronts like eBay and Amazon, delivers like FedEx, handles payment like PayPal, provides banking like your bank, and allows you to invest like your broker. As amazing as WeChat is, Alibaba is, in many ways, even more so because it connects the online and physical worlds to bring it all directly to your phone or your door.

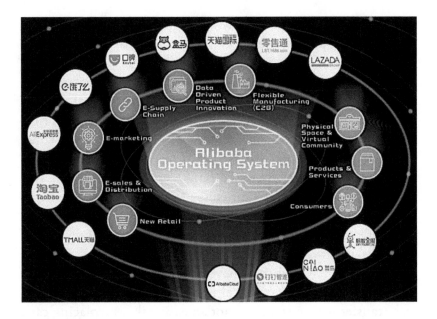

The Alibaba Operating System. A platform of companies enabling one-stop
shopping for services that allow connection between the digital and
physical world.
Source: Alibaba

DIGITAL PAYMENT 1.0

Before going any further, let's make it clear why these are China's
first generation of digital payment platforms. First, let me make
a crucial distinction: they do not use digital currency to transfer funds, but instead use existing banking digital networks.
Nonetheless, their success shook China to its core and inspired
broad-based government interest in advancing digital currencies.
These companies paved the way for China's launch of a fully
digital central bank digital currency (CBDC), and are critical
to the adoption of China's second-generation, or Version 2.0,
digital currency. They are so important that I will cover WeChat
Pay and Alipay over two chapters, with cultural aspects in this
chapter and more technical aspects in the next.

So Alipay and WeChat Pay are digital payment systems by virtue of being attached to the existing banking digital infrastructure. By the way, all modern banking is digital, although you may not have thought of it that way. Banks don't have stacks of cash with your name on them; instead, they rely on digital systems for transactions across all accounts. China's payment platforms' innovation was to democratize access to the existing networks through China's debit card system. This was revolutionary: it created a system that bypassed bank-controlled payment systems while using the debit cards issued by the banks. The irony is unmistakable. Mobile payment systems gave mobile users complete access to their money in the bank—without relying on banks' internet portals or card processing networks, which is something we have yet to achieve in the West.

This Version 1.0 system eliminated the need for physical cash transfer within society—not an easy task, as replacing cash is something that existing credit or debit cards were ill-equipped to do. While credit and debit cards are digital payment tools, they operate on specialized payment processing gateways on the payment receiver's side. Access to these gateways, whether a point-of-sale card swiping device or through online systems, requires paying for the privilege. This system kept the option of digital payment out of the hands of smaller businesses and, of course, private individuals.

China's mobile payment platforms acted as self-contained intermediaries. They were able to handle card-based payments without the need for standalone payment processing. The processing happened within the app, and the user was none the wiser. This brought the possibility of accepting digital payments to everyone, no matter how small, and with minimal charges. I used the term democratization because, in the real sense of the word, China's mobile payment platforms brought the power of banking's digital networks into the hands of every mobile user in China.

It is a revolution that remains elusive in the West. To understand how important it is, look to the fintech unicorn Square.

Square bases its business model on making receipt of credit and debit card payment available to everyone, including the smallest businesses. This has been an excellent business for Square, earning them a six-billion-dollar valuation that is in part based on sales of this service. While I like Square and PayPal, which offer similar services, in China they are as unnecessary as are their card-swiping devices. Using China's payment apps gives users immediate access to bank accounts, simply by using a mobile phone and a mobile payment company as the intermediary. They break the model. While Square charges 2.6% plus US$ 0.10 per charge, China's mobile wallets perform the same service for free or 0.1%, based on universal access. If we consider China's mobile payment as Version 1.0 digital currency, the West is still on version 0.5 due to its limited access to banks' digital networks—a bold statement that I will back up with usage statistics in the next section.

MOBILE PAYMENT ON AN UNPRECEDENTED SCALE

I want to use some statistics to help put China's mobile payment market in perspective. In the year 2019, mobile payments transaction volume in China hit RMB 347 trillion (US$ 51.8 trillion). Put another way, mobile payments in China were more than three times China's GDP of US$ 14.4 trillion. It is essential to understand that this multiple of GDP shows how mobile payments are used not just to buy coffee, but for business-to-business transactions and for an incredible 83% of all payment transactions that flow within the economy.

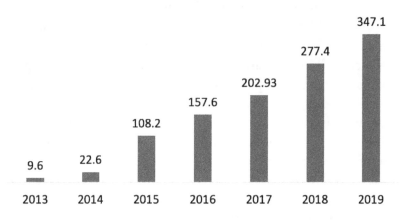

Mobile Payment Transaction Volume
Trillions of RMB

Mobile payments in China have increased thirty-six times from 2013
and more than doubled since 2016 when mobile payment
was already well established.
Source: PBOC

Fifty-two trillion dollars is a big number, so let's put it in context and compare it with US mobile payments as readers may be more familiar with these systems. According to eMarketer data, US proximity mobile payments for 2019 were a mere $98 billion—a pittance compared to its GDP of roughly $20 trillion. P2P mobile payments Venmo and Zelle contributed an additional $309 billion. China's mobile payments are more than 500 times that in the US for this period even though China's GDP is approximately one-third smaller than that of the US. Combining US P2P and mobile payments, as both are combined on China's mobile payment platforms, still makes the US's combined mobile cash transfer market roughly 125 times smaller than China's.

Astute observers will say that Americans use credit or debit cards to pay for the majority of their purchases. After all, contactless payment has made buying your morning coffee with a credit or debit card a breeze. Also, mileage points, cash-back, and other card perks have severely inhibited the uptake of mobile payment. True to a degree, but according to the Nilson Report, the authoritative guide on card use, the purchase volume of US general-purpose brands Visa, Mastercard, American Express, and Discover reached $6.69 trillion in 2019. Why the difference with China? In China, the use of mobile payment is so ubiquitous that money simply flows in cyclic fashion more times through the system because everyone, including business, uses mobile payments.

On a global basis, the comparison is even more impressive with the world's credit, debit, and prepaid cards for all major brands for 2019, racking up $34.8 trillion in payment volume. China's mobile wallet payments were roughly 1.5 times the amount that flowed through all credit cards globally.

NO COMPARISON

WhatsApp is the closest we've got in the West to WeChat, and the messaging system is roughly similar. You can make video or audio calls, send video and communicate in groups, but that's about where the comparison ends. WhatsApp is hard at work, bringing payments to its network and will roll out a version in the UK in 2020 following its successful launch of the service in India. It is not a stretch to say that WhatsApp is copying WeChat's success in combining social and payment services. Even if WhatsApp were to launch tomorrow in any of these countries, including the US, it still would not have WeChat's killer ecosystem of services and retailers that are all united on the platform. For the record, WhatsApp's cousin, Facebook Messenger, does offer person-to-person (no business) cash transfers in the US, UK, and Europe.

Most Westerners haven't experienced anything like WeChat and its compelling ecosystem, which is why it's hard to explain to someone how one app can be so vital. Let me try by sharing my experience hosting business travelers who arrive in Shanghai for the first time without the app. Their difficulty starts when they arrive at the airport and can't reach colleagues or me because we're all on WeChat. Once in the taxi, their full immersion to cashless Shanghai begins because their driver no longer takes cash or has change. Buying tickets to visit clients using China's high-speed rail network means more WeChat for payment as well as checking schedules. Business cards at meetings? Why bother when we can swipe QR codes on WeChat. So whenever I host execs in Shanghai, I usually end up paying for everything—tickets, taxis, lunch—and get paid back in cash. Digitally capable execs visiting Shanghai suddenly find themselves back in the Stone Age, because they're not on WeChat. That's why I always tell visitors to download WeChat long before they arrive.

Similarly, Amazon, for all of its amazing feats, is no match for Alibaba. While Amazon is a master of logistics and is inching closer to providing financial services through credit cards and other consumer finance products, it lacks the depth of services and banking license that Alibaba and its Ant Finance unit provide. No one is getting loans on Amazon or investing just yet. While WhatsApp and Amazon enable important facets of our lives, they can't compare with China's superapps with their built-in ecosystems, payment, and banking services.

WeChat and Alipay control anywhere from 90% to 93% of the $US 52 trillion mobile payment market in China. They are massive, and are the basis for most of China's advances in digital payments and banking because they were the first to popularize mobile payments and the first to acquire digital banking licenses. To put this into perspective, compare Apple Pay and Android Pay, the top two mobile payment methods used in the US, with WeChat and Alipay; the difference is simply astounding. In 2019 WeChat and Ali Pay serviced 2.3 billion customers while Apple and Google Pay just broke 540 million.

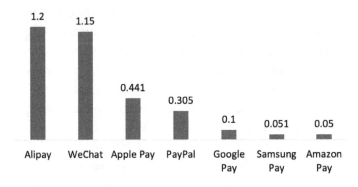

Number of users using leading mobile payment platforms
2018 and 2019 data.
Source: multiple sources

WHY MOBILE PAYMENTS TOOK OFF

Mobile payments exploded in China because they solved the problem of going to the bank for ordinary people. In the city centers, there were undoubtedly plenty of banks, but the wait for service was long, and there was little incentive for banks to improve their service. In rural regions, there simply were no banks because of the remoteness and low income of people in rural China. Mobile payment apps solved both of these problems at a low cost and with little real risk to the existing banking system. Remember, if these apps failed, incumbent banks would simply return to business as usual.

Mobile payment solved the real problems of the Chinese population at a scale that took everyone involved by surprise. Even now, going to the bank in China can be an ordeal. I still go because I have foreign exchange transactions that require my physical presence in the bank. A typical wait is almost always around an hour at one of the better-serviced branches in Shanghai's city center. Back when I moved to China in 2010, before mobile banking took over, the waits were often twice that, and the number of stamped and signed papers passed back and forth to the teller was mind-numbing.

Any mobile technology that could eliminate the need for going to the bank was sure to be a hit because people genuinely hated going. A large amount of business was conducted in cash when I first moved to China in 2010. At any establishment, even a brand-new glossy Apple store, you could always hear the cash-counting machine whirring in the background, counting large bricks of currency. Why bricks? Interestingly, the largest banknote is valued at RMB 100 or around $US 15. Person-to-person cash transfers frequently took place in cash, and it was not uncommon to see people leaving the bank with large bags stuffed with bricks of cash. I did it more than a few times myself and always found it a bit unnerving.

Debit cards are the fuel for mobile payment in China as the entire system is based on using your debit card with the mobile app. China had excellent penetration of debit cards but very few credit cards when mobile payments launched in 2014. Everyone had them, but you simply couldn't use them everywhere. While I could always use my debit card at any of the larger stores, many smaller shops and services were cash-based because they didn't have a point-of-sale terminal for debit cards. The massive economy of more humble shopkeepers in small towns and villages never had the facilities to take cards, and so they remained cash-based. Even when living in downtown Shanghai I always kept a rather large wad of cash in my pocket for services where debit cards would not be accepted.

Another thing about debit cards that helped people make the transition to mobile payment is that most users did not have the same attachment to them as credit cards. Debit cards in China didn't generally have cash-back, mileage points, or affiliations attached to them. Switching to mobile payment didn't mean sacrificing any associated card benefits. Compare this to the West, where the numerous card benefits make for strong card loyalty, and you can better understand why China's transition was so rapid.

For rural areas, mobile payment was positively earth-shaking. Smaller rural shop keepers leaped from isolation to suddenly having the same payment capabilities as their urban peers. Some years before the launch of mobile payment, a government modernization program helped state-owned mobile carriers provide mobile data to smaller villages. These data networks went to work, delivering real-time services to areas that lacked banking services and to small shops that didn't have money for wired connections. All it took was a low-grade smartphone, and suddenly the most remote regions had access to twenty-four-hour banking services.

Another factor that helped drive mobile payments in China was the explosion of online shopping. Alipay existed as an online payment method since 2008, so people were very familiar with online payment and absolutely loved online shopping. Going to the store in China was an experience because, in certain shops, electronics, in particular, the prices of things were flexible. Savvy negotiating skills were required to get the best price, and frankly, not everyone enjoyed the experience. With online shopping, you could search and purchase without the need to negotiate. Online shopping also achieved something far more important: it built the digital logistics and infrastructure systems used during the coronavirus lockdown.

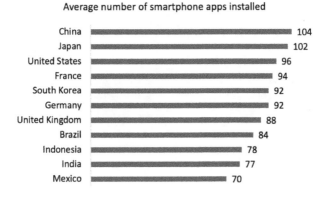

Average number of smartphone apps installed

China	104
Japan	102
United States	96
France	94
South Korea	92
Germany	92
United Kingdom	88
Brazil	84
Indonesia	78
India	77
Mexico	70

China's mobile users are the world's biggest app users highlighting their curiosity for trying something new. Data from 2017.
Source: AppAnnie, 2017 Retrospective Report

The final driver for mobile payment adoption in China is cultural, emanating from China's love of new and modern technology. People simply love gadgets here, and there is a cultural willingness to try something new, which is not evident in many other cultures. In Europe, my cousins praise things as "old and reliable," while in China, the perception of "old" means in need of replacement by something new and ideally digital. Replacing cards and cash with a more convenient system of payment just makes sense, and there was no sentimental attachment to either of those means of payment. Add to that the novelty of using something new, which in China is inherently associated with better, and there was simply no looking back.

5

QR CODES:
TECH THAT CHANGED A NATION

China on QR codes:

> *"The entry point for PC internet is the search box. The entry point for mobile internet is the QR code." (2012)*
>
> Allen Zhang, "the father of WeChat," Senior Vice President at Tencent Holdings

The West on QR codes:

> *"QR Codes are dead." (2012)*
>
> Russell Buckley, "godfather of mobile marketing," Partner at Kindred Capital, former global chairman of the Mobile Marketing Association

The humble QR code is at the heart of both Alipay and WeChat Pay's systems. It is the essential element of technology that allowed mobile payments to explode. Frankly, these systems' simplicity and ability to receive payment without a digital connection is what made them such a tremendous success. It is also why they are so suitable for export to other developing countries.

QR codes are used by mobile payment systems to give each user a digital identity when paying or receiving payment. There are two ways to make a payment using QR code systems. You can pay by simply opening your phone to the payment screen, and your QR code appears on the screen. This code is captured by either another phone's camera or the bar code scanning devices that exist at many stores. There is a ping once the scan is done, password or facial recognition entered, and your cell phone logs the purchase as complete. In this method, some form of technology is used on both sides of the transaction, yet still, the investment in new technology is negligible. The software is designed to work on just about any low-grade smartphone with a camera, making it easy to adopt, and retailers of a certain size already had the bar code scanning hardware on their point-of-sale devices.

MOBILE PAYMENT, NO TECHNOLOGY REQUIRED

Now for the second way to pay using these systems, and the reason why mobile payment conquered China. Vendors or receivers of cash can make use of this system with no technology on their side of the transaction. That's correct: they don't need anything electronic. All they need do is print out their QR code so that the person paying can scan it with their mobile phone and send the money. This made accepting electronic payment within reach of everyone. A revolution in the making, its most significant impact was on small vendors who had been excluded from using debit cards because they lacked the fixed lines and point-of-sale devices.

For simple shopkeepers and dumpling sellers in small towns and villages, digital payments were suddenly and quite miraculously within reach. They were included in this solution because they didn't need to invest anything more than the cost of going to a local photocopy shop and printing out their QR code, to become part of the digital world. Digital technology was finally at the service of all, including those without the resources to purchase access from banks. A phone was all that was needed. It was a revolution in that it allowed everyone, no matter how humble, to participate, and was the embodiment of the high ideals that both the government and private sector had for it at launch.

QR codes are so simple that you can print them out on just about anything, from electric bills to tables at restaurants. There is no limit to what could have a QR code printed on it, and this contributed significantly to the creation of the ecosystem for WeChat and Alipay that I mentioned earlier. As you walk around Shanghai, the adoption is so incredible that almost any financial transaction can be done with mobile payment, and a shocking array of things have QR codes printed on them.

The key to such widespread adoption is that with QR codes, inanimate non-digital objects can join the digital world to build an ecosystem. Consider a bill you receive in the mail from a public utility. Their investment to make use of digital payments is small. They simply need to print the QR code for your account on the bill and add some software in the back end of their systems to link their accounts to either WeChat Pay or Alipay. Restaurants could glue a plastic tag with a QR code directly on the table to allow you to order and pay without a server. Within two years, digital payments exploded in China because building an ecosystem was cheap, easy, and useful.

China achieved a virtually cashless society, something that many of us have only seen in science fiction movies. Best of all, it built it on the humble QR code, technology that was virtually written off as obsolete in the West. If there was one critical message that we need to learn from China's experience building digital currencies, it is that China built its cash-free society from the bottom up. The technology was deceptively simple, and accessible to all. Keep this in mind as we compare this with NFC technology that built from the top down in the West.

An electric bill, with WeChat Pay QR code printed on it. The magic of QR codes is their simplicity. Instructions: 1) In WeChat click scan, 2) Payment complete after confirmed. You can print QR codes anywhere at no cost.

NFC PAYMENTS

Now compare this to Apple and Google Pay's rollout in the US market. If you were an early adopter, both of these technologies required you to upgrade your phone to near field communication (NFC) enabled versions. Apple even launched Apple Pay in conjunction with the release of the newly NFC-enabled iPhone 6—a not-so-subtle message to owners of earlier versions of iPhone that they would have to upgrade and buy into using the cashless lifestyle.

Both Apple and Google Pay also required that shopkeepers update their point-of-sale systems to include the appropriate readers. The outlay in cash for both sides of the mobile payment revolution was substantial, and many smartphone users without NFC-enabled phones were simply left out. During the early years, your Starbucks may have had mobile payment, but did you notice that your smaller local coffee shop didn't? The reason is that switching to mobile payments was expensive for smaller shops, who had to wait for the price to come down and user demand to go up. It was as if the technology manufacturers were intentionally limiting the digital payment dream to those who could afford it, rather than inviting everyone to participate.

Another drawback of NFC technology is that building an ecosystem is far more difficult because it requires that special NFC tags be embedded in, or attached to, the mobile payment-enabled object. By definition, objects without the special NFC tag can't participate. In short, you can't print NFC tags on your electric bill, or paste them to your shop wall like you can a QR code. This is, in part, why some years after their launch, NFC payment is still limited. I fully consent that the use of credit cards in the West also has had an enormous impact on mobile payment use. As mentioned earlier, card users are very loyal to mileage and other card benefits and don't want to give them up. That said, the inability of NFC payment systems to build significant ecosystems of users cost these companies dearly, and it shows in their low payment volumes.

To be fair, some claim that NFC payments are more secure and offer additional functionality when compared to QR codes. NFC's other advantage is that it doesn't require the user to open an app to pay. NFC codes indeed carry about twice the data payload of QR codes, which is an additional advantage. QR codes are easy to fake, whereas NFC codes embedded in a product at the point of manufacture are more challenging to alter. So QR code's ease of use also brings some disadvantages. The new digital RMB is using both NFC and QR codes to facilitate person-to-person digital transfers. So, clearly NFC is not bad tech per se, just ill-suited to building a vast and inclusive payment network.

Indeed, security was very much a problem in early versions of QR-based payment in China. The earliest versions of mobile payment used a single QR code for both payment and receipt of funds. Fraudsters could capture an image of your payment code and then use it to pay themselves. Now both WeChat Pay and Alipay separate payment and funds receipt into two different QR codes. The payment code is generated uniquely per transaction and has a lifespan of less than a minute before it needs refreshing. By changing codes, it makes it difficult for a thief to steal your payment code and reuse it. Facial scanning, biometrics, and passwords are all among the many techniques designed to enhance the security of QR codes and mitigate any inherent security disadvantages. In 2016 Alipay reported fraud levels under 0.001 percent compared to China's bankcard industry, which was about 0.02 percent. For comparison, US credit card fraud was 0.17 percent in 2016. Alipay's experience should sway anyone claiming that QR payment systems are inherently unsafe.

One amusing example of QR code fraud occurred in Shanghai. Rental bike users were warned on TV and radio to double-check the QR code stickers attached to the bicycles. A gang of thieves had printed QR code stickers and carefully placed them on top bicycles' existing QR codes. Users would try to unlock the bike and inadvertently pay into the fraudster's account while the bike remained locked and unusable. The perpetrators were not master thieves and were caught rather quickly after leaving an easy trail of digital breadcrumbs to follow.

BIG TECH'S BUILT-IN NETWORK

It's important to understand that WeChat and Alibaba both had massive built-in networks before the launch of their payment systems, which contributed greatly to their success. Comparing their situation to the analogy of Facebook and Amazon becoming payment providers is wholly appropriate. WeChat was ubiquitous in China even before it launched payments. I have been using it for years in my home in Shanghai and witnessed firsthand the explosive growth from its initial launch in 2011. Alipay had an additional advantage in being the first online payment provider. It built the network to complement its internet sales, and still bests WeChat for payment volume. This is because Alipay tends to be more frequently used for higher-value regular transactions like rent, car or insurance payments, and has the edge over WeChat with retailers due to lower fees.

Yet on the street and within social groups, WeChat edges its older rival. It's easy to understand why: WeChat serves as China's Twitter, Facebook, and LinkedIn combined. Without it, your business and personal life would simply grind to a halt. I was amused when my former employer IBM demanded employees keep business conversations off of WeChat. All of the staff promptly ignored the order because we couldn't reach a client without it. WeChat's white-hot engagement mechanism is in its name: chat. Communication built people's attachment to the service before payment showed up, and when it did, it catapulted the service to levels never seen before in China.

Third-party mobile payment market breakdown by payment volume

- Alipay 54.2%
- WeChat Pay (Tenpay) 39.5%
- 1Qianbao 1.5%
- JD Pay 0.8%
- UMPay 0.7%
- 99 Bill 0.6%
- YeePay 0.6%
- ChinaUMS 0.5%
- Suning Pay 0.2%
- Others 1.4%

Alipay and WeChat Pay (Tenpay) command 93.7% of the mobile payment marketplace. Note Alipay's lead based on its use on higher value payments.
Source: iResearch Q2 2019

Apple and Google Pay also have large user networks. It's interesting to consider why neither of these networks has been as successful as those in China. While the use of NFC technology and the West's love of credit cards stunted their growth somewhat, there is another more insidious reason for their lack of success. Both WeChat Pay and Alipay are mobile manufacturer agnostic. You can use them on any phone, anywhere, and with anyone you choose. A user is not "buying into" anything other than the WeChat social platform or Alibaba services, which are ubiquitous in China.

Compare this with either Android or Apple; both have built walls around their merchants and users. It is evident to all that unless you own their phone, you can't use their service. Just try using Apple Pay to send money to your friend with an Android phone. Why should what phone I buy have a say over where I can spend my money or with whom I can share it? Maybe this is why Apple Pay is in millions of locations but is used for only 3% of eligible transactions by users? Loving the phone doesn't mean you have to love the payment system.

STARBUCKS AND QR CODES

Starbucks' launch of its mobile app in 2009 provides a fabulously successful example of how QR codes were trialed in the US but flew beneath the radar for many. It also shows how early adoption of mobile payment via an agnostic app helped make Starbucks a surprise giant in mobile payments. Just like China, Starbucks designed its app to embrace Apple, Android, and Blackberry users alike, and went with QR codes to defray the cost of launching the system.

To be specific, Starbucks chose QR codes as a way to digitize its physical card system by using their existing bar code scanners. No new hardware was required, and just like WeChat and Alipay, you could use the app on any phone. No new phone required for users, no new tech for Starbucks. It was a win-win for all.

Early version of Starbucks' payment app with QR codes.
Source: Starbucks

Starbucks' payment system was so successful that it eclipsed the number of mobile users of Apple and Google Pay until Q3 2019, when Apple Pay finally overtook them. Critically, Starbucks was not held back by the slow rollout of new NFC-enabled POS systems. Starbucks launched its app in 2009, while the first NFC enabled iPhone 6 models launched in 2014. The company had a five-year lead in collecting digital users, something truly unheard of in the technology space. Who says QR codes never made their mark in the US payment space?

SUPERAPPS' BEAUTY COMES FROM WITHIN

So far, I've discussed how both WeChat Pay and Alipay built substantial ecosystems based on their use of QR codes. I'd also like to devote some time to explaining why their mobile platforms are, in fact, "super." On typical cellphones, single apps cover single companies or services. Changing services means that I need to switch apps. According to the 2017 report by mobile market research firm "AppAnnie," the average smartphone user has more than 80 apps but uses only half to a third of these apps monthly. That means that most people's phones, not just yours, are jammed with them. Each installed to do something different, with each one requiring updates, logins, two-factor verification, and different payment methods. It's a mess.

Both WeChat and Alipay apps use something called "mini-programs" to bring the functionality of an outside app into their own domain. Opening a mini-program in WeChat or Alipay opens a new screen, and the service within functions like an independent program. You are still on WeChat or Alipay, but are now using an app within the app. The power in this arrangement is that the mini-program has access to your payment and user data. So if you are shopping in a mini-program, your payment is automatically handled through the super-app. Mini-programs made it easy for WeChat and Alipay to build ecosystems, because partners wanted to be on the platform, and closer to their customers.

Alipay on the left with the bike sharing mini-program Hellobike (H) in the second row of icons, in the center the Hellobike mini-program, on the right the Hellobike bike locator map opened from the mini-program. Hellobike has a complete app experience

From the standpoint of a developer, these mini-programs are a revolution. If you are designing and building a traditional mobile app to sell a product, you would need to build security, online payments, login, and registration among a host of other services into your coding to make it standalone and complete. In the mini-program world, developers can build within the walls of the super-app, and have most of these services provided ready-made. As a result, Chinese app builders can launch mini-programs quickly and at low cost, maintaining the utility of a standalone app. Mini-programs written for one platform will, with small modifications, work on the other, further reducing development costs. Note that because mini-apps need to be lightweight, there is one potential drawback. They have memory usage limits that may result in fewer features than a standalone version.

Both WeChat and Alipay have large numbers of these pro-grams. WeChat was the first to introduce the functionality, and now offers over one million programs. Alipay launched the function after WeChat, and has over 120,000 apps. While the gap may seem significant, it is essential to remember that besides having a head start, WeChat is a social and gaming platform, so the focus of the mini-programs is much broader. Alipay's mini-programs tend to focus on finance, insurance, bill paying, and practical necessities. What is interesting is that banks—all of whom lost a significant part of their payment business to mobile wallets—built mini-apps with services and advertising on the super platforms, hoping to be nearer to their clients. Capturing their own customers meant swallowing their pride.

One final thought about mini-programs. This is another example of technology the West is copying from China. In the second quarter of 2019, Google announced that it was testing "mini-apps" which would be strikingly similar to WeChat's and Alipay's mini-programs. Google's mini-apps will bring a "new capability" to Google search, opening an "app-like experience" within the search window. The parallels with the super-app's mini-programs did not go unnoticed in China and raised the question: who, exactly, is copying whom?

WHY DON'T YOU HAVE THIS, AND WHEN WILL YOU?

So you're waiting for QR code-based payment systems in your country? QR codes work, and if China and Starbucks have shown us anything, it's that QR codes are simple, effective, and secure. I think that this message got through loud and clear to both PayPal and Apple, who over the course of the writing of this book adopted QR codes in their payment systems. Dare I say another example of Western tech companies copying from China?

It's tough to keep track of the countries that have QR code-based payment systems as the market is changing very quickly, and new products come to market by the day. For now,

QR code-based systems are available in Brazil, Mexico, Singapore, India, several EU countries, and Hong Kong. Australia is developing a QR codes system for its New Payments Platform, as is the Philippines, which will launch its system this year. ASEAN countries also have QR based systems in part due to the influence of nearby China. Many countries in Africa are also using QR codes, again thanks to the influence of China. Kenya's popular M-Pesa app is one example.

A few readers in Europe may already have them, and thanks to Alipay, they are going to get bigger. Alipay recently announced a deal with eight European QR code-based systems to use Alipay's technology to make their systems interoperable as one network. This will create Europe's first QR code-based network. It shouldn't come as a surprise that the Alipay system will also work on that network.

But the biggest news for QR codes comes from Apple, which is making all things old new again, and ensuring QR codes' longevity with its Alternate Reality (AR) app Gobi. AR superimposes virtual information over the real world, and what better way to trigger an AR advertisement or notification than with a QR code? With AR, you use your camera to scan your surroundings, and when it finds a QR code, it triggers the AR event. QR's magic ingredient for our new AR world is that you can print one out and paste it wherever you wish—just like my local dumpling shop.

WATCH INDIA

Today, all eyes in the QR payment system space are on India. It may seem incredible, but WhatsApp, Amazon, and Google have all rolled out a copy of WeChat and Alipay's QR code-based payment system there. So while you can't use these systems, it is probably the most obvious example of how Western tech companies are now copying China's tech. India has become a hotbed for mobile payments since the launch of the Unified Payment Interface (UPI), an instant, real-time payment system by the National Payments Corporation of India. India now appears to be a test market for instant payment systems that may someday be launched by big tech companies in the West. While that's great for India, the rest of us have to wait.

The US, of course, led the charge with NFC payments tied to either Google or Apple Pay, so it may be a while before QR codes come to the US in the form of a standalone system. That said, individual retailers have seen the light and started to build them into their payment apps. Noteworthy users include Walmart, Target, Dunkin Donuts, and Macy's. So don't count QR codes out just yet.

6

HOW REGULATORS
DISRUPTED BANKING

China on fintech vs traditional banking:

> *"The People's Bank of China highly encourages and also cooperates with various industries to promote the development of financial technology."*
> Zhou Xiaochuan, governor of the People's Bank of China, March 2017

The West on fintech vs traditional banking:

> *"I am concerned that fintech will be the source of the next crisis."*
> James Bullard, St. Louis Fed President, January 2019

Fintech in China arose thanks to groundbreaking regulatory changes adopted by the government. In 2013-14, the tech companies Alibaba, Baidu, and WeChat were explicitly granted online private banking licenses, even though their activities would potentially overlap with those of the state banks. To understand the magnitude of the decision, think about Google, Amazon, and Facebook being granted banking licenses in the United States or Europe. The repercussions in China were enormous, just as they would be if a GAFA company were to become both your payment provider and bank in the West.

The liberalization of regulations in favor of tech companies in the financial system was part of a much bigger plan, and did not materialize out of a vacuum. China uses five-year plans to help guide the country's long-term planning and development. China's twelfth five-year plan (2011-2015) emphasized the creation of "next-generation information networks, mobile communication, and the Internet." All digital services were ramping up at a remarkable speed in China during this period, not just fintech.

THE FATHER OF FINTECH

As to digital banking and fintech specifically, the chief architect of China's modernization was PBOC governor Zhou Xiaochuan, a reformer and free-market proponent who served in his post for sixteen years. Zhou has been called "China's most able technocrat." More importantly, he was a vocal proponent of liberalization in the financial sector and, for our purposes, should be called "the father of modern fintech."

During his tenure at the PBOC, Zhou was responsible for granting some 200 licenses to third-party payment providers, creating multiple private banks, and setting up the first research institute for central bank digital currencies among major central banks. Importantly, China's fantastic fintech success was not without missteps. Zhou also presided over the Peer to Peer (P2P) loan debacle, which was so disruptive as to cause social instability. But, back to his successes, Zhou recognized digital currencies as "inevitable" and in starting the PBOC research institute, was responsible for developing China's CBDC. While no longer at the PBOC, Zhou continues to lecture regularly, and is still the consummate insider. He currently serves as president of the China

Society of Finance and Banking, and deputy director-general of the Boao Forum for Asia, China's Davos.

Zhou's decision to allow tech companies to obtain banking licenses is without precedent in the West, where the separation of tech and financial sectors is considered the norm. You may have noticed that GAFA (Google, Apple, Facebook, Amazon) companies all partner with banks to provide their limited financial services. If they were allowed to buy a bank, their tremendous financial resources would allow them to take their pick. But the intricacies of banking regulation in the West, particularly the bank reserve requirements, make these purchases impossible. When you read the fine print on products like Apple Pay, you can see that they are using banking partnerships with Goldman Sachs' digital consumer bank Marcus to deliver financial services. Similarly, Google's new checking account in the US uses both Citigroup and Stanford Federal Credit Union to provide the service. Big tech is unable to provide these services on their own, at least for now.

Market capitalization of big tech compared with US banks
US$ Trillions

By market capitalization, Google, Amazon and Apple are four times the size of all listed US banks combined. Apple alone is more than one and a half the size of all US banks. This challenges the notion held by many that banks are big.

The ability of the PBOC to willingly disrupt its banks with digital entities run by big tech needs to be put in perspective, to understand how revolutionary it is. In the US, almost all new digital banks are forced to partner with incumbents, severely limiting their product offerings and fee schedules. The Treasury Department's Office of the Comptroller of Currency (OCC) proposed a more limited fintech banking license to spur the development of digital financial services, but the proposal met with sharp rebuke by incumbents. It is now mired in the courts of New York State, where incumbent banks are heavily invested in maintaining their lock on the business. So in the US, the idea that big tech could own a bank is almost entirely out of the question, even if we were to ignore the complexity of bank reserve requirements.

Things look decidedly better in both the UK and EU, where there are specialized licensing schemes for the creation of new digital banks. The UK regulators are particularly aggressive in seeking competition to the "Big Four Banks" (HSBC, Barclays, RBS, and Lloyds Banking Group) by creating "challenger banks." The Big Four controlled 87% of personal accounts in the UK in 1987. Sadly, the limited nature of the licenses together with reserving requirements that severely limit their business models, make these initiatives particularly unattractive to big tech companies. So despite the efforts of challenger banks like Monzo, N26, and Revolut, it's hard to conceive of a big tech entity buying one. For all the talk of creating challengers, the wall between tech and banking in the West remains impossible to breach.

FINANCIAL INCLUSION AS A DRIVING FORCE

The driving force for allowing digital banking services in China was the hope that digital services would drive financial inclusion for the rural poor. The plan worked and frankly shocked regulators with the speed of adoption. Mobile payment users nearly doubled in both 2014 and 2015, showing how welcome the system was. Zhou Xiaochuan, with the encouragement of incumbent banks in early 2014, was forced to examine the digital banks' explosive growth; addressing the established banks' genuine fears after the unprecedented exodus of clients who decided to go digital, Zhou announced, "More policies will be implemented to perfect regulation."

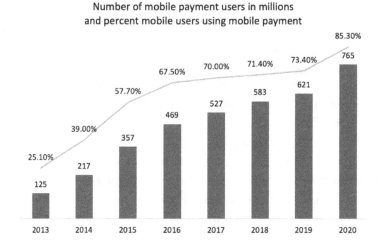

Number of mobile payment users in millions and percent mobile users using mobile payment

Mobile Payment Users in China note the huge leaps in users between 2013 and 2016, signaling the explosion in use of mobile payment.
Source: China Internet Network Information Center

Alibaba, Tencent, and Baidu built China's first truly digital banks. Like the US or EU's "neobanks," they are 100% digital and have no branches. That it took big tech to launch them is no surprise. China's incumbent banks historically had treated clients with chilling disregard. When people who were simply tired of waiting in line had an opportunity to switch to digital payment, they moved en masse.

What is noteworthy is that China was the first country to grapple with the massive regulatory changes that would cause a shock in the heart of our bank-centric financial world. It was a characteristically bold move by the government, showing tremendous faith in digital technology. What makes it all the more surprising is that the government knew the decision would potentially cannibalize profits from the state's banks. Can you imagine the passage of regulation that would sacrifice bank profits in the West?

WHAT HAPPENED TO THE BANKS?

The impact on the banking community of the tremendous migration of people off of bank cards and onto mobile payments was dramatic and shockingly fast. While far short of financially devastating for China's incumbent banks, it certainly caused them to reevaluate both their relevance in retail markets and the threat that digital banking posed. Most importantly, it forced all of their digital transformation programs into high gear.

WeChat Pay and Alipay's most significant impact was to disrupt the payment business that was tied to debit cards carried over the Union Pay network. Union Pay is essentially China's version of Visa or Mastercard, and it is majority-owned by the PBOC with China's banks as shareholders. The problem for the banks was straightforward: while mobile wallets connect to the banks' debit cards, both WeChat and Alipay do not fully use the Union Pay network. They simply created their own. This means that money incoming via the bank's debit card would not flow entirely through Union Pay's network, depriving the banks of commissions, known as interchange fees. Interchange fees are paid by the merchant's bank to the customer's bank for handling the card transaction, and are based on card transaction volume. Interchange fees are a significant source of revenue for banks.

With mobile payments, money is debited directly from the user's bank account to the mobile wallet company, and the bank does not receive an interchange fee for the transaction. Banks quickly lost interchange fee revenue, but they also lost something just as valuable: data. With a typical Union Pay transaction, the bank gets details of the transaction—what you bought, where, and when. With mobile payment, when the bank receives a withdrawal from the mobile wallet company, it only sees that it has paid WeChat or Alipay and does not know any details surrounding the payment. In an era of "big data," the loss of this consumer data might be even more significant than the loss of interchange fees received from Union Pay.

Imagine for a moment that you are a Chinese banking executive specializing in retail payments in 2016, two years after the launch and explosive growth in mobile payments. In your new world, you have to compete with digital companies that already have much more information about clients than you have, and the amount of data you have on your clients is rapidly shrinking as they shift to mobile payments. Also, you have had your revenue from Union Pay card transactions cut by a significant amount. Then of course when the opportunity arose to build mini-programs on WeChat and Alipay, the very platforms that damaged your business, you would swallow your pride and jump at the chance to get your hands on plentiful amounts of customer data.

Kapronasia, a research and consulting firm focused on the Asian financial industry, estimated the losses in transaction fees to Chinese banks in 2015 were RMB 150 billion ($US 23 billion). Further estimates based on data at the time suggested that the number would increase to RMB 400 billion ($US 61 billion) by 2020. It is hard to give these numbers perspective given the enormity of China's banks and the opaque nature of their profitability. Kapronasia estimates that card-based transaction fees represent approximately 5% to 8% of banks' revenue. This loss is not sufficient to "disrupt" incumbent banks, but it certainly hurt. Most importantly, it showed how their grip on clients was more tenuous than they perceived.

We can also look at the impact on banks from the perspective of how much money is held by mobile payments in their banking operations and compare this with actual bank deposits. Total funding in "online payment firms deposits" in August 2018 was RMB 763 billion (from Caixin Financial News), with China's total bank deposits in January 2018 hitting RMB 26,640 billion (from CEIC Data). So roughly 3% of total deposits have moved to mobile payment companies—a significant number when considering that total bank deposits include corporate accounts, but not material to the banks' financial wellbeing.

Interestingly, this data shows that while the Chinese people use mobile payments for their shopping, they still use banks for their savings. This speaks not only to their trust in China's incumbent banks but to the long-term nature of banking relations. While we will never know the exact loss numbers, the impact on banks has been significant but not enough to cause structural damage. In an earlier chapter, I stated that one of the lessons we could learn from China is that even if the West's big tech companies were to become banks tomorrow, they would not "disrupt" the existing banks. This is undoubtedly true, but as in China, competition with tech companies would force banks to reevaluate and refocus on client centricity—a significant impact, even if it falls short of disruption.

FIGHTING BACK

China's banks are, of course, fighting back. They enlisted the assistance of regulators with whom, as fellow state-owned entities, they have had long and solid relations. In January of 2019, the PBOC required that mobile payment companies hand over all payment deposits that are held on account by the payment systems. Payment deposits are monies temporarily held as the transactions wait to clear. Estimated at $US 200 billion, it was invested by payment companies in overnight deposits or short-term money markets, further contributing to their revenue.

Under the new regulations, the money is required to be transferred to the central bank and held on account. While done in the name of protecting users' funds, it removed a significant source of revenue from mobile payment providers. This revenue was used both to reduce the cost of transactions to customers, and to give the payment providers less of an advantage relative to banks. After enacting this law, both Alipay and WeChat Pay started to charge a small amount (0.1%) for certain card transactions on their platforms, to recoup costs that had been covered by this payment deposit interest income. Just as in the West, in the end, it's the customer that pays.

While it may be convenient to see Ant's thwarted IPO and run-in with regulators as motivated by banks, the real reasons are much more closely related to the regulator's responses to the P2P loan crisis. More regulatory issues relating to the P2P loan crisis and Ant Group's thwarted IPO are covered in chapters 7, 8, and 18.

7

P2P LENDING:
PART 1 THE SET-UP

China on P2P loans:

> *"It was a mission impossible ... as the number of P2P platforms was so large at the time."*
> Anonymous, China Banking and Insurance Regulatory Commission

The West on P2P loans:

> *"We go after the nearly half of Americans that have credit card debt and tell them, you have a loan, and not a very good one,"*
> Scott Sanborn, CEO, Lending Club

In 2012 my trusty Blackberry started to ping with SMS messages, a few at first, then more with increasing frequency as the year progressed. While my command of Mandarin was limited, it was clear that 15% returns were on offer and that if I acted quickly, they could be mine for the taking. My first exposure to the peer-to-peer loan (P2P) market came from this minor intrusion, but as technology progressed, the offers moved to WeChat and became even more insistent. The investment of a lifetime was waiting and now was the time.

As a foreigner lacking a China ID card, I couldn't buy, but friends assured me that an ID card could be made available by one of the less scrupulous salespersons if I asked. There was no shortage of salespeople pushing these products because there was no regulation or enforcement of who could sell them and take your money. A WeChat message from Mr. Yang, your mom's best friend, and a WeChat money transfer, was all it took to get you in on the ground floor. I knew a few expats who boasted of their investment prowess by buying into these products. I've lost touch with all of them, but more than a few Chinese friends now tell me they regret the day they invested.

NOT ALL OF CHINA'S FINTECH TURNS TO GOLD

China's P2P lending disaster shows that China's fintech industry does not have a golden touch in all sectors. This is a riveting story of the domino effect when fintech goes wrong. It also dispels any notion that the Chinese government can control and predestine the outcome of their fintech experiments because of their ability to strongarm the marketplace. If anything, the P2P crisis is an extreme example of laissez-faire government policy. What may have seemed like an excellent idea at the start eventually led to social unrest, suicides, and other human tragedy. The point is this: for all of China's fintech and digital prowess, the outcomes of any of these "fintech experiments" are not a given, and carry real risk. These lessons, learned at a high cost in China, serve as warnings to others.

P2P lending is not a new concept. It has been around since 2005, with the founding of Zopa in the UK. However, tech showed its real potential in 2006 with the launch of giants Prosper and Lending Club in the US. The goal of P2P loan platforms is to offer borrowers loans that are provided by "peers" who accept repayment risk for a fee. (While this sounds deceptively simple, the actual programs are complex.) Several benefits make P2P lending an attractive alternative to traditional financial service providers. The first is that P2P loans don't require an interview or going to the bank. You can apply online, and in general, the terms are more flexible, with better rates and shorter closing times. In many cases, the borrower can go from application to receipt of funds within several days.

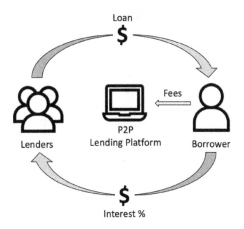

P2P lending platforms match borrowers and lenders.

In theory, P2P lenders can offer better rates than traditional banks because they digitized the lending process. Application, evaluation, and collection from delinquent accounts became more efficient. Moreover, eliminate brick-and-mortar locations and highly paid loan officers, and you've got a stripped-down internet loan machine that works 24/7 to connect borrowers and lenders. This internet-based efficiency compresses the costs ordinarily sunk in a middleman, allowing for reduced rates to the borrower and increased returns to the lender. Compared with applying to a bank, home equity loans, or running up credit card debt, P2P lending represents an efficient and practical way of obtaining a loan.

What makes P2P even more compelling is that it readily takes on individuals with bad or no credit scores, those who are underserved by traditional banks, and digitally inclined younger people. It makes credit accessible to groups who were previously overlooked by banks and does it non-judgmentally. P2P is an ideal example of how fintech can disrupt incumbent banks with a product that does the job more efficiently, and reaches people that the banks had frankly ignored.

US REGULATORY WARNING IGNORED

The P2P concept is straightforward, but the history of P2P in the US should have been fair warning to China that this market was best not left to its own devices. Starting in 2006, P2P lenders in the US operated without much regulation. The early versions of these companies had few restrictions on borrower eligibility. This caused adverse selection, attracting borrowers who would default on their loans, resulting in high loss rates. Still, according to the Federal Deposit Insurance Corporation (FDIC), by the end of 2007 the P2P market had an estimated volume of $600 million. Perhaps not enough to ruffle the incumbent banks, but certainly enough to draw the attention of the Securities and Exchange Commission (SEC).

> *The SEC admitted that P2P had no regulatory home, a problem that would also plague China's P2P market.*

By early 2008, the SEC closed shop on all P2P lenders, including Prosper. In what would later turn out to be a stroke of genius, Lending Club voluntarily ceased operations in 2007 just before SEC closure. The SEC closed these lenders because it deemed that the notes issued to the lenders could be considered securities offered to the general public, and as such, amounted to investments. Consequently, the P2P lenders would have to be registered by the SEC and cease operations until they received the necessary certification. In another interesting twist, the SEC commented that there was "no alternative regulatory scheme" that could adequately reduce investor's risks. The SEC was essentially admitting that P2P had no regulatory home, a problem that would also plague China's P2P market.

Timing and context are crucial; it's important to note that P2P lenders in the US may have been victims of circumstance. The global financial crisis and "Great Recession" of December 2007 to June 2009 played a significant part in changing the course of the US's P2P markets. One reason why the SEC came down so hard was the prior abuse of sub-prime lending that contributed to the financial crisis. The optics of allowing comparable lending to low-credit borrowers without regulation may have been too much for the SEC to bear at a time of global economic upheaval. Unwittingly, raising the stakes for P2P lenders by requiring them to acquire a costly SEC registration resulted in the closing of all but Lending Club and Prosper.

When Lending Club reopened in 2008, it was a different world, one that was desperate for credit. Following the financial crisis, home prices were in free fall, and the home equity loan market, once viewed as a "credit card" for your house and a popular way to borrow, was gone. Given the rise in foreclosures and the decrease in loan collateral value, banks and lenders of all types were reeling and simply curtailed lending as they did their best to reevaluate their risks. Borrowers had no place to go, and P2P exploded. When Lending Club opened in 2008, it was the only game in town. Prosper opened six months later but was never able to overcome the delay.

The reason this is so important is that it demonstrates the efforts the SEC made in 2007 to regulate the P2P market in the US. Interestingly, these steps were taken after the lending market was launched, reinforcing the point that the speed of new technology adoption may exceed regulators' ability to react. The irony? Sub-prime lending was conducted in a heavily regulated market, yet still collapsed. Perhaps this was not lost on the Chinese government, who knew about P2P regulation in the US market but chose not to implement it themselves. We will never know why, but what becomes clear at the end of China's P2P crisis is that this mode of lending—as had been the case in the US—did not have an obvious home amid China's regulators.

CHINA'S NEED FOR CREDIT

Now imagine we are in China and it's 2007. This is not the China of today, at the fore of digital invention. In this year, China's internet companies were still searching for the right formula for success, and copying from the US was a way of life. The US's early successes with P2P made it an obvious target. Paipaidai (PPDAI Group Inc.), the first P2P loan company in China, was born in 2007 and would list on the NYSE. Unlike their US counterparts, the playing field was unregulated. Anyone could set up a platform, as the underlying technology was not particularly hard to replicate. The seeds sprouted like weeds, and by 2015 the market peaked with 4,000 P2P lenders.

The factors that made P2P so popular in the US helped propel it to even greater heights in China. The ease of using online platforms (in a country with a significant unbanked population) made it an immediate success. Consumer credit in China was highly underdeveloped when Paipaidai launched. While almost the entire banked population held debit cards by this time, the penetration of credit cards was, and remains, very low. Getting a credit card in 2007 was a lengthy process reserved for the upper echelon of the wealthy who traveled abroad and had ready access to considerable funds. For everyone else, credit was hard to come by. The government loved P2P as it would help to cover the gap in lending promulgated by largely unresponsive state-owned banks. The ability of P2P to provide credit for the masses of SMEs was both practical and essential in speeding China's development, and senior officials publicly praised the new system. Sadly, much of this praise would later be manipulated by P2P lenders to entice investors.

> *Bank lending was next to impossible for ordinary people, who had no data for the banks to evaluate.*

As noted previously, a critical feature of P2P lending is its availability to those with low credit scores. This is perfect for China, where there were no credit scores for the majority of the population. While this may seem odd to readers who know their credit score by heart, national credit scoring didn't exist in China until the founding of government-sponsored Baihang Credit arrived in 2018. The PBOC did have the Credit Reference Center, founded in 2006, but it had access only to bank data on personal account balances. This limitation meant that it had an incomplete picture of people's financial history and did not have data on the large part of the population without accounts. The lack of credit rating technology contributed to making bank lending next to impossible for ordinary people, who had no data for the banks to evaluate.

That P2P lending could circumvent the banks and deliver a loan to someone who had never borrowed before and had no history was, and remains, a significant accomplishment. To fill this gap, Ant Financial and Tencent are devoting tremendous resources to developing credit scores based on big data on their internet platforms. In the absence of credit ratings, big data is a logical alternative, and precisely why Baihang Credit aggregates data from eight privately run credit rating systems. It will ultimately become the collection machine for all credit data in China.

The real fuel for P2P in China was mobile phones. By 2010 the Chinese government had rolled out mobile data connections to the country's most remote regions, and within a few years, residents started converting to smartphones. For the first time, data was available on mobile devices, even in villages that never dreamed of having a bank or investment services. Mobile data is the final and most crucial piece of the puzzle that contributed to P2P's explosive growth in China, as well as the great success of payment apps WeChat Pay and Alipay.

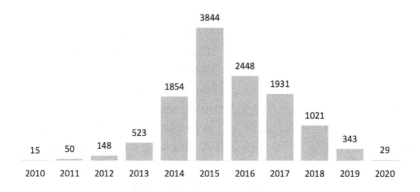

The number of online P2P lending platforms in China from 2010 to 2020. In total, the market had as many as 6,600 platforms.
Source: WangDaiZhiJia

The first and only computer many will ever own in China is their mobile phone. Once P2P went onto mobile platforms, everyone had access to a loan, regardless of their intent or ability to pay it back. Similarly, on the investor side, a love of investing and following the booming stock market made high yield P2P investments a viable option for investors who could easily earn 10% to 15%, when savings accounts were yielding roughly 2.5%. Many Chinese did not understand that the loans might not be repaid, and that they shouldered significant investment risk. Unscrupulous platforms touted the high returns, safety, and convenience of P2P lending, but never the risks.

What is fascinating is that the perfect storm of the global financial crisis and recession, which contributed to P2P industry regulation in the US, worked to help keep it unregulated in China. It is almost as though the global financial crisis acted in opposite directions in these two countries. The global financial crisis caused the US to crack down and restrict lending due to wide-scale abuses in sub-prime mortgages, while in China it created a rapid drop in factory orders, which caused the government to rely on credit to compensate for the loss of industrial production.

China needed credit in two very different places. First, credit was required by state-owned entities and private sector construction companies to pay for massive infrastructure and housing development programs, to keep employment and growth at high levels. Next, on a smaller scale—one that was perfectly suited to P2P lending—the government stimulated its nascent service sector to reduce the economy's reliance on manufacturing. This required opening credit lines to small businesses throughout the country to help them finance new ventures.

THE DIGITAL PONZI SCHEME

How people lost money in P2P loans closely mirrors age-old Ponzi schemes, brought to the digital age with a few new twists. In the most basic case, P2P lenders simply stole the money outright through creating fraudulent loan entries and would then route the funding for these loans into their accounts. To pay back early investors, the P2P lender would simply issue more loans and repay investors with new funds—proof that twenty percent returns were possible. This was a Ponzi scheme for the digital age, with predictable results.

The high-profile closure of P2P lenders using this fraudulent scheme shook China. Shanghai's Shanlin closed in 2018 and stole an estimated $US 9 billion from some 500,000 investors. Ezubao closed in 2016, taking an estimated $US 7.6 billion from some 900,000 investors. The lethality of these fraudsters and the ease with which they could create ersatz digital loan requests on their systems was a direct result of the absence of any government supervision or control. In retrospect, this makes the US's requirement that P2P lenders register with the SEC seem more than prudent.

Add to this fraud a uniquely Chinese part of the sales pitch, making investors, who could invest as little as one RMB, feel secure. Their returns were "guaranteed" by the P2P company—in fact, both interest and principal were guaranteed. Now, given that the P2P companies were operating as Ponzi schemes, these guarantees cost the P2P company nothing and brought in investors by the millions. Guarantees offered by honest P2P companies, and there were some, were paid from the enormous spread that they were making between borrowers and lenders.

GOVERNMENT GUARANTEED: "AS SEEN ON TV"

As if the P2P companies' guarantee wasn't enough, many P2P platforms touted that the investments clients were buying had the government's implicit support. In China, investments traditionally involved state-owned enterprises that came with an unwritten guarantee that the government would step in and rescue investors if the entity failed or faced difficulty. To illustrate, there were no corporate debt defaults in the China markets up through 2014. So local investors felt that outright losses were not only unlikely, but wouldn't be allowed by the government.

P2P platforms played with this historical assurance of government support to gain investor confidence. Every trick in the book was in play: associating themselves with local politicians, touting the government's praise of P2P lending, partnering with state-owned enterprises, and running advertisements on state-run TV. For unsophisticated investors (and it is essential to remember that for many in China, investing in private companies was then and still is a relatively new concept), the close relationship with the government was proof of tacit government support for the P2P investments.

> *Many saw state TV running ads featuring the government and a P2P lender.*

Unlike in Western markets where "As Seen On TV" has become a warning to stay away, the state-owned broadcasting networks in China are rightly perceived as extensions of the government, and are trusted. That state-run TV had changed to an advertising-based model and willingly ran P2P advertisements to raise revenue was lost on many. Many simply saw state TV running ads featuring the government and a P2P lender, so it must be a good deal. At the same time, the government was issuing warnings that the P2P companies were private, and like all new forms of private investment, including the stock market, were not subject to government support. So to the government's credit, they were advising investors that this was a brave new world, but old mindsets die hard.

Other changes made to the P2P model helped to further the fraud. Most of the P2P companies did away with the direct matching of borrowers and lenders, and instead used a portfolio of loans (fund pools) whose constituents were impossible to check. Investors received returns based on the portfolio's performance, essentially a black box, and as long as the returns kept flowing, no one ever asked what was inside. Perpetuating this particular fraud is even easier for the P2P company, as a company did not need to show actual borrowers' personal IDs. Dangerously, it gave the P2P company total control of the value of the pool. There is a certain irony that the assembly of these loan portfolios closely resembled sub-prime loan securitization in US markets, which had similarly disastrous results even with considerable regulation.

CHINA'S P2P AND US SECURITIZATION CONVERGE

Many P2P platforms did not intentionally defraud their investors with fraudulent loans, but pushed the P2P concept to the brink with exotic risk and questionable investment structures. As intermediaries, P2P lenders should not have taken any actual positions in the loans on their platforms. They were meant to simply match borrowers and lenders and receive a fee. However, during the run-up to the disaster, many P2P lenders moved out of matching personal loans and into business lending, creating securitization-like structures reminiscent of notorious Collateralized Debt Obligations (CDOs) in the US market. P2P lenders had gone full circle to become quasi-banks, and all of their activities were "guaranteed."

> *The entire P2P sector became known as the "shadow banking system."*

The transactions grew so large that the entire P2P sector became known as the "shadow banking system," given that they supported China's corporate debt from companies large and small. P2P lenders would regularly make loans to sizable companies who had been rejected by banks or could not even apply. To be fair, the problem for small and medium enterprise (SME) businesses in China was not one of creditworthiness. Many SMEs were simply not well served by banks and had no other route apart from P2P lenders or local loan sharks.

For the private investors in P2P, these high-value loans to corporate entities were fraught with risk that far exceeded that of lending to private individuals. Worse, investors took these risks with relatively little underwriting information. Neither the investors nor the P2P company made an informed decision as to the appropriateness of the investments. In many cases, high-yield loans from companies nearing bankruptcy were lumped into loan portfolios to add short-term returns at the expense of the investors' long-term capital preservation.

This highlights the final problem with P2P lenders: duration mismatch. P2P lenders used short-term investments to fund long-duration loans. This creates a fundamental problem when clients want to cash out of the fund. Liquidating longer-term illiquid assets was often impossible or required selling at a substantial loss. When clients are all buying into the fund, this does not present a problem, but given a run on the fund, where large numbers of investors seek to cash out simultaneously, it's a death sentence. Of course, P2P lenders did not necessarily have an equity stake in the loan pool, so by stuffing their portfolio with these larger, riskier loans, they would increase their fees with no personal risk. Interestingly, the lack of equity stake and duration mismatch problems parallel the failure of sub-prime loan markets in the US.

8

P2P LENDING:
PART 2 THE KNOCKDOWN

China on P2P regulation:

> *"The authorities had no toolbox to supervise the firms; there was no offsite surveillance. This is why it all went wrong."*
> Anonymous, China Banking and Insurance Regulatory Commission

The West on regulation during the global financial crisis:

> *"In addition, our regulatory system was Balkanized, outdated and lacked the infrastructure to oversee these markets."*
> Hank Paulson, former Secretary of the Treasury, CEO of Goldman Sachs

The Chinese government's reaction to the P2P crisis was step-wise, logical, and reasonably planned. Each year saw additional regulation heaped on P2P lenders to curtail their activities. At all points, the government took reasonable steps, any one of which might have worked to rein in the crisis, if P2P markets weren't digital. For the first time in China and probably in the world, a large-scale retail fintech solution came off the rails, and regulators were left trying to pick up the pieces with tools designed for a non-digital era.

2015 AND THE SHANGHAI MARKET CRASH

P2P started to show signs of stress toward the second half of 2014. The government knew it had a problem, but when "Wangdaizhijia" (网贷之家—"Online Loan House"), a P2P lender information site, showed troubling statistics at the start of 2015, things became ominous. Wangdaizhijia reported that of 1,575 total P2P platforms, 275 were reported by users to have liquidity problems, sixty reported owners that ran away with funds, and seventy-one were labeled as scams. By June, as many as a quarter of all P2P lenders had closed, but ironically enough, people continued to invest. Believing that P2P lenders were both guaranteed and, in some cases, government-supported, the message that P2P wasn't "as advertised" didn't reach the populace.

Monthly transaction volume for online P2P lending platforms from 2014 to 2019. Note growth in 2015 and 2016 after P2P problems were fully evident.
Source: WangDaiZhiJia

As if the news of P2P failures wasn't disruptive enough, it was followed by the 2015 summer Shanghai Stock Exchange "turbulence" that removed about one-third of the market value. This shocked the system, laying bare P2P's excesses and removing any hope of piloting the P2P market to a soft landing. The market disruption stressed both sides of the P2P equation. Borrowers flush with cash from the rising stock market suddenly found themselves unable to repay loans. In contrast, lenders suddenly found themselves hit by losses driven by borrower defaults that they could ill afford after the "turbulence." The crisis also abruptly signaled regulators that there was another problem hidden in plain sight with the booming economy: many of the P2P loans had gone to finance purchases of equities and housing down payments that helped fuel bubbles in both markets.

One has to wonder if Chinese authorities could have managed the P2P crisis to a less dramatic ending were it not for the stock market disruption. Instead, the market turmoil forced massive regulatory changes, in an interesting parallel with US regulators and the sub-prime crisis. While I grant that the markets are very different, in both cases regulators were aware of market excesses but lacked the regulatory control to correct them until after the crash. In both cases, technology was critically able to evade the state's regulatory power.

China's regulators started with simple laws requiring that P2P platforms use the custodial services of established banks and provide better disclosures to customers of the potential risks. Most importantly, it made the crucial decision to put P2P lenders under the China Banking Regulatory Commission. While prudent, this move would not result in the speedy resolution that one might assume. China's regulators also began an extensive campaign to warn investors about the perils of P2P loans. These warnings fell on deaf ears due to China's extraordinarily high growth, nearing eight percent in prior years. People were still investing.

2016 AND EZUBAO COLLAPSE

2016 saw even more dramatic laws enacted following the dramatic collapse of Ezubao. With losses estimated at $US 7.6 billion impacting nearly a million investors, mostly common people, Ezubao laid bare the full extent of the crisis. The introduction of new regulations came in several waves. The first called for province-level agencies to stop registering all new companies with "finance" (金融) in their name as a way to prevent the formation of new P2P companies. While this may seem an odd strategy, the majority of P2P companies did use the term "finance," so this measure would act as a stopgap.

The law also prohibited using portfolios of loans and required that P2P companies return to their origins of matching individual borrowers and lenders. Later in the year, further regulations forbid P2P lenders from accepting deposits, guaranteeing principal on loans, and using any structure to mimic securitization. Also, P2P platforms could no longer finance their projects, depriving them of the ability to build Ponzi schemes. Rules also put caps of RMB 200,000 and RMB 1,000,000 on personal and company loans, respectively.

Average P2P Investment Return

The average annual return of online P2P lending platforms in China from 2014 to 2020.
Source: WangDaiZhiJia

These laws fundamentally deleveraged the P2P business model and were prudent. They forced P2P lenders back into their traditional role of intermediaries rather than acting as shadow banks. While better-run P2P lenders focusing on SME and personal lending could survive under these constraints, it was a death sentence for others. Many P2P lenders found it impossible to support their existing business with such a highly constrained portfolio. The problem was that for some lenders, closure was a last resort, and they would continue to defraud until regulators locked their doors.

In addition to the changes described above was one deemed by a special working group formed under the banking regulator. It would require provincial-level licensing for all P2P companies, with a deadline of 2017. The decision to pass the licensing requirements to the provinces would prove to be a critical misstep, as many provinces were ill-equipped to handle this task.

PROVINCES AND P2P

In 2017 the message was clear that the new regulations passed in 2016 would make the business models of many P2P lenders unsustainable. Enforcement teams authorized by the banking regulator curtailed the activities of the more outrageous companies, who were doomed by the prior year's regulatory changes. At the same time, new laws from 2016 were phased in to end P2P companies' investment guarantees. Investors were shocked to discover that their "surefire" investments were anything but.

At the provincial level, the lenders' licensing did not go well and required postponement until June 2018. Many of the provinces simply didn't have the workforce to deal with hundreds of new lenders. Local regulators also did not want to be in a position of "approving" a P2P lender when there were no countrywide standards to follow; understandably, provincial officials did not want that responsibility. Adding to the problem, P2P lenders had financed many province-level infrastructure projects, forging relationships that local officials were uncomfortable about disrupting. This delay proved fateful as it kicked the problem down the road for another year.

Amusingly, the big banks also have a part to play in this story. According to the new rules, P2P lenders had to keep custodial accounts of customer funds. Big banks, however, were reluctant to open their accounts for fear of becoming involved in eventual blow-ups. Regulatory efforts to reel in P2P lenders and force them to place assets in custodial accounts and registration fell behind schedule. From a regulator's perspective, both of these measures were entirely rational and reasonable for traditional banking or financial services firms, but not so for P2P.

THE CRISIS HITS THE STREETS

In July of 2018, people's frustration with P2P markets reached the boiling point. Protestors in Shanghai and Beijing took to the streets over the default of some 250 P2P lenders in June and July. While mild by external standards, the protests were shocking for China and laid open the depth of the problem. The dramatic closure at the end of April of Shanlin Finance, with US$ 9 billion in losses, also fueled raw fear that *all* P2P lenders were fraudulent. In total, 1,738 P2P lenders were closed from the start of the new regulations in 2016 to July of 2018. An estimated forty percent of all P2P lenders were Ponzi schemes. A once-respected fintech industry was in free-fall.

It is crucial to understand that the majority of P2P lenders were closed without incident. While their business models may have been flawed, they did not defraud investors so much as they provided poor returns. Still, millions of investors faced significant losses as the lenders closed, and for many, this was a shock. The sudden realization that the government would not guarantee the returns on these products and that no help was forthcoming drove them to protest.

The concept of expecting the government to pay for investment losses may seem strange to Western readers, but that had been the Chinese government's policy for many years with state-run enterprises. Another factor that may be considered strange is that citizens held the government's power in such high regard that it was inconceivable for the government to let this happen. Just to make the scenario more chaotic, the founders of some of the P2P platforms disappeared, and others were arrested as they attempted to escape to foreign countries. It was an unsettling moment for a government that prides itself on providing social harmony.

PICKING UP THE PIECES

In August 2020, the China Banking and Regulatory Commission chairman, Guo Shuqing, announced that investors lost more than RMB 800 billion (US$ 115 billion) in P2P markets. Asset recovery for defunct P2P lenders may eventually return some funds to investors, but this is a long and arduous process. Four years after Ezubao's spectacular crash, its 900,000 investors received a paltry 35% of their investment. Part of the problem is that each of the lenders had its own unique tangled web of investments, which must be painstakingly sorted. A government analysis of problem P2P platforms showed that 42% simply ran off with customer funds. In 33% of cases where investors had "difficulty withdrawing," most lenders will be allowed to run off their loan books or work with asset managers to return some principal to investors. While this may be inconvenient, at least there is the prospect of resolution and the return of some funds depending on borrower repayment.

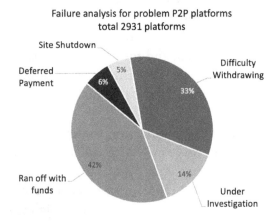

Failure analysis for problem P2P platforms
total 2931 platforms

A government analysis of 2,931 problematic P2P platforms found 42% of P2P lenders simply ran off with the funds.
Source: WangDaiZhiJia

Stolen assets from China's P2P companies were sent offshore to buy properties in major cities or were hidden in foreign banks and are difficult to trace. In 2020, the jailing of executives involved with P2P is still a regular occurrence, and the scandal reaches into the highest circles. Recently the head of the Zendai Group in Shanghai, a prominent billionaire property tycoon who founded one of the city's more significant art museums, surrendered to police. One of Zendai's units was a P2P lender that collapsed with RMB 3.3 billion in outstanding loans. Arrests are ongoing, and the wound is still open.

DEATH AND BIRTH OF INDUSTRIES

China's P2P lending business is now completely gone, with the last P2P lender having closed in November 2020. The final blow came exactly a year earlier when the government gave the five hundred or so remaining players one year to clear out all loans on their books and two years to convert to regulated lenders. PingAn's subsidiary Lufax, an industry leader with a stellar history, exited the business in late 2019, finalized its transformation into an asset manager, and listed on the NYSE in November 2020. With lending technology rivaling Ant or WeChat, Lufax was one of the few to successfully transition out of P2P and certainly the only to list abroad. Government statistics show that as of December 2019, of 3,339 P2P lenders, 76% were closed, 20% were in run-off, and a mere 3% transformed into new entities like Lufax.

In the aftermath, the People's Bank of China is requiring all lending records from active and inactive P2P lenders to be sent to the state-run credit database Baihang Credit. The actions are a strong signal from the government that it will act against defaulters and proceed with the arduous process of collecting defaulted loans. As in the West, where credit rating is ubiquitous, those who defaulted can expect reduced access to financial services in the future. The problem is that in the aftermath of P2P lending, this may take a while.

The end of P2P loans is by no means the end of digital credit in China. Loan platforms based on big data operated by WeChat and Alipay, among others, have already filled the gap for SME and personal lending that P2P lenders once hoped to fill. Fans of agile software development are familiar with the "fail fast" philosophy. When something doesn't work, you cut your losses and move on and try something else as quickly as possible. China fintech markets are the embodiment of "fail fast." P2P's failure meant simply that it needed to be replaced with something better. We will cover these new lending platforms in chapter 17.

The final element of the P2P debacle has more profound social ramifications. Many who obtained loans from P2P companies that failed have now decided that they don't have to repay because the companies have folded. In fact, during the crisis, reports indicate that people intentionally took loans from lenders that they thought would fail, with the express intent of non-payment. The government is working to inform everyone that debts have to be repaid, or face the consequences. The impact on the social fabric is severe— many who lost money are friends, relatives, and neighbors of those who took loans but don't want to repay them. P2P loans shattered the dreams of millions of ordinary people in China, many of whom regard the event just as Westerners view the global financial crisis.

The government does have a solution for this; it's called the social credit system. Yes, China's social credit system is controversial, but it was partly born out of the chaos of the P2P crisis and the desire to hold people accountable for their debts. Credit rating systems are an essential part of life in the West, with societal emphasis on credit scores bordering on maniacal. It's essential to understand why China's social credit is considered vital to repairing the damage caused by the P2P crisis, and why ordinary Chinese support the strict penalties imposed.

DIGITAL VERSUS ANALOG REGULATION

Why did Chinese regulators allow the P2P lending crisis? There is no single answer, but the best explanation is that digital technology clashed with analog regulators. Seeing P2P as a potential solution to a real problem of providing credit, senior officials were willing to give it a fair amount of freedom in hopes that the technology would work. China needs solutions that efficiently distribute credit to its people in the absence of banks which, in 2007 when P2P started, were unable to fill that role. So to say that the government had a laissez-faire attitude toward P2P lending is correct.

China's government also loves high tech, and I believe that they were willing to treat this new technology gently since all previous digital investments had worked out so well. It was simply not on the radar as something that could blow up and not be under the purview of any specific regulatory body. It was a digital solution in an analog regulatory world and simply fell through the cracks.

The fateful moment came in 2016 when regulators in Beijing treated P2P lenders like a traditional bank and pushed lenders' registration back down to the provinces. A perfectly reasonable decision when dealing with conventional banks. P2P lenders, though, weren't banks, and the provincial regulators were unprepared to deal with these new digital companies. It delayed reform for about a year and allowed fraudulent P2P lenders to amass even more funds. Lack of guidance or criteria as to what these new and untested digital lenders should have in their accounts also added to the general state of confusion. There was simply nothing for regulators to enforce. Traditional regulatory methods ran into the digital age and clashed.

Whether regulators could have avoided the events of the summer of 2018 is anyone's guess, but I think so. The regulators' inability to quickly defuse the P2P bomb in a way that investors could understand was a key factor, especially following the stock market crash of the summer of 2015. Allowing tension to build up with investors, who lived for a full year with stress-inducing uncertainty about their investments, could not have helped and certainly aggravated the outcome.

> *P2P was China's first attempt*
> *at fintech at scale*

Remember that P2P launched before e-payments on WeChat and Alipay, which were both required to become licensed financial institutions. While not commonly recognized as such, P2P was China's first attempt at fintech at scale. It conducted business relatively quietly for five years from its launch in 2007 to 2012 before it caught on. This would support an argument that it quietly slipped through the slow-moving analog gears of China's regulatory system until it exploded at such a pace that it outstripped regulators' ability to keep up.

WHAT THE P2P CRISIS REVEALS TO THE WEST

The P2P crisis reveals three critical points that will surprise some in the West. First, the Chinese government is not omnipotent. In the West, many view China's government and substantial bureaucracy as all-controlling. It most decidedly is not, and P2P lending is perhaps one of the better examples of its vulnerability. Second, China took a laissez-faire approach toward P2P lending for the first eight years of its existence. P2P's development shows again how China's fintech markets don't obey the top-down "command and control" philosophy many people associate with this nation. Finally, analog regulators are ill-equipped to deal with problems that occur at the shocking speeds of digital technology. China's regulators made some good decisions, but they came too late or were too slow to implement. If there is any lesson to be learned from China's experience, it is this above all others.

MORE REGULATION?

The P2P crisis would appear to be a strong case in favor of regulation of fintech activities to ensure that they do not create market bubbles. That sounds logical and would have helped avoid some of the problems faced with China's P2P market. However, when we examine the undeniable parallels with the US's sub-prime mortgage crisis that occurred in heavily regulated markets, the argument weakens.

Further defusing this argument, in 2016 the Lending Club, which was subject to significantly more regulation than its China-based counterparts, also managed to get in hot water when it pumped up its loan sales by selling large blocks of loans with fraudulent data to institutional investors. The CEO of Lending Club was fired along with several senior managers, and the stock price collapsed. So while it may seem facile to say more regulation is necessary, the more significant issue is that digital technology accentuates the potential to defraud and reduces regulators' time to react. In October 2020, Lending Club threw in the towel and stopped offering investments to private investors, marking the near end of P2P lending in the US.

Perhaps it is not further regulation that is required so much as more diligent confirmation that new digital technology is used "as advertised." In both sub-prime and China's P2P markets, the use of technology transformed into something unrecognizable from their original intent. P2P started as a benign matching engine, just as sub-prime began as a means of securitizing competently underwritten loans. The problems started when these technologies morphed into something not envisioned when they first hit the market. So more regulation? Sure, but the kind that monitors the use of these products, to ensure that they do not deviate too radically from their original intent, and which also has the ability of reacting with lightning speed to digital markets.

Chinese regulators just may have taken this lesson to heart. Their admonishment to Ant Group in the aftermath of its failed IPO to "return to its roots of electronic payment" bears this out. The regulator's response to Ant's IPO is far too frequently viewed in isolation. Instead, it should be seen as a direct result of the P2P crisis. Regulators shell-shocked from P2P could not bear to sit idly by and run the risk, however remote, of repeating the same mistake. We will cover this topic more thoroughly in chapter 18 on Ant.

PART 2

Version 2.0
Digital Payment
Central Bank
Digital Currencies
(CBDCs)

9

WHAT IS A CENTRAL BANK
DIGITAL CURRENCY?

China on the evolution of digital currencies:

> *"It is an irresistible trend that paper money will be replaced by new products and new technologies."*
>
> Zhou Xiaochuan, former People's Bank of China Governor

The West on the evolution of digital currencies:

> *"Central banks should issue their own digital currencies to replace a crisis-prone banking system and shut out cryptocurrencies."*
>
> Nouriel Roubini, Professor of Economics, New York University

COVID-19's greatest legacy to the financial system may be that it made us all question the need for cash. Let's face it, when a potentially deadly disease is spreading across the globe, no one wants to reach over the counter for change, stick a wad of cash in their pocket, or enter their PIN on a touchpad with an ungloved hand.

In February 2020, the Guangzhou branch of China's central bank announced it would destroy banknotes collected from hospitals, wet markets, and buses to ensure the safety of cash—disinfecting all other notes before circulation. Similarly, the US Federal Reserve announced that it would quarantine all US dollar banknotes repatriated from Asia for seven to ten days before being reintroduced into the banking system. If governments were concerned about the transmission of coronavirus by cash, the message is clear: we should be too.

The quarantine measures were not unfounded. Researchers from Australia's National Science Agency report that SARS-CoV-2, a strain of virus related to COVID-19, can live on banknotes for up to 28 days. While the chances of getting a virus from cash may be small, it is certainly not zero, and prudence dictates that we avoid contact. Concerns over banknote contamination made contactless payments increase worldwide, with Visa announcing a 150% increase in contactless usage in the US between March and May 2020. MasterCard provides the definitive answer as to the cause of the shift. In a global poll conducted in April 2020, MasterCard found 82% of its users see contactless payments as cleaner than cash. Coronavirus is radically accelerating the pre-existing trend of going cashless.

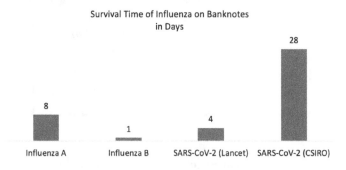

Influenza survival time on banknotes.
Source: Thomas et al (2008), Chin et al (2020) Lancet, Australia National Science Agency (CSIRO)

The rise in contactless payment instigated by COVID-19 spurred governments worldwide to hasten their plans to introduce digital currencies. According to a Bank of International Settlements (BIS) study conducted before the pandemic, some 80% of central banks were working on CBDCs—up from 70% the year prior. The BIS is an international financial institution owned by central banks that serves as a bank for central banks and provides important research on central bank policy. That increase was due to China and Facebook's efforts in digital currencies. After COVID-19, central banks went from studying CBDCs as a nicety to accelerating their launch in earnest. Even the BIS, which before the coronavirus advocated a cautious approach, later stated in a bulletin that "The pandemic may amplify calls to defend the role of cash—but also calls for central bank digital currencies."

The European Central Bank also slightly altered course. In May 2020, Yves Mersch, a member of the Executive Board of the ECB, announced that "a retail CBDC, accessible to all, would be a game-changer," despite seeing the "lack of a concrete 'business case' for a CBDC at present." The most surprising development arose in the US. An initial version of the coronavirus stimulus bill included a plan to create a digital dollar to speed payment of stimulus checks. While not a true CBDC, this development stunned the fintech world. The plan didn't survive to the final bill, but it put everyone on notice that a digital dollar was not just a pipe dream.

CBDCs have both advantages and disadvantages relative to the existing banking system. But before we examine the China initiatives in particular, it's important to understand the underpinnings of central bank digital currencies in general, to better grasp why they are essential to our digital future. We need to understand the big picture before making a case for (or against) their use.

WHAT IS A CENTRAL BANK DIGITAL CURRENCY?

CBDCs, as the name implies, are digital currencies that have the backing of the central bank of the governments that issue them. They have the same value as the currency of the country of issue because they are the digital representation of that currency. So one euro or Chinese RMB of digital currency is the equivalent of one unit of that currency in paper money. One critical aspect that is often misunderstood: CBDCs are not the same as cryptocurrencies (even if they share some characteristics).

> *CBDCs are not the same as cryptocurrency*

Cryptocurrencies like Bitcoin, Ethereum, or Tether are digital assets that function as a medium of exchange and exist only on digital ledgers. They exist independently of governments, and they trade on exchanges that convert their value into local currencies. CBDCs owe their existence to cryptocurrencies, but they couldn't be more different. The former is the official currency of a country, the later an independent asset or store of value. Enthusiasts of cryptocurrency follow CBDCs with great interest. They ascribe the development of government CBDCs as a validation of cryptocurrencies. The intertwining of the two is so tight that the price of cryptocurrencies may go up with the announcement of new CBDC projects. That cryptocurrencies and CBDCs regularly arise in the same conversation creates a connection that does not exist apart from some shared technology.

As I mentioned in the chapter on Alipay and WeChat Pay, apart from cash, our money is already digital. China's mobile payment systems might be called Version 1.0 digital currency because they are already, in fact, completely digital. They move account "balances" through the existing payment networks digitally. Note the term "balances." In our current systems, we are not shifting digital currency per se when we make a mobile payment.

Instead, we are shifting account balances, figures on digital led-gers in banks. Using Apple Pay to pay a friend means that ledger items are moved at two corresponding banking institutions, with Apple Pay as the conduit for transmitting the change in entries. Our phone shows us the bank balance, but of course the money is not in the phone.

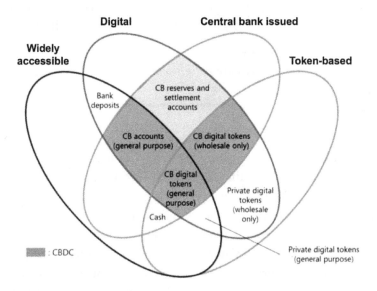

The "money flower" helps to define the role of CBDCs relative to other forms of money. The Venn-diagram illustrates the four fundamental properties of money- issuer: central bank or not; form: digital or physical; accessibility: widely accessible or restricted; technology: token or account.
Source: BIS

With "Version 2.0 digital payment," individual balances shown on our phones recognize the units of currency physically stored on your device, rather than the balance in a bank account. When you transfer money from person to person, actual digital money is moving from one storage place to another. Payment is instantaneous with ownership tied to your unique digital ID. The digital currency is self-contained, with security features to ensure that each unit is separate and distinct from all others without the need for an account.

That may sound like a semantical difference. But our current ability to digitize cash makes for profound changes in how we wire our financial system. Are you tired of waiting for a check to clear before seeing it in your account balance? In the US, customers still wait two to five days for check clearing. It is an archaic holdover from the banking system before digitization. It's still in use, even though the majority of transfers are entirely digitized. With the new digital currencies, payment is immediate.

> *CBDCs are not always built on a blockchain.*

A quick aside: by now you are well aware that I've used the word "digital" repeatedly, but I have not yet mentioned the word "blockchain." Blockchain is a type of immutable shared digital ledger commonly used in cryptocurrencies like Bitcoin. The reason is that unlike cryptocurrencies, which by definition all use blockchain, CBDCs may or may not employ the technology. This is a design decision we will discuss later. For now, it's important to understand that CBDCs are not *always* built on a blockchain. The reason? While blockchains have features that make them perfect for cryptocurrencies with limited distribution, those same features can make the technology ill-suited to a mass-market currency.

In sum, the most profound innovation inherent in CBDCs is that you can pay electronically without using a third-party intermediary like a bank or credit card. It's as easy as sending a text message or using your favorite messaging app. That is the real power of digital currencies, and frankly, is what financial institutions find slightly unnerving. What is their role to be if you don't need to use a bank to make a "wire transfer?" The very term speaks to a technology from the past century. Digital currency opens opportunities for fintech and other providers of digital wallets to provide new services, and ecosystems like those built by WeChat Pay and Alipay. Yes, you will still need a bank, but your relationship with them will change for the better. Service and competitive products will be the only things keeping banking clients loyal when it only takes a few clicks to change providers.

ADVANTAGES AND DISADVANTAGES OF CBDCS

Digital currency will change how we transfer money, and will present both advantages and disadvantages. These manifest at three distinct levels. The first, and of most concern to you and me, is what is known as the retail level, meaning payments for individuals and businesses. The second is the wholesale level, which encompasses cash flow between banks and large financial institutions. At the third level are supranational organizations that use and issue currency.

Our focus here will be on retail and wholesale use of CBDCs. Their use at the supranational level is complex, and may add little practical efficiency given the high value, low-frequency nature of these transactions. For example, the proposed use of digital currencies in the International Monetary Fund (IMF) is of academic interest, but still many years away from practical implementation.

Because of the complexities involved in "disrupting" the money systems, governments are spending a tremendous amount of time researching CBDCs before launching them. Getting it wrong could be expensive and potentially dangerous to financial stability. What follows is a list of the advantages and disadvantages they are considering in regard to CBDCs. These are the critical considerations that governments need to design around when developing a novel currency. The list will clarify why governments consider issuing CBDCs to be a bold move and not something to be rushed. It's not that CBDCs are inherently dangerous; rather, it is their potential effects on the financial system. The unintended consequences could be severe, so the journey is not for the faint of heart.

CBDC ADVANTAGES

Disintermediation

For retail users, of all the potential benefits of CBDCs, disintermediation is potentially the most beneficial. They allow instant digital payment to a receiver of choice, bypassing the bank or credit card network. This means savings, depending on how much your credit card network charges. Typical credit cards charge merchants from 1.5% to 2%, with small business owners paying PayPal and Square around 3%. In 2019, Visa's gross revenue was US$ 29 billion, based on card processing alone. This sum notably does not include interchange fees paid to the bank sponsoring the card, which would be multiples of this figure. CBDCs would adversely impact these card fees and represent a "disruption" in the payment industry.

Similarly, the need for bank wires would also be significantly reduced. Bank income from "float"—the two to three business days when your money is in the bank but not yet accessible to you—would disappear. These are profound systemic changes that threaten entire lines of business within banks and credit card companies. While most retail payment users would welcome disintermediation, it would be a severe blow to all companies in the payment sector who extract "rent" for transferring cash.

Improved tax collection and anti-money laundering

Readers may wonder why I saved this most obvious advantage of CBDCs to the government for second. The answer is that for most of us, the advantage happens to be moot. For people paid by direct deposit into bank accounts and who use credit cards for the majority of payments, a transition to CBDCs will have a negligible impact on taxes. We are already participating in a highly digital tax collection process that leaves little room for evasion unless, of course, you happen to have the good fortune of receiving large gifts of cash.

There are certain businesses, both illicit and legitimate, that depend on cash, and CBDCs will undoubtedly impact them in different ways. Legitimate companies that pay taxes may find conversion to CBDC a welcome relief, as the time and effort spent controlling the flow of cash will be eliminated or sharply reduced. As we will see in a later section, there are real costs to managing cash. Meanwhile, illicit businesses that hide cash for tax evasion purposes (and I have no direct experience with such entities), will phase out cash and phase in cryptocurrencies as their means of moving ill-gotten money. It will certainly be more challenging to "misplace" CBDCs—which are digitally tracked through the system—than cash. Money laundering and tax evasion, however, have more to do with false contracts and invoicing that may still be fraudulent regardless of the form of payment.

So while a significant selling point to regulators, and a significant perceived advantage of CBDCs, is "bringing in cash from the cold" and ending money laundering, I argue that its effectiveness in this role is somewhat overstated. History suggests that the technological acumen of those seeking to avoid taxes will simply ratchet up to match the government's digital efforts. Cryptocurrencies are already in use for hiding and trafficking illegal funds. That these efforts will only increase as cash is weaned out is a given.

Financial inclusion

Another great advantage of offering a CBDC is that it provides those who are as-yet unbanked a safe and secure means of holding currency. Hiding money under the mattress will be a thing of the past, as will carrying large rolls of cash and its associated security risks. While you may assume that this is a problem of developing nations, even Western economies have large unbanked or underbanked populations. The FDIC 2017 survey shows that 6.5% of American households were unbanked, while 18.7% were underbanked. CBDCs offer these populations a safe and convenient way of joining the financial system. One need look no further than the tremendous success that China had in drastically reducing its unbanked population with Version 1.0 digital currency products, to see digital's effect on enhancing financial inclusion. World Bank statistics show that between 2011 and 2014, the percent of Chinese adults with a "store of value" account increased from 64% to 79% due to the availability of mobile payment systems.

Financial stability

The 2008 global financial crisis embedded the term "too big to fail" into the vernacular. No one will ever forget that financial institutions such as Lehman Brothers were excluded from this category, while institutions like AIG were deemed systemically important and worthy of a bailout. This memory is still fresh for many who have paid in various ways for the industry's excesses.

The COVID-19 market crash also brought an influx of cash into the US's largest banks—also deemed "too big to fail" and, therefore, a safe haven. Ironically, this flight to larger institutions makes them even more systemically critical, and potentially imperils the entire financial system. In holding a CBDC, you are no longer dependent on a financial institution's size to protect your money. You need not use a financial institution at all because CBDCs are supported by the reserve bank and are not dependent on your bank's liquidity. CBDCs would make this perceived flight to safety irrelevant and stem cash outflows from smaller institutions perceived as less safe.

Cryptocurrency deterrent

When looking at the relative ease of transferring money using digital currency, it should be no surprise that many individuals and entities are not waiting for a CBDC. Instead, they use cryptocurrencies as both a store of value and as a convenient means of moving money. As of January 2021, coinmarketcap.com listed a total cryptocurrency market capitalization of around US$ 1.1 trillion, up from US$ 250 billion in May 2020. With new highs a daily occurrence, this is a considerable sum that is, to some degree, outside of government control. Not surprisingly, governments everywhere are displeased at this development.

The ultimate irony is that while cryptocurrency markets were, in part, the inspiration of CBDCs, it is now considered a government priority to reduce people's exposure to them. In theory, the risks posed by cryptocurrencies can be reduced by providing a government-backed digital currency with similar convenience, and greater security.

Fans of cryptocurrency will be either chuckling or grimacing as they read that. Most will not see dissuading people from buying crypto as an advantage, and I'm not sure I blame them. Owners of cryptocurrency see it as a good investment and a hedge to inflationary national currencies. In the eyes of the government, however, cryptocurrencies are the "bogeyman," running wild and free of regulation, and are therefore a danger to the populace and, not incidentally, an existential threat to tax revenues.

Monetary policy

Central banks fine-tune interest rates and the money supply to target inflation or deflation in an economy. If a CBDC were designed to be interest-bearing, and not all CBDCs will be, then digital currency itself could allow for immediate adjustments to accommodate a country's monetary policy. A change in interest rate could be as instantaneous as the press of a button on the central bank's computer. The ability of a central bank to enact negative interest rate policies would be just as easy. While this intrigues central bankers, most of us see making it easier to enable negative rates as a dubious benefit.

CBDCs could allow for configuring interest rates based on a number of factors that are not currently actionable. For example, rates could vary depending on whether a corporation or a person holds the currency, or which country is holding it. The possibilities are limitless. They all depend on what data is captured within the currency, and whether this data is transmitted back to the central bank. Digital allows for monetary policy considerations far beyond the one-size-fits-all policies of analog systems.

Fiscal policy: stimulus and UBI

COVID-19 brought economic suffering to many. Governments responded with stimulus checks in the US and other countries. At the same time, the long-term nature of unemployment in the wake of the crisis is leading to serious discussions about the provision of universal basic income (UBI). Overnight, as I was writing this section, Spain announced that it would implement a "national minimum income" of €462 per month, with increases depending on the number of family members. CBDCs would make the payment of benefits of any form to the populace both cheaper for government and more efficient. That the US considered launching a digital dollar speaks to CBDC's efficiency for this purpose.

Cost of cash

While this might not come readily to mind as an advantage, there is a significant cost associated with printing and managing paper money. The US Treasury's annual budget for producing and managing its currency is an astounding US$ 877.2 million. Granted, this won't break the US's budget, but for smaller countries, the cost of custom-printing banknotes can be high. Much more expensive, and rarely reported, is the massive human effort expended annually in counting and caring for cash. IHL Group's research on this topic showed that in 2017 in the US and Canada, an estimated US$ 96 billion was spent on managing cash. The estimated cost was from 4.7% to 15% of face value depending on the retail segment. In the UK, the cost of running the country's cash infrastructure is estimated to be GBP 5bn annually. These are real costs and time expenditures that digital payment effectively eliminates.

CBDC DISADVANTAGES

Disintermediation

Readers will recall that disintermediation was high on the list of advantages for CBDCs. It is equally a disadvantage, because the very freedom to keep your money where you want adversely impacts financial institutions. Your bank needs deposits to fund its reserves. If CBDCs are too popular, many people may choose to keep their money elsewhere, brokerage accounts being one potential option, depriving the bank of significant funding. Worse, banks may need to pay increased interest rates to lure clients into parking money in their repository. This is clearly an unwelcome change in their business model. While this may seem inconceivable now, with a CBDC, your currency becomes very much your own; what you do with it will be your choice, unhindered by transfer fees and the bother of securing cashier's checks.

I do not anticipate an outpouring of sympathy for large financial institutions by the majority of readers. Still, the possibility that CBDCs will disrupt banks' and credit companies' business models is a real concern for financial regulators. To reduce potential system shock, countries launching CBDCs should do so gradually, under tightly controlled circumstances.

The effects of disintermediation will, to a great degree, be ameliorated by what new and innovative services financial institutions can develop for a CBDC economy. This is a true challenge for incumbents, who will no longer have captive customers but instead need to offer them a business rationale to stay.

International transfer

The ease of transferring CBDCs is either one of their most significant advantages or disadvantages, depending on your point of view. The international transfer of money outside of the confines of the established banking system is a significant concern for governments. All rely on the system to track where and how much money flows through the financial system. Banks and money transfer agents like SWIFT (the Society for Worldwide Interbank Financial Telecommunication) are vital components in the enforcement of sanctions, anti-money laundering, and anti-terror activities. Of course, it's possible to design a CBDC that allows for tracking, and for the disruption of illegal flow. Facebook's second-generation Libra stable coin was forced to enable this capacity after governments railed against its lack of know-your-client (KYC) control in the original design. While companies like Facebook may be forced by governments to abide by their rules, it is already evident that other sovereign nations may not be so accommodating. Controversy over CBDCs' use in international trade is virtually guaranteed.

Another problem is that universal agreement isn't necessarily guaranteed about which country or company is deserving of sanctions. Consider that the EU defied the US by using the INSTEX transfer system rather than SWIFT to send humanitarian aid to Iran during the coronavirus pandemic. The use of CBDCs in some cross-border transactions will bring cries of "sanction busting," when, or if, they occur. Contesting them will be even more complicated given an absence of readily accessible evidence from the banking system.

Sanctions have the potential to become a hot-button issue because CBDCs based on an independent digital transfer system can't be stopped or monitored. For this reason, CBDCs could usher in an era of increased economic conflict. Countries may do battle over CBDC usage in traditional banking markets, causing greater friction in a system that has worked relatively smoothly since the end of WWII. Ultimately, CBDCs may lessen cooperation in international banking, but such a development will be gradual, because as CBDCs gain in popularity, public policy will evolve to match their use.

Run risk

While we don't think much about bank runs anymore, after the failure of Lehman Brothers they are still very much a concern to regulators. CBDCs could in fact make bank runs easier if bank patrons with a sizable portion of their holdings in CBDCs suddenly decided to move them from the bank holding them. Bad news about a bank's financial health could panic customers, triggering a sudden transfer of assets, further destabilizing the bank. In practice, this would be far easier than a more traditional "run on the bank," where patrons queue to withdraw their deposits. With CBDCs, all it would take is a few clicks to move money to perceived safety. From a practical standpoint, the bank could mitigate this risk by limiting the amount of CBDC that can be transferred, or mandating that only a portion of deposits be held in CBDCs. In the extreme, the government could issue additional CBDCs to the bank, collateralized by bank reserves, to ensure liquidity.

In developing countries, there is also the concept of a "run on the currency." Here the "run" isn't on the bank, but instead, a race to transfer assets into a more stable currency. Sparked by devalued currencies, the potential ease with which users could switch in and out of national currencies with CBDCs could be a significant benefit to developing countries. Facebook's Libra made much the same argument when promoting its stablecoin as a boon for developing countries. The fact that currency substitution represents a benefit to users—at the cost of destabilizing nascent governments—gives rise to a hot debate about the pros and cons of CBDCs.

Easy way to print money

Many fans of cryptocurrency are sensitive to fiat currencies (government-issued currencies not backed by commodities), and the historical practice of governments printing so much money that it devalues and destabilizes the currency. Ironically, the same technology that makes it impossible to mint new Bitcoin makes it possible for a government to quietly mint new CBDCs at the stroke of a keyboard. Practically speaking, CBDCs do not give governments any greater powers to print currency than they already have, using traditional central banking systems. The difference, according to some, is that CBDCs make it easier to conceal the practice—a belief not fully supported by the mechanics of CBDC issuance. Many governments created money for stimulus packages during the pandemic, and there was no need to use CBDCs to do this. Suffice it to say that debasing a currency through CBDCs is far less efficient and more complicated than more traditional means like printing cash or issuing more debt.

Reputation risk

Getting it wrong would be tremendously embarrassing and expensive for a central bank. Once a CBDC launches, it will be tough to recall it and ask for a "do-over." Because CBDCs have so many second- and third-order effects on the financial system, the central bank must get it right the very first time. Consider the US's position. As the issuer of the world's reserve currency, it is already in a position of immense power, with a profound impact on financial markets across the globe. Issuing a CBDC and getting it wrong at this scale could cause a global crisis.

It is less of an issue that a government might make a mistake issuing the CBDC, and more so that it may not anticipate the rapid adoption of the currency and ancillary effects. This was a genuine concern and practical problem that occurred in China. Mobile payment adoption was so shockingly fast there that it left the central bank, and indeed the entire banking system, stunned. While there was no destabilization, traditional bankers were left aghast and leaned on the central bank for more favorable regulation.

Loss of privacy

There is a heated debate about the loss of privacy with CBDCs, and I agree with all who see the beauty of cash's anonymity. The problem is that the debate over whether CBDCs rob individuals of privacy is generally used as a strawman attack on CBDCs. The reality is that the vast majority of us already coexist with digital money, and the fear that CBDCs will suddenly obliterate privacy is misplaced. CBDCs will likely have little real impact on your privacy, which is determined by the currency's design and the amount of privacy programmed into it. CBDCs are not, by definition, tools of government oppression.

> *Before proclaiming that CBDCs invade privacy and are a disaster, or conversely, that CBDCs are harmless, it is essential to consider the exact design of the CBDC in question.*

CBDC privacy will vary significantly by country. Those with more robust privacy policies will probably base their design on mirroring your limited privacy in digital banking today. Most countries will have big-data-assisted analysis of you and all your spending habits—as your credit card and credit scoring companies do now. That is sobering to many for sure, but unless you use cash for most of your transactions, we all have very few secrets when it comes to finance. On the positive side, however, some countries are discussing complete anonymity for all CBDC transactions below a threshold amount.

A generic discussion of CBDC's impact on privacy is challenging because as digital instruments, programming them for no privacy, complete privacy or anything in between is a relatively easy undertaking. So before proclaiming that CBDCs invade privacy and are a disaster, or conversely, that CBDCs are harmless, it is essential to consider the exact design of the CBDC in question to understand its degree of data transparency. Don't fall for either argument until you see the details.

10

STRUCTURING A CBDC

China on the purpose of digital currency:

> *"The digital yuan is used to spend, not for speculation. It does not have the characteristics of bitcoin speculation, nor does it require a basket of assets to support its value like stablecoins."*
>
> Mu Changchun, Deputy Director of the PBOC's Institute of Digital Currency

The West on the purpose of digital currency:

> *"To date, our observation is that many of the challenges [CBDCs] hope to address do not apply the US context including disuse of physical cash, narrow reaching or high concentrating banking, or poorly developed payment infrastructure."*
>
> Jerome Powell, Chair of the Federal Reserve, 2019

So far, knowing what we do about CBDCs, let's think about how we could build one, intuitively. Let's consider ourselves assigned to a central bank, one that is mid-tier and digitally sophisticated. We've got computers, account creation software, and many of the tools found in a large commercial bank. But as a central bank, our clients are financial institutions. Also, being a government entity, we'd have access to taxpayer lists, retiree and pensioner lists, and with the birth of new citizens, their unique state ID number. We can presume this because most modern governments have a reasonably accurate picture of who is living in the country and making or receiving payments.

The simplest CBDC we could envision would see an account opened for every citizen, and the central bank would process each transaction that comes in. For sure, a massive undertaking, but at least theoretically possible. The central bank would have to revise its money laundering and KYC standards to the level of those at a retail bank—again, difficult but not impossible.

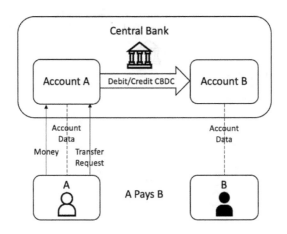

Account-based CBDC
All funds pass through accounts held by the central bank. This type of CBDC is also referred to as "single tier" as both issuance and distribution occur at the central bank.

With this type of CBDC, a user's payment is immediately sent from their account to the account of the intended receiver, all under the central bank's oversight. It's simple and technically feasible, but would require a significant investment to scale up the bank's internal systems. It would also require the bank to take on a role in retail banking that most would not be comfortable with, even if the regulatory and technical requirements were achievable.

This design successfully creates an "account-based direct retail CBDC." But it also disintermediates the entire banking system, causing widespread chaos in that industry. They would be justified in claiming that the central bank was nationalizing much of their business.

So while this first idea for a CBDC is technically viable, it's also overreaching. To scale back the ambition and reduce the massive computational load and systems changes required to handle retail clients, we could limit transactions to a select group of account holders: banks within our country. This would create a "direct wholesale CBDC." It is still a valuable tool as it would speed cash transmission between financial institutions.

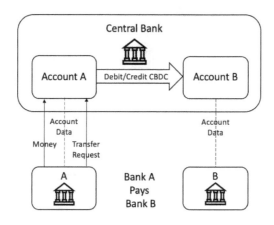

Direct Wholesale CBDC

This "account-based wholesale CBDC" is a more workable project. Payments fly through the network and are immediate for those financial institutions that hold accounts, but there's still something missing. According to our innovation and IT teams, we're ignoring the latest technology imported from the cryptocurrency space: blockchain and its ability to create tokens.

As simple and useful as our CBDC is, we are going to make it better. Rather than dealing with accounts, we will use blockchain technology to issue and track the ownership of "tokens." Tokens are digital equivalents of cash that we can pass between users who are attached to a blockchain that records ownership. This will solve two critical problems. First, by tokenizing our currency, the central bank no longer has to monitor accounts for every individual. Once tokens are issued, the tokens themselves pass between market participants, and the central bank's responsibility is limited to running the blockchain system that issues, redeems, and follows their flow. Second, now that the bank uses tokens, our system requirements are significantly reduced, just as our IT and innovation teams predicted. The reduction is so substantial that the bank could consider launching this solution to retail customers, something deemed technically challenging with an account-based system. The only problem that remains is bank disintermediation, and angry bankers who feel left out.

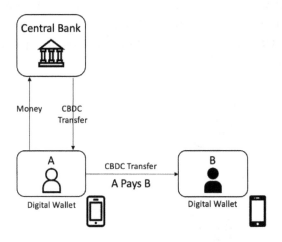

Token-Based Wholesale or Retail CBDC
Replace figures in A and B above with banks for the wholesale version.

For our final project as central bankers, we're going to keep the retail financial institutions happy by keeping them in the picture. For practical purposes, they're set up to deal with retail clients, and their branch networks could be valuable assets to help with the transition to a CBDC. Using their systems dramatically reduces the burden upon central bank systems and, most importantly, assuages their fear of disintermediation.

With this version, we maintain the banks as an intermediary between the central bank and the retail client, to maintain existing financial systems as part of the solution. Our new and final CBDC is called a "tokenized indirect retail CBDC."

We're also going to add a novel feature, something central bankers have wanted for decades. This is the ability to raise or lower interest rates immediately. To this end, the tokens will be programmed to bear interest. Now with full control over interest rates, enacting monetary policy will be as easy as pressing a button on our central bank computer. So our new CBDC is fully able to provide instant retail payments, includes existing financial institutions as part of the solution, is technically feasible for the central bank, and allows for immediate changes in monetary policy. As a bonus, if we've used "blockchain" to issue the tokens, we'll be considered technically avant-garde and hailed as heroes. Everyone wins, and we can all celebrate with champagne—purchased, of course, with our CBDCs.

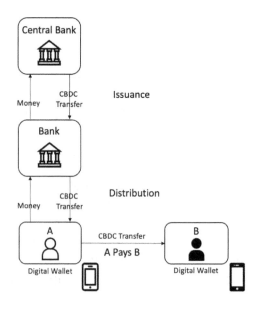

Tokenized Indirect Retail CBDC

This structure is commonly referred to as a "two tier" CBDC where issuance by the central bank occurs in tier 1 and distribution by banks is in tier 2.

I used the story above to explain in an intuitive fashion the options central banks have when creating a CBDC. There are only four fundamental configurations: 1) Direct, or Indirect, 2) Account-Based, or Token, 3) Blockchain, or non-Blockchain and 4) Interest-bearing, or not. That said, each central bank will have to determine which of these options suits its use case, technology limitations, and most importantly, willingness to disrupt the financial system. The process is necessarily introspective as each will have to weigh the advantages and disadvantages of each of these decisions relative to their economy. Let's look at each of these decision points in more detail.

DIRECT OR INDIRECT PROVISION

Here the CBDC design decision is whether the central bank should provide CBDC to the users directly, or through retail bank intermediaries. Indirect CBDCs are also commonly called two-tier, or tiered systems. For practical purposes, most retail CBDCs that you read about are of the two-tier or indirect type. There are two primary reasons for this.

First, with an indirect structure, central banks do not have to deal with the general public and the creation and management of retail accounts, a role for which they are both ill-suited and ill-equipped. In an indirect CBDC, the central bank keeps accounts only for the intermediaries who handle claims arising from CBDCs. That said, in smaller countries, island nations, for example, direct retail CBDCs are not only possible but may provide an opportunity to increase financial inclusion. For countries with large populations like China and India, it is impossible to conceive of central banks being able to reach such large populations.

The second reason tiered CBDCs are more popular is that they are far less disruptive to incumbents in the financial system.

With a tiered system, the existing financial infrastructure is reused and repurposed. All of the banks, brokers, and money transfer services will have a role and an opportunity to innovate new services in support of making the new CBDC a success. They will provide digital wallets, and already have the infrastructure in place for KYC checks, to ensure that users are who they say they are. Tiered CBDCs do not set the central bank in conflict with incumbents. While there would undoubtedly be a role for incumbents to participate and innovate in a direct system, diminishing that role creates the potential for significant disruption.

Direct CBDCs are most commonly associated with interbank transfers within the wholesale financial system. In this use, CBDCs take on the precise role that central banks have always played in facilitating cash transfers within the financial system. In this use case, CBDCs may provide an advantage over existing systems, but that is highly dependent on which systems the country uses. Intrabank transfers for most large countries already have digital cash transfer through "real-time gross settlement" (RTGS) systems. For example, the US and EU handle some interbank transfers through RTGS Fedwire and Target2 systems, respectively. At the same time, the US, EU, and Canada also operate the CHIPS, EURO1, and LVTS systems, which rely upon near real-time "deferred net settlement." The problem with the use of CBDC technology in this role is that because all central bank transfers are already digital, swapping existing cash transfer methods for a digital currency may offer only limited advantages.

In contrast, single-tier direct CBDCs for interbank transfers may be advantageous in developing countries, where real-time payments are not yet in use by the central bank. One of the first CBDCs in the world, ready for launch in 2020, is single-tier and designed specifically for intrabank transfers. The National Bank of Cambodia (NBC) is launching a single-tier, or direct, wholesale CBDC serving eleven banks in the country. According to NBC's director general, the system provides "smooth, efficient, safe, and affordable interbank transactions which will ultimately benefit end users." Cambodia has an active mobile payment market, meaning that payments are immediate on the retail side. Now interbank payments will be instant on the wholesale side of the banking system as well. This is a great use case of a single-tier or direct CBDC, which ultimately puts the entire country on digital speed transfers with minimal technical resources and no disruption to incumbent financial institutions.

TOKEN OR ACCOUNT BASED

Tokens are quite the celebrities recently. I'm sure most readers received offers to purchase tokens that convey fractional ownership of such diverse assets as real estate, stocks, fine art, and the deservedly maligned initial coin offerings (ICOs). Tokens are all around us, and clearly, the general intent is that tokens convey ownership. While most skirt the boundaries of legality, tokenization is now offered at more progressive financial exchanges and can be wholly legal. Most digital tokens are the byproduct of blockchain systems, but digital tokens can also be created without blockchain, using advanced cryptographic techniques.

Looking deeper, we may consider cash as a "non-digital" token. It can be passed freely from user to user as it changes ownership, and we accept a bill only after we verify it is authentic through testing. Counterfeiters may make "fake tokens" (bills); we unconsciously test banknotes by their feel, weight, and look to ensure they are real. Conveyance entitles ownership, and no ledger entry is required to attribute its value to your accounts. Digital tokens in CBDCs function in much the same manner, with one exception. The tests for verifying that the token is real are digital. A digital currency token is verified on a network, which may or may not be blockchain-based, to assure that it is authentic, to prove the identity of the owner, and to ascertain that it has not already been spent—a practice commonly referred to as "double-spending."

For practical purposes, users do not care, and would not know, the difference between an account-based and token-based CBDC. As long as they can use it to pay, there is no practical difference, even if the underlying technology is very different. The RTGS payment systems Fedwire and Target2, for example, while not CBDCs per se, are model, real-time, account-based payment systems that function without the need for blockchain and the use of tokens. So while the hype that "everything with blockchain is better" may make blockchain-based tokens appear to be the natural solution for CBDCs, this is not always the case. The Canadian Central Bank goes so far as to say that "It may, therefore, be preferable to avoid framing the scope of a CBDC in terms of notions of accounts and tokens."

Turning currency into tokens in CBDCs does have one small advantage worthy of discussion. Tokens are actual digital money held in your digital wallet and are usually transferred only when the network is accessed to verify the token's identity. For low-value transactions, we can reduce the required verification criteria and allow a transfer with a lower level of security. This technique can allow two wallets that are disconnected from the network to pass tokens using the wallet's more basic verification. Of course, this can only be used for low values, but it solves a fundamental problem of using digital payment in remote areas where no network is available. What limits to place on such low-value transactions is a matter for central bankers. To claim that you could not replicate this feature in an account-based CBDC would be wrong. It is fair to say, however, that this feature is far easier to build with token-based systems.

BLOCKCHAIN VS. NON-BLOCKCHAIN

I am a resolute fan of blockchain, but not the hype that surrounds the technology. The mantra that blockchain will cure all problems is repeated all too frequently without a real understanding of the technology's limitations. When discussing CBDCs, most assume that blockchain will be the foundation technology. While the odds are in favor of this being right, it would be an error for the architects of a CBDC to blindly make this assumption. CBDC designers need to perform an impartial analysis to see if blockchain's capabilities meet the CBDC system requirements before leaping on the blockchain bandwagon.

Much of blockchain's fame is related to cryptocurrencies, of which the most popular is Bitcoin. Bitcoin, among others, works on a "public" blockchain meaning that anyone can join the network and read, write, and participate. There are no "permissions" for joining the network—no identification checks or documentation required. Public means just that: everyone. Public blockchains are, by definition, "decentralized," meaning there is no single entity controlling the network. This is a critical distinction because with decentralized networks, decisions on how to run the network are made by the peers voting.

Decentralized networks like Bitcoin need to use and pay for significant computational resources, which give rise to their other famous feature, mining. Mining is the process of being paid in Bitcoin for providing the computational engine for the Bitcoin network. Bitcoin by design uses intentionally inefficient "proof of work" calculations to generate new blocks on the blockchain. For their investment in servers and electricity, miners receive a reward of payment in Bitcoin when they solve equations which generate a new block on the chain.

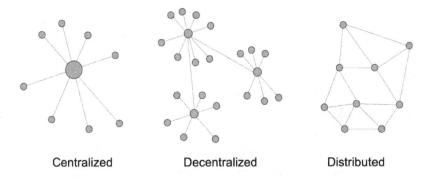

Centralized   Decentralized   Distributed

Decentralized networks used in Bitcoin and other cryptocurrencies have many properties that central banks would consider undesirable.

While there are undoubtedly other facets of bitcoin and cryptocurrency worthy of discussion, I've highlighted decentralized networks, mining, and voting by peers in order to emphasize the difference between the use of blockchain in cryptocurrency compared to CBDCs. Imagine for a moment a CBDC blockchain network that is public and without "permissions." Does that sound like the kind of network a central banker would use? Of course not. Central bankers want to control access to their networks, so they will use "private blockchains." Private blockchains are run by a central authority and users must receive permission from the central authority to participate.

Voting and mining are also not high on the list of priorities for central bankers. To them, voting is unnecessary because the central bank or a consortium of leading participants control the rules that govern the passage of funds on the blockchain network. Mining is also deemed unnecessary because computational power will come not only from the central bank but also from the other financial institutions that participate in the "decentralized" network. Clearly, the type of blockchain network a CBDC requires is substantially different than that used with cryptocurrencies.

Blockchain truly is a natural fit for CBDCs, and there is no argument that its high security, programmable levels of confidentiality, and tamper-proof recording of data fit the basic design specs for CBDCs. It also provides a ready means of tokenizing assets and replicating its data across computer clusters. That said, I hesitate to endorse blockchain unequivocally due to its high computational requirements, which may not meet *every* CBDC's design specifications.

Many have heard that Bitcoin's annual electrical consumption is comparable to a small country like Switzerland. While the latest high-speed blockchain systems will consume a small fraction of the electricity used by Bitcoin, it is crucial to understand that blockchain networks are computationally heavy. As a result, they are slower and more expensive to run than traditional databases like those used in credit card processing. This is a serious design constraint and one that has to be calculated in earnest rather than glossed over. CBDCs may require high-volume, high-speed transaction processing that many blockchain systems cannot deliver.

We will see in the next chapter how blockchain performance will be a significant factor in the design of China's CBDC.

One final note: blockchain systems are all governed by underlying cryptography. Traditionally, "blockchain" denotes that the system stores records on a growing number of blocks, which increase with the size of the data set. Increasingly, high-speed distributed ledger technology (DLT) systems have done away with blocks and relied more on cryptography to increase the computation speed of the systems. So is a DLT solution without blocks a blockchain? To purists it is not, but it is still common practice to call these DLT systems blockchain even when no blocks exist.

INTEREST OR NON-INTEREST BEARING

Most, if not all, CBDCs will have the built-in ability to manage interest rates, regardless of central banks' stated intent to use them. Being able to control interest rates on CBDCs gives the central bank a potent tool to help control the issuance of CBDCs upon launch, and then later to impact monetary policy once they become widely distributed.

Setting interest rates above or below the rates offered by banks for cash deposits allows a central bank to encourage or discourage the demand for CBDCs. The ability to set an interest rate on a CBDC is an important policy tool that can help regulate their use after launch into the system. Interest-bearing CBDCs also present a potential threat of increased commercial bank disintermediation. If rates for the CBDC are sufficiently close to bank rates, people might avoid bank deposits, depleting bank reserves. Ironically, some proponents of CBDCs see this as their ultimate goal, reducing the individual's dependence on "too big to fail" institutions, which in turn makes the financial system safer. I doubt that bankers will agree.

One of the concerns about CBDCs is the potential for increased deposit volatility due to "runs on the bank." Interest rates on CBDCs are a hidden policy tool that can in fact dissuade such runs. By setting punitive rates for converting or using

CBDCs, central banks could mitigate the relative ease of turning deposits into CBDC and moving to another institution. This is one of the primary reasons why all CBDCs will have interest rates built-in; think of it as an insurance policy.

CBDCs will only come into their own as a tool for managing monetary policy once they have extensive distribution within the financial system. Once this occurs, setting the rates on CBDCs would be the primary tool for adjusting monetary policy. Interest rates for CBDCs are indeed a sensitive topic. They primarily function as shock-absorbers, built into CBDCs in order to smooth unforeseen bumps in the road. Most countries will set their CBDC interest rate to zero at launch as a means of neutralizing their impact on the banking system. For example, Sweden's Riksbank has stated precisely that: it plans to set its CBDC rates to zero at launch.

Basic CBDC Design Decisions

Role of the central bank?	Direct provision	Indirect provision
What is money?	Account Based	Token Based
What technology?	Blockchain	Non Blockchain
Role in creating money?	Interest bearing	Non-interest bearing

The basic design decisions central banks need to consider when designing a CBDC.

HYBRID AND SYNTHETIC CBDCS

There are two final forms of CBDC, called "hybrid" and "synthetic," which will complete our discussion on CBDC architecture. The hybrid CBDC is the easiest to visualize, being. a form of direct CBDC with the use of third-party intermediaries to help manage KYC, user onboarding, and cash payments. What is important to note in the hybrid CBDC structure is that, like direct CBDCs, the central bank creates and manages accounts for individual CBDC users. The benefit to the central bank with the hybrid structure is that it can outsource much of the servicing role while maintaining accounts for all users. Hybrid structure is potentially beneficial to central banks in less populous countries, where direct CBDCs are reasonable options.

Synthetic CBDCs are, strictly speaking, not central bank-issued digital currencies. Instead, they are the result of a central bank partnering with a third party to issue a digital currency backed by the central bank. The technology behind the issuance of the digital currency is immaterial in synthetic CBDCs. What is critical is that the partner issues the digital coin with the backing of the central bank, whose reserves provide trust in the currency. Partners might be banks, tech companies, or payment providers. It is even possible for the central bank to engage multiple partners who would compete among themselves for users.

Stablecoins like Diem (Libra) and Tether currently tie their digital currencies to the US dollar, but of course, have no government backing. Stablecoins like these provide the best examples of digital currency that could be used in a synthetic structure. The principal advantage to the central bank of synthetic CBDCs is that they can launch very quickly. The central bank's role is limited to transferring fiat currency to the digital currency provider, then monitoring that they do not issue more currency than was allocated. The assumption is that the digital currency is one-to-one backed by fiat currency. It is essentially a way for a government to go digital without launching its own CBDC. Facebook CEO Mark Zuckerberg highlighted this benefit in his testimony to the US Congress when he unsuccessfully tried to get them behind Libra. Zuckerberg told a US House of Representatives Committee that "Libra will be backed mostly by dollars, and I believe it will extend America's financial leadership."

In the US, the government's desire to share power by issuing digital currency with the assistance of private companies appears to be exceedingly low. The US response to Facebook's Libra was the aptly named "Keeping Big Tech Out of Finance Act." While still undergoing revision, its name makes no secret of its intentions to regulate cryptocurrency and privately issued digital dollars.

The global outcry surrounding Facebook's Libra showed the intensity of the government's wish to fully control the monetary system. So while synthetic CBDCs may be technically possible, it is hard to envision all but the tiniest of countries adopting them anytime soon. Another big stumbling block is the irreparable damage to a central bank's reputation if a synthetic CBDC has issues. Compare this with the limited downside in delaying CBDCs and digital currencies, and the choice for central bankers is clear.

11

CHINA'S DC/EP

China's motives for digital currency:

> *"The idea behind the digital currency is to enable anyone, across and beyond the nation, who doesn't have an account in the Chinese banks, to use a digital wallet and enjoy mobile payment services in China."*
> Mu Changchun, Deputy Director of the PBOC's Institute of Digital Currency

The West's motives for digital currency:

> *"The demand for and use of such instruments [CBDCs] need further consideration in order to evaluate whether such a central bank digital currency would allow for quicker and more ubiquitous payments in times of emergency and more generally."*
> Loretta Mester,
> Cleveland Federal Reserve President

These are exciting times for China's CBDC—or what it refers to as Digital Currency / Electronic Payment (DC/EP). The testing phase is finished and the currency is in trial use in a number of cities, and planning to launch by Q4 2020. The People's Bank of China (PBOC) is striking a balance between being fairly open about the significant design challenges and overall features built into its new DC/EP, and being justifiably secretive about precise DC/EP design details. While additional specifications may be revealed at launch or soon after, we know enough now to understand both how it works and what it will look like from a user perspective.

> *China refers to its CBDC as*
> *Digital Currency / Electronic Payment*
> *(DC/EP)*

It's also important to acknowledge that the PBOC's new digital currency is a work in progress, a continuously evolving product that will never be static. While the digital RMB may always look the same in a user's digital wallet, big-data and KYC systems will be ever evolving behind the scenes, just like they do at your bank. Understanding the DC/EP's architecture at launch will help the reader understand how new changes and emerging details fit into its evolution.

> *One Coin, Two Repositories, Three Centers*
> 一币，两库，三中心

Yao Qian, the former head of PBOCs Digital Currency Research Institute, succinctly described the architecture of China's DC/EP as having (一币，两库，三中心) one coin, two repositories, and three centers. This is a beautiful example of China's love of enumeration to illustrate essential concepts and is a great starting point for understanding the design of DC/EP.

We will use this model as a template throughout our discussion. It is a very effective shorthand for understanding the high-level structure of the DC/EP. Moreover, this is the model the PBOC uses when describing the currency in progress updates, or when announcing new details. Sticking with this model makes it easier to understand the PBOC's announcements, and where any new features may fit in.

ONE COIN (一币)

The RMB is China's legal currency, and the digital RMB is a digital equivalent of the paper RMB in all ways, including its value. Most importantly, the new DC/EP maintains the PBOC's centralized control over the currency, just as it did with paper money. PBOC Deputy Governor Fan Yifei makes this clear: "Currency issuance is the basic responsibility of the central bank, and digital renminbi should adhere to central bank management." China's digital RMB is the equivalent of cash or "M0" in the financial system and is not included in "M1" or "M2." As the electronic heir to cash, it is seen by the PBOC as the natural evolution of currency following the success of privately run mobile payment. DC/EP's introduction will bring even greater digital currency use within society, increasing financial inclusion and spurring economic growth while maintaining paper money as an option for all citizens. DC/EP is to all intents and purposes cash, and cannot be refused for payment.

To be cash's rightful heir, the DC/EP was designed to maintain two of cash's primary functions:

1. Using it does not require network connectivity.
2. It retains the anonymity of cash when transacting.

> *China's DC/EP does not pay interest and is 100% reserved.*

Neither cash nor China's DC/EP pays or receives interest, and both require 100% reserving. This means an RMB in cash, held by your bank, cannot be loaned out and may not be included as part of the bank's fractional reserves. With bank fractional reserving, used in China and the West, a bank can lend out deposits, and the proportion of deposits lent versus held in reserves against loans is the reserve ratio. Through lending, the bank generates new revenue through the receipt of interest payments. China's DC/EP, however, is treated just like a paper banknote, and cannot be held in reserve against loans. By requiring 100% reserving, banks are incapable of creating additional digital RMB through interest, credit, or lending.

Full reserving is a crucial concept for the DC/EP. When banks exchange account RMB for digital RMB, they will be changing the amount of cash available to satisfy regulatory reserving requirements. A massive rush to using DC/EP could potentially suddenly reduce banks' reserves (M2). The PBOC is avoiding this scenario by placing limits on DC/EP conversion in the digital wallets of users. The impact of digital currency on the financial system can be profound, and is often conveniently overlooked when comparing CBDCs with cryptocurrencies and stablecoins.

Another important reason for keeping the digital RMB interest rate at zero is to avoid competition with the existing banking system. If the PBOC were to issue an interest bearing RMB, it would potentially attract money away from the traditional banking system and disintermediate commercial banks. With the DC/EP directly backed by the PBOC, an interest-bearing digital RMB would be a less risky asset than accounts offered by banks, again potentially disruptive to incumbents. So while China's DC/EP will have a programmable interest rate feature built-in, it won't be switched on, at least for domestic use, for some time to come.

The PBOC also built in one more feature to avoid bank disintermediation. When banks issue DC/EP, it is the issuing bank that guarantees payment of the digital RMB issued, not the PBOC. This eliminates any incentive for users to accumulate digital currency with the thought that it is risk-free because it is PBOC guaranteed. It is also likely that this is why China calls its digital currency DC/EP as opposed to CBDC. In the strictest technical terms, China's retail digital currency is not central bank issued. The PBOC states that the issuance method was borrowed from Hong Kong where bank notes are issued by the major banks. It was adopted with DC/EP issuance to ensure incumbent banks' role, eliminate any speculation that DC/EP could replace banks, and ensure currency stability.

TWO REPOSITORIES（两库）

Here, the repositories or warehouses manifest the two-tier or indirect style of DC/EP (see chapter 10). One of the warehouses for the DC/EP is the PBOC; the second is the issuing commercial bank. The partnerships signal that the PBOC is striving for minimal disruption within the banking system. The two-tiered system allows commercial banks to retain their traditional role in providing cash to clients, and ensures China's massive populace the best possible user experience. Commercial banks, both digital and physical, will be critical in the conversion process.

Note that restricting DC/EP issuance to commercial banks leaves WeChat Pay and Alipay out. They may transfer digital currency, but will not issue it directly on their apps. This is not a slight against the mobile payment systems as much as adherence to current policy. Account-based RMB transferred by the payment apps also had its origins in the banking system. In any case, this does not place the payment giants at a disadvantage, because both currently own commercial banking units that will likely issue DC/EP.

In the two-tier system, the central bank controls the amount of DC/EP issued, and triangulates that amount against the issuance of paper money and account-based RMB to control the country's money supply. By balancing these three cash flows, the PBOC can effectively modulate the impact of the DC/EP on the PBOC's monetary policies.

To issue DC/EP to a commercial bank, the PBOC creates DC/EP and simultaneously deducts an equal amount of account-based RMB from the bank's deposit reserves. The commercial bank then holds the digital RMB until a conversion from account-based RMB to DC/EP is requested by a client. Redemption of DC/EP follows the same process in reverse, with the direct matching of account-based monies to digital RMB. The two-tier structure requires upholding 100% reserving at both the commercial bank and central bank levels.

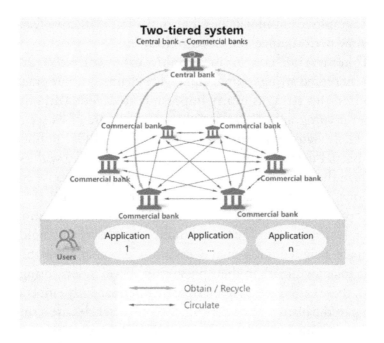

China's DC/EP uses a "two-tiered" design that minimizes the DC/EP's impact on the banking system. The PBOC issues DC/EP to commercial banks, which in turn issue DC/EP to clients who circulate it among themselves.
Source: PBOC

Now let's take a deeper dive into the key components of the two-tiered DC/EP system.

1. Tokens without blockchain and loosely coupled accounts

Our "two repository" system is ready to pass DC/EP among the PBOC, commercial banks, and clients, but we have not yet defined how or what to transfer between entities. China's DC/EP will be token-based, as opposed to account-based, but in a twist that some may find odd, will not use blockchain technology. Instead of using blockchain to create tokens, China's DC/EP will rely on the cryptographic techniques at the core of blockchain to create tokens in a centralized rather than decentralized ledger. The PBOC is choosing a hybrid approach that takes tokens and cryptography from blockchain but omits less attractive features like slow performance and decentralization.

Tokenization is a cryptographic process that creates a long-encrypted string of undecipherable characters. For practical purposes, this string is nearly impossible to decode without the proper cryptographic keys, which are at the core of its security. As a likely deterrent to hackers and attacks, PBOC publicized only partial details of the cryptographic system they will use to tokenize their DC/EP. Even without knowing the precise specifications, the use of tokens is relatively straightforward.

Once encrypted, a DC/EP token holds data on the amount, owner, issuer, and a unique serial number. All users who hold the token are assigned individual decryption keys that allow the use of the token while it's in their possession. Besides decrypting the token, these keys leave a digital signature permanently embedded, adding to the history of ownership. Cryptocurrencies use a similar system—it's obvious where China's DC/EP drew inspiration.

Blockchain-based cryptocurrencies also inspired the DC/EP's controls for double-spending, divisibility, transferability, and the potential for forgery. There is, however, one key feature that China's DC/EP will not borrow from cryptocurrency. Most of these systems promise anonymity and contain no reference to the actual owner's identity. China's DC/EP will register each token to an identifiable owner on PBOC systems.

```
00000000   01 00 00 00 00 00 00 00   00 00 00 00 00 00 00 00   ................
00000010   00 00 00 00 00 00 00 00   00 00 00 00 00 00 00 00   ................
00000020   00 00 00 00 3B A3 ED FD   7A 7B 12 B2 7A C7 2C 3E   ....;£íýz{.¹zÇ,>
00000030   67 76 8F 61 7F C8 1B C3   88 8A 51 32 3A 9F B8 AA   gv.a.È.Ã¯ŠQ2:Ÿ.ª
00000040   4B 1E 5E 4A 29 AB 5F 49   FF FF 00 1D 1D AC 2B 7C   K.^J)«_Iÿÿ...¬+|
00000050   01 01 00 00 00 01 00 00   00 00 00 00 00 00 00 00   ................
00000060   00 00 00 00 00 00 00 00   00 00 00 00 00 00 00 00   ................
00000070   00 00 00 00 00 FF FF FF   FF FF 4D 04 FF FF 00 1D   .....ÿÿÿÿÿM.ÿÿ..
00000080   01 04 45 54 68 65 20 54   69 6D 65 73 20 30 33 2F   ..EThe Times 03/
00000090   4A 61 6E 2F 32 30 30 39   20 43 68 61 6E 63 65 6C   Jan/2009 Chancel
000000A0   6C 6F 72 20 6F 6E 20 62   72 69 6E 6B 20 6F 66 20   lor on brink of
000000B0   73 65 63 6F 6E 64 20 62   61 69 6C 6F 75 74 20 66   second bailout f
000000C0   6F 72 20 62 61 6E 6B 73   FF FF FF FF 01 00 F2 05   or banksÿÿÿÿ..ò.
000000D0   2A 01 00 00 00 43 41 04   67 8A FD B0 FE 55 48 27   *....CA.gŠý°þUH'
000000E0   19 67 F1 A6 71 30 B7 10   5C D6 A8 28 E0 39 09 A6   .gñ¦q0·.\Ö¨(à9.¦
000000F0   79 62 E0 EA 1F 61 DE B6   49 F6 BC 3F 4C EF 38 C4   ybàê.aÞ¶Iö¼?Lï8Ä
00000100   F3 55 04 E5 1E C1 12 DE   5C 38 4D F7 BA 0B 8D 57   óU.å.Á.Þ\8M÷º..W
00000110   8A 4C 70 2B 6B F1 1D 5F   AC 00 00 00 00            ŠLp+kñ._¬....
```

Bitcoin's "genesis block," showing how a Bitcoin token is a cryptographically coded string of characters.
Source: Wikipedia

By tokenizing the DC/EP, the PBOC will enable a critical feature called "loose-coupling," which allows for the offline transfer of tokens. This feature is considered key to the broad adoption of digital currency within China. Token-based "loose coupling" is best illustrated by comparison with account-based systems.

Version 1.0 mobile payment systems require a constant connection to a data network to make or receive payment. As such they are "tightly coupled" to accounts. Tight account-based coupling is strict and simple: no connection, no payment. The money isn't in a token form on your phone, but instead in an account, and you need to connect to the account to make or receive payment.

> *Loose coupling enabled through tokenization allows payment to take place without connection to a network.*

Loose-coupling, which is possible only through tokenization, allows payment to take place absent connection to a network. How is this possible? Tokenization means the digital currency can be stored in a cryptographic form on a mobile device, and can be transferred to another device independent of network connection. This is the most highly touted feature of China's DC/EP. This, above all other features, makes the DC/EP the rightful heir to cash. It allows for the replacement of cash in even the most remote environments, as it effectively reproduces the transferability of paper money.

2. Spending tokens using UTXO

Our two-tier DC/EP system is beginning to take shape. We've got tokens and now need to understand how to spend them. Once again, the PBOC will go to the blockchain and cryptocurrency world, this time adopting the Unspent Transaction Output or (UTXO) model. Unlike account-based systems that use serial transaction processing to track payments, UTXO enables the processing of large numbers of transactions in parallel.

The easiest way to visualize UTXO is through its similarities with cash payment. Imagine paying five vendors simultaneously, when all you have is cash, and no coins for making exact change. Depending on the sum, you'll overpay most if not all vendors with a combination of bills, and then receive change in return. Each vendor processes the banknotes independently of the other. In effect, each payment works in a parallel processing system.

Compare that to an account-based transaction system. Paying five vendors with Alipay, for example, requires they be paid serially. One is paid the exact sum required, that money is subtracted from the account, which is updated, then the next paid, and so forth, until all five transactions are complete.

UTXO allows the use of DC/EP to pay multiple vendors, with each transaction independent of the other. There is no dipping into an account (remember, this works like cash). Unlike cash, our UTXO "notes" have odd values depending on how much prior transactions have left in our wallet. When we spend DC/EP, some combination of UTXO that exceeds the amount spent is bundled together, spent, and UTXO change returned.

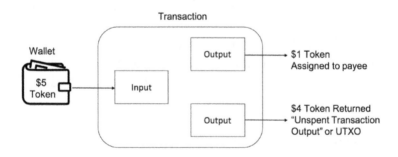

A UTXO transaction where $5 token is input resulting in two outputs. A new $1 token is created and spent, and a new $4 token returned as change or UTXO.

While UTXO is a bit complicated, it offers great advantages in transaction processing speed. Payments are independent of one another on the system. A user can theoretically make simultaneous mobile transactions, without one holding up the next. UTXO also allows for asynchronous payments, where the processing happens after the payment. This occurs with offline payments where payments are made and accepted but only processed by the system after a mobile device returns online. As with all things digital, there is always a trade-off.

Not surprisingly, UTXO technologies must avoid "double spending" where a digital instrument is sent to two parties, and accepted by both. Cryptocurrencies handle this problem through "consensus" algorithms where the nodes on the blockchain agree and record the token, preventing it from being spent twice. China's DC/EP avoids this blockchain issue more efficiently, by relying on a single centralized system which is less susceptible to double spending and impervious to 51% attacks, a problem in the cryptocurrency world. In a 51% attack, malicious nodes comprising more than half of those on the blockchain, reach consensus on a fraudulent transaction to rob the system.

3. Wallets

Our two-tier DC/EP system's final component is the wallet, the user interface where digital currency is stored, expended, or received. Interestingly, this component of technology, the one connecting the DC/EP with the user, is not provided by the PBOC. Instead, the PBOC has tasked commercial banks and payment companies with developing it. This design decision makes sense, given that the DC/EP will come from the conversion of account-based RMB in commercial banks. The bank interfaces are all unique, so a wallet that requires a direct connection with the user's account for exchanging DC/EP with account-based RMB is better left to the bank. Users can have multiple wallets provided by their commercial banks, just as they can have multiple bank accounts.

Agricultural Bank of China's digital wallet,
used in DC/EP trials, with English translations.

From a technical perspective, the wallet's primary job is to hold the keys that allow for encryption and decryption of tokens stored and transferred by the user. The system uses two specific keys, a public key and a private key. Public keys are shared when transacting between two wallets, and form the cryptographic basis for a confirmed, and therefore trusted, relationship.

Public keys allow:

1. confirmation that your private key signed a token from your wallet, and
2. encryption of my token to send to your wallet.

Private keys allow:

1. decryption of a token encrypted with my public key, and
2. signing a token that can be confirmed by my public key.

It's not as complicated as it sounds. It's sufficient to say that for two wallets to transfer DC/EP between them, the public and private keys confirm the players in the transaction, and encrypt and decrypt the tokens for secure handover. This procedure makes falsifying a transaction a practical impossibility, and happens behind the scenes without the users' awareness. As you may have guessed, this procedure was borrowed from cryptocurrencies, and is the basis of the cryptographic "trust" you may hear fans of cryptocurrencies tout.

The concept of using a digital wallet is second nature in China, where all Version 1.0 payment systems use a wallet or app to send and receive funds. Typically, users have both an Alipay and WeChat Pay wallet, but may also have any of the other half dozen or so payment company wallets available. All of these apps will likely be adapted to handle DC/EP, meaning they will accept DC/EP or make payment with them, but they will not be able to convert or retire DC/EP into a commercial bank account.

Under this system, DC/EP use is not directly tied to either the payment networks or the originating bank. Third-party companies therefore can and will build DC/EP payment apps. It's important to quickly note that under PBOC nomenclature, the payment apps that handle DC/EP may not in fact qualify as "wallets" in their strict definition of the word. Instead, they are considered DC/EP custody accounts or simply apps; the distinction is based on payment apps' inability to create or retire DC/EP. This may seem like a fine point, irrelevant for users who will use whatever app or wallet that makes payments most easily. It will make only a minor difference if the PBOC limits or restricts the number of DC/EP "wallets" a user may have.

The coming battle for the customers' DC/EP app of choice will be interesting. Commercial bank wallets and lesser third-party apps will have to beat the convenience of the superapps to pull clients away. Right now, innovation teams at Alipay and WeChat Pay are trying to figure out what "killer" features will motivate users to forsake the new bank digital wallets, and stick with the payment apps they use and love.

China Construction Bank (CCB) recently launched a trial version of a DC/EP wallet, and seems to have unwittingly revealed the transfer limits for DC/EP wallets. CCB's wallet documentation offers four tiers of wallet service. Tier 1 wallets are reserved for non-mobile users and have the greatest cash transfer limits, which were not published. Tier 2-4 wallets are for mobile users, and CCB was kind enough to post the wallet limits.

Tier 2 mobile wallet limits taken from the trial app are a DC/EP balance of up to RMB 10,000 max (US$ 1,480) with a cap per single transaction of RMB 5,000 (US$ 740), a maximum daily spend of RMB 10,000, and an annual maximum spend of RMB 300,000 (US$ 43,000). Tier 3 users are limited to an RMB 2,000 balance, with an RMB 2,000 maximum spend and an annual limit of RMB 50,000. Finally, Tier 4 users would have a maximum wallet balance of RMB 1,000, RMB 500 maximum spend, and an annual limit of RMB 10,000. These Tier 4 wallet limitations likely encompass offline transactions between two phones exchanging funds by tapping.

CCB's leaked figures are not out of line with the personal limits for WeChat and Alipay mobile payments, which are RMB 10,000 per transfer and RMB 200,000 per year. So it seems likely that CCB leaked actual figures rather than trying to confound competitors. The most interesting part of these limits is the RMB 10,000 DC/EP balance limit. This relatively small limit on DC/EP holdings seems to ensure that large RMB conversions from user accounts do not adversely impact the bank's reserves.

While most of the discussion about DC/EP wallets focuses on mobile versions, there will also be two variations. First, a computer-based version for business, which presents a clear opportunity for commercial banks to win back users. Banks will build systems that seamlessly integrate with account-based RMB, and they hope this will coax some clients to reduce their reliance on superapp payment systems. A "Tier 1" terminal-based wallet can be expected to have transfer amounts in proportion to the company's size and client base.

The second variation of DC/EP wallet is a credit card-like device referred to in PBOC patent applications as a "Digital Currency Chip Card" or "IC Card." The card would likely be purchased from a bank and tied to an individual user through thumb print recognition to allow for offline transfers of DC/EP using the card. The chip card frees the user from using a cell phone and would allow the DC/EP to be transported and used directly from the chip card. The chip card will likely be the way elderly and tourists use the DC/EP to make small purchases offline without buying or using a mobile device. These small offline purchases may be included in the "Tier 4" service level referenced above.

Mobile wallets are one area where blockchain may finally enter the picture. Wallet transfers to and from the commercial bank may use blockchain technology if the bank so chooses. While we've seen diagrams of the bank's test version wallets, we do not yet know if any individual banks use blockchain on their wallet apps. The selection of wallet technology and design will be solely at the discretion of the commercial bank or third party, and it seems likely that some will use this technology.

4. Smart contracts

Smart contracts are a way of embedding a programming language into the DC/EP to allow the token to think for itself and carry out its program. They enable the DC/EP to expand its functionality and go beyond being a simple carrier of value and become intelligent by carrying out embedded programs. Simple coding may put limits on the ability to spend a token, for example: "The holder may spend no more than RMB 100 per day." More sophisticated smart contracts could encode insurance or investment policies within the token, specifying complex payouts dependent on multiple contingencies. The possibilities are endless.

Smart contracts are an "optional feature" and not strictly necessary for the DC/EP to do its primary job of being a cash replacement. The smart contract feature is included in China's DC/EP as a means of future-proofing and will be "turned off" at launch. The PBOC recognizes that simultaneously launching its DC/EP and enabling smart contracts contains substantial risks. For one thing, smart contract operating code can be complicated and difficult to debug. An error in a contract that causes a loss of confidence in the PBOC's new DC/EP would be a disaster. So while fans of smart contracts may disagree, the PBOC's perspective is that the feature could cause more problems than it's worth, at least in the early stages of the DC/EP launch.

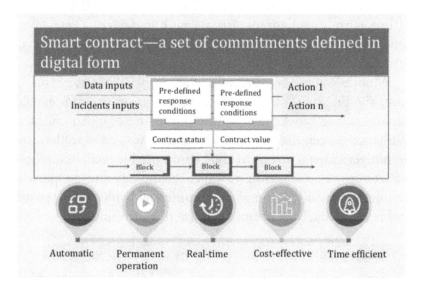

Smart contracts will be turned off in China's DC/EP at launch but will be enabled in the future. Smart contracts offer tremendous functionality, but can potentially cause legal and systems issues if not developed carefully.
Source: PBOC

Ethereum, an open-source blockchain platform for decentralized apps, has some of the most advanced smart contracts going. This capability has been used to create decentralized autonomous organizations (DAO), crypto exchanges, and the deservedly maligned "initial coin offerings" (ICOs). Errors in coding in one DAO (aptly named "The DAO") caused cryptocurrency losses of US$ 50 million. Meanwhile, ICOs continue to raise legal issues because they are considered illegal securities offerings in many jurisdictions. I mention Ethereum to illustrate the potential for unintended consequences in smart contracts. Their potential to bring unwanted scrutiny to a government-sponsored digital currency is certainly cause for concern. If the PBOC learned anything from smart contracts on the Ethereum network, it's that they have tremendous power and, as such, need to be treated with tremendous care.

That said, one day the PBOC will realize its dream of using smart contracts in its DC/EP. One example of potential use that would fit with the PBOC's goal of internationalizing the RMB is Ant Group's recently launched trade finance network, named "Trusple" (an amalgam of the words trust and simple). The system uses smart contracts for international trade finance to embed order placement, payment, logistics, and tax policy for quick and seamless cross-border transactions. It is not a stretch to think that use cases like this could help promote international adoption of the RMB someday. In the meantime, the PBOC will continue to monitor smart contract use cases very carefully.

Even without the use of smart contracts the DC/EP will still be able to think for itself to a limited but useful degree. It will deploy a different form of intelligence that is not embedded in the DC/EP as code so much as contained within its network. As we will see in the next section, China's DC/EP will be tightly monitored using "big data." Big-data systems can control the use of RMB and create the semblance of intelligence even if it's not directly built into the token.

A simple example of how this might be used is in blocking the exchange of the DC/EP by certain parties or in certain jurisdictions. In this case, the big-data center attached to the network would detect that one of the parties is not approved to receive or send and simply block the transfer. The DC/EP isn't programmed for this action; instead it is the big-data center on the network controlling the transfer. More exciting examples are far more subtle. Big data could be used to control exchange rates, turn on the interest rate function built into the DC/EP, or create special conditions for DC/EP use between two specific counterparties.

The options for a form of intelligence are limitless and imbue a degree of "smart" behavior due to control built into the network rather than embedded in the token itself.

5. Anonymity

When we think of anonymity, we all think of the suitcases full of (usually) untraceable cash that are a staple of gangster movies in both the East and West. Cash is the quintessential form of anonymous payment as it has no record of provenance. Digital anonymity in almost all forms is inferior to that of cash. Even Bitcoin is far from anonymous. The FBI can well attest that Bitcoin transactions are difficult to trace, though not untraceable. Arrests of the founder of the notorious "Silk Road" drug trafficking site or the former CEO of failed crypto exchange Mt. Gox provide examples of Bitcoin's traceability.

China's DC/EP has taken an approach to anonymity that is undoubtedly useful but certainly no match for cash.

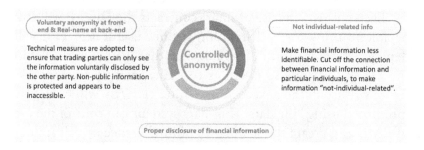

Controlled Anonymity allows the buyer to remain anonymous to the seller, just like cash, improving on existing mobile payment systems.
Source: PBOC

Let's be clear: China's DC/EP has an ownership record built into each token that follows it throughout its life, automatically limiting its anonymity. Furthermore, the PBOC is clear that behind each DC/EP transaction, data flows to PBOC's data centers, which register each coin to a real user. China's DC/EP is far from anonymous. This makes the PBOC's solution to limited anonymity all the more ingenious.

The PBOC recognizes that, as with cash, "individual-related information" may be withheld from the counterparty on a DC/EP transaction. When I buy dumplings in cash from a street vendor, the vendor does not know who I am or my personal information. Similarly, with China's DC/EP, the buyer can select whether to reveal personal information to the seller when purchasing. This is a form of counterparty anonymity replicating that of cash. This feature does not exist in Version 1.0 payment methods, where the dumpling vendor knows, to a limited degree, who is making the payment.

The PBOC further recognizes that access to the financial and personal information contained in the DC/EP must be limited to the minimum required to suit the transaction counterparties' needs. For example, while the payee may not need personal information when I purchase dumplings, they certainly want to log the transaction details—the how much and when of my purchase, in order to keep their records in order. For their part in this transaction, commercial banks will need to see the user's identity information with every transaction, as they may place digital currency into personal accounts, but not the details of the counterparty with whom they transacted. Banks also do not get to see prior transaction details encrypted within the token, only the most recent transaction relevant to their needs.

The PBOC is setting up a system to sequester privacy by giving the related parties only the amount of data required for each to do their job. It's a sophisticated solution that improves the existing payment systems that dole out the same data for every transaction. Of course, it will never satisfy those fixated by the anonymity of cash or pseudo-anonymity of cryptocurrency. Cash isn't going anywhere in China, despite launching a DC/EP, and if people still want to use cash for privacy reasons, they most certainly can and will.

Relative to the existing mobile payment systems and credit cards used in China, the DC/EP privacy system represents a significant improvement. From the user perspective, the new DC/EP will afford greater counterparty anonymity when making payment. That the PBOC will have near real-time payment data is irrelevant, as this data is already available to PBOC and law enforcement (with a slight delay) from the payment companies. In the end, as far as China users are concerned, the DC/EP represents a net improvement in privacy over existing payment methods.

6. Why no blockchain?

The PBOC is essentially creating a hybrid system building upon what it considers the best features of blockchain systems: tokens, loose-coupling, UTXO, and cryptographic security. Simultaneously, it is very consciously leaving behind what it perceives as the worst elements: poor performance and decentralization. The PBOC's attitude toward blockchain is rooted in practicality rather than a religious conviction toward blockchain as a technology.

Mu Changchun, Director of the PBOC's Digital Currency Research Institute, makes the PBOC's agnostic attitude toward blockchain crystal clear. His statement is so compelling that it is worthy of publication in full:

> Our (PBOC) payments network during last year's Singles' Day [November 11th shopping holiday] sale at its peak handled 92,771 transactions per second. In comparison, Bitcoin and Ethereum handle seven and 10 to 20 transactions per second, respectively. [Facebook's] Libra, based on its recently released white paper, is 1,000 transactions per second. For a country as big as China, it's impossible to achieve high scalability by purely relying on blockchain. As such, we have decided to remain technologically neutral and do not necessarily rely on one fixed technological path.

The exact transaction-per-second figures attributable to blockchain may be debatable, but not to the orders of magnitude required to handle the tremendous payment flows within China. During the 2019 Singles Day peak, Ant Group's systems processed an amazing 544,000 transactions per second. For comparison, the Visa network peaks at around 65,000 transactions per second. Based on technical rather than ideological views of blockchain, it is unlikely that current blockchain systems, even with improvements, can supply the processing power required by China's digital payments of 300,000 transactions per second.

A second quote by Mu Changchun explains why, in further detail: "The blockchain at the cost of synchronous storage and co-calculation of a large amount of redundant data, sacrifices system processing efficiency and some of the customer's privacy, and is not yet suitable for high-concurrency scenarios such as traditional retail payments." While his comments on customer privacy issues are certainly open for debate, his comments on co-calculation and concurrency are not. The key to decentralized blockchain networks is that each transaction is shared across the network and registered only after redundant calculations across nodes on the chain are completed and compared. In high volume scenarios, this can create a backlog as UTXO transactions pile up, just as they do with Bitcoin today. Throwing more computer processors at the problem can alleviate some of the backlog, but rapidly becomes expensive and technically impractical.

To be sure, fans of cryptocurrency and blockchain will scoff at China's DC/EP use of limited anonymity and centralized networks. Many fervently believe that decentralized blockchain's most significant contribution is currency's anonymity, even if imperfect, and that money should remain private. Anonymity brought by decentralized networks is anathema to the PBOC, which contends that it is solely responsible for controlling and monitoring currency flow within the country, whether paper or digital. These are the starting points for a philosophical debate that will not be easily resolved, and is certainly not unique to China. Nations designing DC/EPs will wrestle with the degree of anonymity to provide on their systems, and whether blockchain is the correct path to take. The profound implications for tax collection and money laundering, known issues with cryptocurrencies, will lead many countries to follow a path not too dissimilar to China's.

THREE CENTERS (三中心)

The final components of our DC/EP are the "three centers," which refer to the three major central processing centers run by the PBOC that make the DC/EP work. They constitute the "secret sauce" of China's DC/EP, and we know the least about them. It is very likely to stay that way for some time to come. The reasons for this are not so much that the PBOC is worried about leaking top state secrets; it is more that their internal workings—like those of your bank or credit card company—aren't open for discussion. Certainly, this has something to do with security, but also because these systems are subject to frequent upgrades and change as technology evolves.

The three centers are "Verification," "Registration," and "Big Data." While their internal workings may be unpublicized, there is no great mystery to what is going on behind the scenes, as the jobs they do are comparable to those in banking, credit card, and cryptocurrencies. These centers represent the back end of the DC/EP and are out of sight and mind for most users, just like credit card security systems are—until a transaction is blocked. While they may not be the most eye-catching part of the DC/EP, they are its nerve center and brain and thus are truly where the magic happens.

THE VERIFICATION CENTER

The verification center is responsible for verifying the identity of DC/EP users. It is essentially a centralized KYC platform to ensure that DC/EP users are authorized. It is directly analogous to those used by the West's financial institutions. Its responsibility is verifying the identity of users who use DC/EP both at an institutional and personal level. Just like your credit card or bank verifies that you are who you say you are when making a transaction, the PBOC will do the same. How it happens, of course, is different, because this is China. Let's examine KYC for two groups of users—those within China and those who are not.

KYC within China is a straightforward process. For the most part, the government knows who you are, via several large databases. The first, of course, is the central government's database of identification (ID) numbers for both citizens and corporate entities. This is the base level of KYC in China and is roughly comparable to state IDs such as identity cards in the West. As in the West, the database is flawed, because changes of address are frequently not registered, so the ID of a supposed Beijing resident may turn up living in Shanghai.

The next database is that of the cell phone carrier. While registration of cellphones to state-issued IDs is increasingly important in the West, it is mandatory in China. A critical difference between China and the West is that in the former, every mobile device is linked to a state-issued ID card, and starting in 2019, to a facial ID scan for those who register phones. Here again, there is some room for misidentification. Many mobile users use phones registered to family members or other third parties. Vanity phone numbers with multiple repeating eights, meaning good luck, are frequently sold to small businesses and may be registered under another ID number.

Finally, the third principal database is the KYC performed by the individual's bank, which links accounts, IDs, and phones. Physical bank branches still have in-person identity checks for all of these three pieces of information. Digital banks do not have in-person registration, and instead use ID cards and facial recognition gleaned from mobile verification to open an account and ensure that the phone, ID card, and person all match up to the same user.

The combination of these three data sets comprises the core of digital KYC in China. It's not particularly new. These systems are in place and already at work for Version 1.0 payment systems, all of which tightly tie the mobile device to users and their payment history. If it isn't abundantly clear by now, China's DC/EP provides the convenience of cryptocurrency but not the anonymity.

From a digital perspective, the registration center serves another critical function: checking one crucial piece of information that is the byproduct of tokenization. As noted previously, every DC/EP transaction token is signed cryptographically by a "public" and "private" key, which are unique digital identifiers for each user. In essence, the keys are a digital signature that identifies every user and "signs" every transaction from the user's wallet. Even payments using controllable anonymity, where the user's name is not identified to the payee, include this cryptographically encoded signature. The system recognizes you as a permitted user at the token level through this signature. The verification center provides the critical link between your physical identity, name, and address with your digital signature as defined by your keys. The registration and big data centers have only your digital signature but do not know who you are, unless they connect with the verification center.

For international users of the DC/EP, KYC will become decidedly more complicated for the PBOC. It will be a difficult problem for them to solve and is likely related to the PBOC's surprise announcement of a JV partnership with SWIFT. When the DC/EP first launches into international markets, the PBOC will likely restrict use to clients within their foreign network of state banks, allowing the PBOC to rely on the bank's KYC processes for new users. Severely limiting DC/EP use is antithetical to the PBOC's intent, so eventually they will have to build KYC profiles based on a combination of local IDs, public databases, and facial scans. Given that China will be targeting small business users in developing countries, KYC is going to be a significant issue that will require specific solutions for each country.

It's likely that the base level of KYC for foreign users of the DC/EP will be a combination of mobile phone identifiers combined with face and ID card scans. This system is well established in China, verifying new users within a low DC/EP transaction limit. Raising the limit would require additional levels of KYC confirmation.

Example of identity confirmation using a passport and facial recognition scans. AI facial recognition compares the ID photo with the photo of the person registering. Here the system is used on a Shanghai household registration form.

THE REGISTRATION CENTER

The registration center confirms and records the ownership and flow of DC/EP transactions. While centralized, it takes its inspiration from cryptocurrency networks. The registration center is where DC/EP tokens are born and die, and it is the engine room of the system, providing the processing power to both encrypt and decrypt transactions at high rates of flow.

DC/EP is created and destroyed in the Registration Center. It registers the PBOC's conversion of every account-based RMB into DC/EP tokens and their reconversion. It also validates all transactions, and as it functions on a "loosely coupled" basis, the registration process may be asynchronous with the actual transaction. The best example of this is found in the off-network phone-to-phone transactions. The registration center also traces the flow of tokens through the system, retaining a record of their entire life, including all transactions and owners. Imagine following a cash bill throughout its life from printing through destruction with a history of every hand it passed through and every transaction conducted.

Above all, the registration center is an authentication engine, providing the computing power that allows transactions coming into the network to be confirmed. What is critical to understand is that it is very different from an account that tracks balances. Instead, think of it as a database that identifies each coin. The registration center authenticates UTXO transactions in parallel by performing a series of cryptographic calculations. The calculations confirm that the UTXO transaction is valid, rather than checking a balance. The tokens are the money, and the concept of account is irrelevant.

All authentication is not created equal, and the different levels of mobile wallet Type 2, 3, and 4 we saw in the earlier section are directly linked to different types of authentication processes. Mobile device processing power and the ability to collect biometric data will directly impact the authentication process. Also, the end-point connection to the network may change, and all of these factors will potentially impact the calculated level of certainty in token authentication. The direct result of this process is that differing wallet types have different spending limits. Naturally, the lowest level of authentication found in offline transfers has the lowest limits.

Compare this with blockchain networks, which spread this computational work out over a network of computers and require each independent node in the chain to perform the same calculation and agree on the answer. This is called "consensus" and is required to confirm a transaction and form a new block on the chain. The process is computationally slow and redundant but allows for decentralizing the computer network with some genuine security enhancements. In contrast, with China's DC/

EP, centralized systems perform the calculations, eliminating the need for redundancy, which allows for faster processing. Of course, the cost is that the network is centralized, which bears on security, but so are the networks of major credit card processors who also need centralized computing's speed advantage. The lack of blockchain does not mean that the process is inherently less secure.

I acknowledge that some blockchain systems' security can be superior to centralized systems. Yet this is certainly not always the case. Blockchain and cryptocurrency's security comes not just from decentralization but from the cryptographic algorithms built into blockchain systems. Commercial "blockchain" systems in the West, such as those offered by "R3," no longer use traditional blockchain architecture, but instead opt for advanced cryptographic techniques.

While we likely will never know the exact algorithms for China's DC/EP, research papers from the PBOC's Blockchain Research Institute confirm that China's highly advanced SM2 cryptographic signature algorithms may be in play. SM2 is an algorithm published by the Chinese Commercial Cryptography Administration and is already at work in commercial and government applications in that country. SM2 is a replacement for RSA cryptosystems commonly used on the web in the West.

As stated, the PBOC's DC/EP system appears to borrow more from modern cryptography used in blockchain systems than the blockchain concept itself. This puts the PBOC in good company with some commercial so-called "blockchain" companies, as mentioned above. PBOC systems will be state of the art and run message authentication codes (MAC), hash algorithms, and ciphertext, as do other high-security encrypted messaging systems. These techniques all have the goal of making each token unique, confidential, secure, and tamperproof. Each of these cryptographic techniques consumes system processing power. The PBOC's system designers will need to preserve a delicate balance between security and the massive throughput speed the system requires.

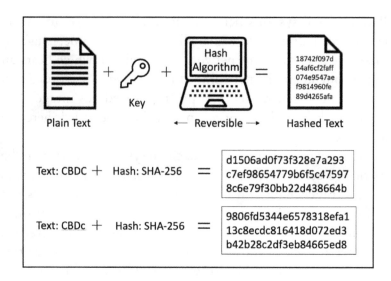

Hashing is one of several cryptographic processes used to create tokens and render them secure and unique at the cost of system processing power. Tiny changes in the text string result in an avalanche of changes in the hashed text.

One feature of note is that PBOC systems can de-encrypt all DC/EP tokens to log and maintain a registry of their use. Cryptocurrencies such as Bitcoin, in contrast, use a one-way form of encryption that you cannot decrypt without your key. The result is one of Bitcoin's least favorite features: losing your key means your cryptocurrency is gone forever. The PBOC system is cryptographically reversible at the PBOC level, meaning it is technically feasible to recover DC/EP if you lose your phone. While there are no procedures for doing this just yet, it should allay fears that DC/EP balances are like cryptocurrency balances that can vanish forever.

THE BIG-DATA ANALYSIS CENTER

If the registration center is the engine room of China's DC/EP, think of the big-data center as its brain. It provides the DC/

EP with a form of intelligence that does not exist in cash or account-held currency.

The big-data center is responsible for analyzing the massive amount of data generated by the registration center. With in-depth data mining, the PBOC can see DC/EP use in near real-time, including spending details that include where, who, and how. From the PBOC's point of view, this will give it tremendous real-time insights into currency use in support of macro-economic policy decisions and the more mundane task of tamping down fraud, money-laundering, and crime.

Clearly, from the users' perspective, spending DC/EP means that their financial life is an open book to the central bank, causing chills among the privacy-minded. This raises the obvious question: does the loss in privacy merit the use of DC/EP? In China, paradoxically, the DC/EP will bring an improvement in privacy relative to the current mobile payment systems.

The PBOC is not releasing technical details of the big-data center, but it will likely be similar to cloud-based centers in the West that use big-data analysis for fraud prevention in all bank and credit card transactions. The checking process must map transaction-to-acceptance criteria within milliseconds, so as not to unduly delay flow through the system. What makes China's system different is the granularity of data available on individual transactions.

Frankly, the potential for big data to make the currency "smart" is almost unlimited. Not only can the system use data contained within the DC/EP, but it may also collect virtually any other network data or app data associated with the transaction. Let's examine a few use scenarios where this might be beneficial.

- Fraud and money laundering: The technology for spotting payment irregularities is already well tested in the mobile payment space. Using existing systems in the DC/EP environment should not be technically challenging. Here the parallels with Western credit card and bank security systems are clear and relatively standard.

- Crypto-Exchanges: "The currency is not for speculation," said Mu Changchun. Fans of cryptocurrency, however, are already trying to better understand how they can get their hands on DC/EP and trade it in exchange for popular currencies like Bitcoin. The problem is, for an exchange to use DC/EP, it needs a valid DC/EP account. In this use case, the massive flows of DC/EP required to build an exchange would make it an easy target for the PBOC's big-data systems. Any DC/EP crypto-exchanges seeking to find an illegal loophole on WeChat or Alipay, as some currently do for Bitcoin, would find themselves quickly detected.

- Location: Anyone trying to watch Netflix from abroad is well aware of how digital services' location restrictions work. Given our age of TikTok and WeChat bans, it is likely that China will block some countries from using its DC/EP due to political or legal concerns. If the PBOC doesn't wish a given state to use the currency, it can turn it off within that region, even if the location is not a data packet contained within the token. The PBOC's big-data center can simply ban traffic originating from designated IP addresses, just like Netflix. The PBOC can also use network location data to turn on certain functions or deliver certain benefits, based on the country of use.

- Special issue or usage DC/EP: Big data enables the PBOC to designate special issues of DC/EP, say for rural farmers, or tokens that have tax or other benefits attached. An example might be a tax credit attached to DC/EP spent within underprivileged regions in China. These development schemes already exist, but could be streamlined via digital programs.

- Stimulus payments: I include this one as it's a timely topic. Big data will allow China to precisely target who should receive DC/EP stimulus, delivered in a matter of seconds. This might pertain to residents in areas of natural disaster or other calamities, and would be of utility and social benefit to all.

The concept that the PBOC will suddenly become omniscient, given its access to countrywide DC/EP transaction data, is patently far-fetched. It's likely the PBOC will run into the "fallacy of big data." This is thinking that any additional data you collect gives you increasingly more significant insights. The fact is, there reaches a point where additional data becomes noise and adds little to overall understanding.

I am willing to bet that new means of defrauding the system will be developed despite the use of big data. Perhaps the DC/EP's greatest weakness is that the PBOC's big-data center only works with what's on the system, but can't verify whether it got there legally. This is analogous to cryptocurrency exchanges that are prone to hacks and fraud, while the cryptocurrency networks are untouched. Meaning that ill-gotten gains from account-based systems will be effortlessly conveyed through DC/EP systems. Besides, the very exactitude of DC/EP can, in the hands of the right money laundering magician, potentially be used against it. No one knows how just yet. Soon after DC/EP launches, we should all look for a series of relatively quiet PBOC announcements restricting use or reducing payment amounts in specific sectors. These acts may just be in response to new types of DC/EP-related money laundering.

A POTENTIAL DC/EP TRANSACTION

Now that we've outlined the essential features in China's DC/EP, let's look at a transaction to try to put it all together.

Imagine we want to spend RMB 150 in DC/EP to buy xiaolongbao (soup dumpling) from our favorite vendor. Our digital wallet already has RMB 100 in currency remaining.

1. We go to our wallet and convert an additional RMB 100 in account-based RMB to DC/EP, making a 200 RMB balance. Simultaneously the bank takes DC/EP out of its

accounts in a 1:1 ratio with the DC/EP RMB transferred to you.

2. Our digital wallet now has RMB 200. We do not know that the RMB 100 already in our wallet contains UTXO of RMB 29.51, RMB 40, and RMB 30.49—"change" left over from previous transactions.

3. When we buy our xiaolongbao, we have the choice of remaining anonymous to the vendor or not. As we regularly buy from this vendor, we allow the vendor to receive our details and opt not to use the anonymity feature while using QR codes to scan and transfer balances.

4. Our wallet using UTXO sends tokens in the amount of RMB 100, RMB 29.51, and RMB 30.49 for an overpayment of RMB 10 returned to us from the seller's wallet. The mobile phones use cryptographic keys for the first level of security on the transaction.

5. The transaction is completed and as we are online, the payment data is sent to the "three centers." The registration center verifies our account and key, the verification center simultaneously decrypts the token information and validates the spent and received tokens. The big-data center checks to see if users have any restrictions on their accounts or the tokens have any special characteristics associated with them that impact their use. For fully offline transactions, this step is delayed until the devices reconnect to the network.

6. At the end of the day, the xiaolongbao seller would like to deposit his sales in the bank and takes the digital RMB in his wallet and transfers them to account-based RBM in his bank. Simultaneously the bank adds the tokens to its balance and returns a like amount to the seller's RMB account.

7. At the end of the working day, the bank has an oversupply of digital RMB and would like more account-based RMB to satisfy its reserving requirements. It sends digital

RMB to the PBOC, and both organizations adjust their balances of account-based and digital RMB. The "three centers" make a note of the transfer. The PBOC then destroys the returned digital RMB and removes them from the registration system's active list.

This simplified version lays out the basic steps for processing China's DC/EP. What I have intentionally left out are the device-level security protocols that would potentially change the internal workings. For example, what if the person buying did not use a cell phone but an IC card without network connectivity. The transaction would still go through but hit the verification center using a specialized set of cryptographic functions and limitations to transaction size. If the transfer were made offline, by phone-to-phone transfer, the verification center would not even see the transaction until one of the phones goes online, and the transaction is processed after the fact.

DC/EP IS PURPOSE-BUILT FOR BLOCKCHAIN

So far, the PBOC has been clear that its DC/EP is blockchain-inspired, even if it will not use blockchain as its core technology. This does not mean that it will always be sidelined, indeed the PBOC has been issuing new patents to transport DC/EP across blockchain networks. These patents give us a hint as to a potential role for blockchain in the DC/EP's future. China's mandate to promote blockchain was stated by no less than General Secretary and President Xi Jinping; it is only natural that DC/EP will synch with both government policy and the massive new "Blockchain Service Network."

> *"It is essential for blockchain technology to play a bigger role in building China's strength in cyberspace, developing the digital economy and advancing the economic and social development."*
>
> Xi Jinping, General Secretary of the Communist Party of China and President of the People's Republic of China

China's Blockchain Service Network (BSN) is a groundbreaking infrastructure project that will create the world's largest global network for hosting blockchain applications. The project has nodes in some 128 Chinese cities and eight foreign nodes, spanning six continents. The vision is to create a global network of over two hundred nodes and to turn blockchain into a new kind of global infrastructure, just as the internet's TCP/IP is today. The BSN's objective is to reduce the cost of developing and deploying blockchain applications at scale "to near zero" and will run most Western blockchain protocols on two separate networks.

The first network, for consumption within China, will run permissioned networks that comply with government policy. The BSN white paper is clear: "According to the requirements of current Chinese laws and regulations, it is very difficult to legally operate permission-less blockchains in China due to their lack of administration and liberal nature." The second network, for global consumption, runs full permission-less blockchain networks. The two networks are entirely separate, meaning that the BSN's permission-less blockchain network will have limited China availability.

China's DC/EP is purpose-built to be carried by blockchain and BSN. The BSN's launch is creating thousands of new blockchain companies, and inasmuch as the apps they build will transport currency, they will all use the new DC/EP. So the intersection of blockchain and DC/EP is assured. A few use cases are already turning up in PBOC projects, such as a blockchain trade finance platform sponsored by its research institute, where the BSN and digital RMB are combined.

Patent ID number	Name
CN201611208947	A method, device and system for the regulation of digital currency transaction information based on blockchain
CN201710056081	A method, system and terminal for digital currency based on blockchain
CN201710496296	Method and system for the management of nodes
CN201710494860	A method and device for the transaction of digital currency
CN201710495156	Method and device for the usage of digital currency and transactions
CN201810922484	A method and device for the management of blockchain-based digital currency wallet addresses
CN201710056081	A method, system and device for the secure usage of blockchain-based digital currencies

PBOC Blockchain patents for use with DC/EP.
Source: Digitalchamber.org

THREE POTENTIAL USES FOR BLOCKCHAIN IN THE DC/EP

Three direct uses of blockchain and the BSN may come up in future announcements by the PBOC. The PBOC has not mentioned any just yet, but they appear to be supported by the

PBOC's blockchain patents. Leaving them out here would be an omission.

The first is a blockchain system used for large-scale bank-to-bank or business-to-business transfers of DC/EP. The platform may be used to streamline transactions occurring within specialized bank transfer networks. Two examples of these are tax payment and social benefit transfer networks that send money from banks to specific government agencies. Either may benefit from using DC/EP for real-time payment.

Though it's a small chance, the PBOC may use a second blockchain network to transmit DC/EP to commercial banks. Remember that this transfer is the first of the two-tier DC/EP system. PBOC has other means of moving the currency, but a blockchain network would suit the low transaction throughput required and provides additional network security. It is also in keeping with the PBOC's desire to continuously push the boundaries of digital innovation.

The third possibility for using blockchain, and potentially the BSN, is to hold identity documents and data input pertaining to the KYC portion of the verification center. This use makes some sense because it would guarantee secure transmission over the BSN from China's more remote provinces, or even potentially from international users. This use case is perhaps the most speculative, as unlike the prior two it is not supported by PBOC patents.

THE RISK OF WRITING ABOUT NEW TECHNOLOGY

I am confident that within several months of this book's publication, I will face the dreaded realization that something I wrote in this particular section is wrong or outdated. New details on the DC/EPs construction will be coming to light, and I am preparing for surprise announcements by the PBOC, as should you.

I've taken substantial risks in writing, and you in reading, a technical breakdown of a highly sophisticated digital product that has not yet launched. My rationale is that the greater risk is not understanding the basic principles of how China constructs its new DC/EP, and what it means for our common cashless future.

To deal with inevitable design changes, I've made a great effort to stick very closely to the "one coin, two repositories and three centers" model proposed by the PBOC. I've broken each of these individual sections into their component pieces to make it easier to visualize the DC/EP's structure. When the PBOC invariably announces further design details or changes, the reader will understand which component pieces will change and their effect on the overall structure. Rest assured, your investment today in time spent understanding China's DC/EP will have long-term value.

To keep up with these changes, I'll be posting modifications and notes here and hope you can visit to keep up to date:

QR Codes for updates
www.richturrin.com

12

CBDC IN DOMESTIC USE

China on Digital Currency:

> *"Shifting to a government-run digital payment system will help combat money laundering, gambling, and terror financing."*
>
> PBOC, unnamed spokesperson

The West on Digital Currency:

> *"A digital currency issued by a central bank would be a global target for cyberattacks, cyber counterfeiting, and cyber theft."*
>
> Jerome Powell, then-Federal Reserve Governor, 2017

In the future, for the Chinese people, the launch of the CBDC will be viewed as a footnote rather than the "Sputnik moment," as it may be perceived in the West. Given the gravity of the project, this may seem surprising, but as previously stated, most of China's population is already using Version 1.0 digital payment systems. The evolution of these systems to something newer and better will be seen as another step in the march of technological advances. CBDCs will bring new capabilities and advantages for sure, but the population is already enlightened to the benefits of digital payment.

As evidence, consider a trial of the CBDC in October 2020 in Shenzhen. It was met with great enthusiasm as it used a lottery system to disburse RMB 10 million in CBDC (or as it is referred to locally, DC/EP), in allotments of RMB 200 to the winners. Certainly free money is always a crowd pleaser, but two million applicants far exceeded everyone's expectations. Interestingly, after the trial was concluded, users commented that while they enjoyed using the DC/EP, they didn't see much difference from existing payment apps. Their response was, as predicted, blasé. With two great payment options already on their phones they weren't overly impressed by yet another. Still, that the digital currency reproduced the ease of use of the payment apps was regarded as a great success by the PBOC. Similar lotteries are planned for trials in Suzhou and other cities.

Another incident shows how enthusiastic users are for the DC/EP, even absent the lure of free money. In August 2020, China Construction Bank made a test DC/EP wallet available to users of their mobile app, and was quickly overwhelmed by applicants. They took down the trial and limited it to invitees only. This is a clear indicator of how popular the DC/EP is in the public imagination, and how keen people are to understand how this new payment method will better their lives.

The CBDC represents a fundamental change in the financial system's gears. Users desire to learn how to use it and what new services and changes in payment workflow they can expect. Innovators in every realm of the private sector are already doing their best to please them, by working out new uses for CBDC-based payment. Expectations are high, as they expect the CBDC to exceed the possibilities of Version 1.0 payment systems, already a high bar to clear. And it isn't just the private sector that is innovating. The PBOC is setting up a new fintech subsidiary to explore new uses of CBDCs, and investigations are underway about building a fully digital central bank, preparing for a day without cash.

If I'm writing fast enough, the CBDC will still be in the testing phase as you read this and not yet in final production. Many have expressed concern over, or simply noted, the PBOC's long testing phase. Every announcement of a new city testing the CBDC heightens expectations that the currency's launch is imminent. Some find the testing phase and city-by-city rollout painfully slow, especially observers accustomed to the relatively fast launch of cryptocurrencies, which go to market in a matter of weeks. CBDCs, as we've seen, are substantially more complicated than cryptocurrencies. They must integrate with existing central bank and commercial bank systems. They also require new back-end systems that the central bank has to build from scratch. It's laborious, and there is a tremendous risk to the PBOC if it gets it wrong.

> *The PBOC's test phase of the CBDC should not be seen as slow, but as meticulous.*

Rather than seeing the PBOC's CBDC testing phase as markedly drawn out, people would be wise to see it instead as meticulous. The risks of failure are enormous, as the world's attention is focused on the first-ever launch of a digital currency by a major economy. The PBOC is doing everything in its power to get it right, as there are no "do-overs." The cost of a public failure would be embarrassment with far-reaching implications, both internally with loss of public confidence in the institution, and externally to its global reputation. The risks are being managed with a prolonged city-by-city rollout, where new features are tested and tweaked to perfection before the full launch.

Compare this with Facebook Libra's (Diem) first proposed launch cycle, and the promises "to change everything" in about a year. Fans of stablecoins and cryptocurrency must remember that they are issued and traded in isolation, without direct connectivity to an active financial system. Their sole point of contact with the fiat currency is through crypto exchanges, which the issuers do not control. They may closely monitor issuance volumes (or in Bitcoin's case, have preset issuance limits), but there is no amalgamation with an existing banking structure, as with a central bank-issued currency.

Central banks will be responsible for interfacing with their own systems and ensure that the entire system from central bank to commercial bank, the retail point-of-sale system, and users' wallets works the first time, every time. This is in addition to the task of removing cash in circulation and replacing it with digital currency, to avoid excessive money creation. This is only one reason why the PBOC has every incentive not to rush, and to produce a perfect product.

BANKS VERSUS WECHAT PAY AND ALIPAY

The most significant innovation for domestic users of China's digital RMB is that it provides an alternative to using Alipay and WeChat Pay for domestic cash transactions. Instead, users will pay directly from their bank "wallets," with no fees attached. The bigger question remains: do people want to be free from these apps, when they are so useful?

The PBOC's goal has always been to replace free cash or, in central bank parlance, M0, as opposed to M1 or M2, which include short-term bank deposits. To back this point, the PBOC has been steadfast in declaring that the CBDC would not be interest-bearing. The PBOC has taken great pains to make the new digital cash replacement behave like cash. The best example of this is the ability to transfer money directly from phone to phone without using a network. It's the digital equivalent of handing a friend a banknote, or having the actual cash stored in your phone.

For ordinary people—"retail users" —paying directly with the new CBDC is not a massive advantage as the costs of sending cash through alternate payment systems is either free or hidden in the price of goods and services. Businesses, however, will welcome it as a way to receive payment without the small fees (.1% to .6%) paid to either of the payment giants. In the West, an equivalent would be companies liberated from credit card processing fees.

While their revenue streams will undoubtedly take a hit, WeChat Pay and Alipay will remain an integral part of the payment system. Their diversification can be seen in Ant Group's semi-annual report ending in June 2020. They report that digital payment and merchant services accounted for only 36% of their YTD total revenue. This is less than their take from CreditTech (loans), which accounted for 39%. InvestmentTech at 16% and Insurtech at 8% round out Ant's portfolio. These percentages show how fees on cash transfer are only a single revenue component on what are now highly diversified platforms. The impact of CBDC will be real to these payment platforms, but hardly destabilizing or threatening.

BANKS VERSUS "STICKY PLATFORMS"

Banks have suffered greatly at the hands of WeChat and Alipay, and frankly, there is no love lost between them. The "pause" of Ant's IPO and recent antitrust investigation into Alipay and WeChat by the PBOC may in part illustrate the degree of animosity. The timing of the pause—days before Ant's IPO and an antitrust investigation the month before—were more a product of genuine regulatory concern than the revenge of banks, but still the timing gives the impression that banks are getting even. (More on this topic in the chapter 19 on Ant.) That banks will imminently be able to offer direct digital payment is fundamentally a good thing, and will help embed digital payment more deeply into the financial system. The digital payment giants played their part by bringing instant payment to life; in turn, banks will soon share the spoils.

What the banks can't replicate, however, are the ecosystems WeChat and Alipay have developed. As I am fond of saying, "None of us goes to look at our bank website for fun on a Friday night." WeChat and Alipay have tremendously "sticky" platforms that allow you to handle most of your life needs, and draw you in to spend hours on their sites. Just because a bank has a digital payment system doesn't mean everyone will suddenly stop surfing elsewhere. Both WeChat and Alipay will support the digital RMB, so if users prefer, they will be able to use the new currency directly on these platforms for payment.

In fact, from this vantage point it appears that unless vendors start to offer substantial discounts to entice customers to leave the Alipay or WeChat platforms, there is little incentive to change payment habits. My household is a typical example. My monthly bills are already on both of these platforms, and without a financial incentive, I won't bother switching to my bank's new digital platform unless someone makes it well worth my while. Changing without that incentive would produce little benefit, only additional hassle.

Another essential feature of the digital platforms is the security they provide. They act as a middleman between transacting counterparties, holding funds in escrow until the package is delivered or service received. Any problems that develop during the transaction have a neutral intermediary to help resolve disputes. This feature is what put Alibaba's Alipay on the map. Banks may opt to develop a similar function as an intermediary. However, this necessitates setting up a new entity that would compete with the already established giants. Possible? Sure. But unlikely, given that China's banks have shown somewhat limited interest in redefining banking's traditional product lineup.

Alipay and WeChat Pay's stickiness and utility as an intermediary make them resistant to banks' efforts to dethrone them as kings of digital payment. With market share nearing 95% of all mobile payments, they have a formidable advantage. Banks may opt to woo the population with cash-back or other points schemes, just as the credit card industry has done elsewhere. But if you live in China, you'll have either WeChat or Alipay already open on your phone when it comes time to pay for something. Convenience may trump all when it comes to staying put or taking the time to open a bank's app.

NO VENDETTA

A small yet vocal group views China's CBDC as a nefarious government effort, hellbent on destroying Alipay and WeChat Pay's market dominance. While patently absurd, the notion bears brief discussion.

There is no question that China's CBDC is building on the shoulders of these giants. The creation of a CBDC should not be seen as a government vendetta, but instead as the next logical step in the digitization of money. China's digital economy now represents an astounding 36.2 percent of its total GDP, so creating a digital currency to match this economy is simply prudent. Similarly, a surmised initiative by the PBOC to develop a universal barcode (to streamline the QR code payment system) is also seen by conspiracy theorists as a threat rather than a basic convenience—as if one bar code, capable of working on both systems, were somehow a death blow to the payment giants.

> "WeChat and Alipay are wallets, while the digital yuan is the money in the wallet"

Both of these firms are systemically critical to China's economy and together wield tremendous influence. Both proved the value of digital payment and, more important, contributed mightily to China's GDP growth. As a means of dispelling any lingering question of their continued importance, Mu Changchun, head of the research institute for digital currency at the PBOC said, "WeChat and Alipay are wallets, while the digital yuan is the money in the wallet." That some see China's CBDC as built expressly to destroy Alipay and WeChat Pay's franchises seems blind to the fact that as great as these companies are, their mobile payment systems are only the first step in the broader evolution of digital currency.

As stated, the CBDC will surely impact the payment giants' revenue and decrease their lock on digital payment in China. People will have more choice, and a new form of legal tender, which is a good thing. What the CBDC will not do is reduce the societal relevance of these two digital platforms or present banks with an unwarranted gift. It bears repeating: China's CBDC is the next logical evolutionary step in the digitization of money, not a vendetta.

HOW TO SPEND IT?

Not surprisingly, the new DC/EP app or wallet looks quite a lot like the Alipay or WeChat Pay interfaces. This familiarity is arguably the most significant advantage China will have over other countries that desire to launch a CBDC. There is no training or acclimation for the general public. From the very start, everyone will know how to use the DC/EP wallet or app, and how to transfer money.

Note that I have referred to the app for WeChat or Alipay as a "wallet." I have so far used this term sparingly for fear of potential conflict with PBOC nomenclature, which may limit DC/EP wallets to the commercial banks. WeChat and Alipay, for their part, may be bestowed a different term, owing to their inability to create digital currency from a bank account. Granted this is a fine point but one that might become important if the PBOC limits users to a single "wallet"—meaning commercial bank app.

Agricultural Bank of China's (ABC) test wallet or app for DC/EP on the left, with Alipay app in the middle and China Construction Bank's (CCB) test wallet on the right. Note similarities of the top row of buttons on the ABC and CCB apps with Alipay; no question people will know how to use it.

When looking at the ABC app's test wallet, we can see how similar the technology will be with Alipay. The Alipay screen shows the reach of this superapp, with everything from Didi, an Uber-like car service, to tickets, utility payment, and Yu'e Bao (a money market investment fund) on the app. No doubt banks will copy parts of this functionality, particularly with micro-investment, insurance, and other financial products. Another function that bank wallets will copy will be the ever-popular mini-programs. The banks know a good thing when they see it, and will try to imitate the superapps in as many ways as possible.

HOW DO YOU GET IT?

Everyone in China—with or without bank accounts—will get access to the digital RMB. As the official new legal currency, ease of access and use is a top priority. Those using the currency without a bank account, however, will be strictly limited in how much they can transact. If you look again at the ABC wallet, you'll see two noteworthy buttons that are distinctly different from the Alipay wallet. These buttons indicate how bank account holders can obtain digital RMB.

The first is a button marked DC. This converts RMB held in the bank to electronic, or eRMB, spendable via the app. A client who receives salary in RMB by direct deposit, for example, can convert RMB to eRMB, then send it using the eRMB payment system. The conversion process requires network connectivity to the bank. This protocol is familiar to users of existing payment systems, for these wallets already distinguish between funds held in a bank account and those stored in a separate account on the app.

Stepping back from the CBDC for a moment, to see the current state of affairs with the superapps, consider the following example. When paying from a WeChat account (see the illustration below) we have a choice among three sources for funds. The "balance" indicates the amount remaining in the WeChat account (as opposed to funds in debit or credit card accounts). Note that I am careful to call all of these "accounts" because the amounts shown represent account balances, not money held on the phone as is the case with digital RMB.

WeChat wallet showing three potential sources for payment. The "Balance" consists of funds in the WeChat account. On WeChat, there is a small fee to transfer funds back into your bank account. Payment is free. When WeChat and Alipay get the DC/EP, a fourth payment source will be available.

Back now to the ABC screen, in the comparative illustration just above this one. The second button of interest is the one with two cell phones held at an angle to each other, first row far right. This engages the near-field communication system (NFC), which allows for direct cellphone-to-cellphone transfer of funds, no network necessary. This feature is critical to China's rural population, who may not always have a cellphone signal.

A similar direct transfer function will also make it possible for those without a bank account to get ahold of limited quantities of DC/EP. While we do not yet know all the limits for offline transactions and wallets, the lowest, Tier 4 mobile wallet users, can currently hold a maximum of RMB 1000 on their wallets. This figure is likely not far off for DC/EP amounts that can be held independent of a bank account. The digital RMB's ability to be used as a store of digital cash independent of a bank makes it no different than carrying a wad of cash in your pocket. This will likely be the norm for many rural Chinese, and the PBOC hopes that DC/EP will be an entry point for many into the banking system.

While as yet unconfirmed, a special tourist digital wallet is likely to be part of the DC/EP launch. There is great speculation that the DC/EP launch will take place prior to the 2022 Olympic games, making a tourist wallet in the form of an integrated circuit or IC card a showy demonstration of the new currency's potential. The wallet could be filled by a bank and used for payment and (limited) DC/EP receipt. This limited wallet would suit many travelers' needs in China, as many find it difficult to pay for things without access to digital payment. I already have this problem when I host guests in Shanghai. Many complain that they cannot pay for taxis and other essential services without access to WeChat and Alipay. Both launched tourist services in 2019, which allow limited use of the payment apps through foreign credit cards.

WHERE TO SPEND IT?

Under the "one coin, two repositories, and three centers" system, the digital RMB is digital legal tender in China. It will be legally accepted everywhere, and adoption by vendors and citizens will be as easy as updating an app. The infrastructure for digital banking and payment is already well developed, so adoption will be virtually effortless. Acceptance of DC/EP will be mandatory throughout China. This is a change from the current system where a shopkeeper can, at their own risk, refuse to use one or both of the payment apps. With DC/EP as the national currency, declining to use it will not be an option.

WeChat and Alipay will be critical to the success of the CBDC, because both systems will build on the currency's functionality, and are already widely adopted. At launch, the payment giants will dominate CBDC usage, because that is where people are already making digital payment. With time, people may decide to use bank apps with their CBDC, but it is hard to find a compelling reason why.

The shift may take place because the payment apps will not be able to access a bank account directly and convert RMB to CBDC; this is a privilege reserved for commercial banks. So frequent users of CBDC might want to keep their CBDC holdings only on their bank apps to simplify creation and conversion. Beyond that there is no compelling reason to use the bank's app. Of course Alipay and WeChat Pay users who have accounts with the companies' associated commercial banks, MYbank and WeBank, will also have the ability to convert account RMB to CBDC.

What is unknown today is precisely how CBDC will make it onto the payment apps from the banking apps where it is created. The easiest route would be to simply transfer funds from your bank app to your WeChat or Alipay app. Another possibility is that the apps will have some direct connectivity allowing the WeChat and Alipay app to access digital currency on the bank app. There isn't an example just yet of how this would work, so this detail is still an unknown. What we do know is that it will be easy. It is not in the PBOCs interest to make this hard as it would only delay CBDC adoption, their highest priority.

Now imagine if you were to launch a similar CBDC in a country without an existing digital cash transfer network. Much of what China takes for granted would have to be built, and then people trained to use and trust the system. Countries without an existing digital cash transfer network will have a significantly longer lag time due to the need to change people's habits and familiarize them with digital payment.

COMMERCIAL PAYMENTS

China already has direct bank-to-bank real-time payment for most commercial transactions, so the digital RMB's immediate impact will be minimal on business-to-business (B2B) transactions, at least at first.

The "China National Advanced Payment System" (CNAPS), run by the PBOC, is the primary means of transferring electronic payment within China. Greatly simplifying the multitude of cash transfer options in the country, it is fair to say that CNAPS has three main subsystems, two of which are real-time payment, the third is not. The High-Value Payment System (HVPS) (minimum, RMB 500,000) and the Internet Banking Payment System (IBPS) for debit and credit cards (max RMB 50,000) are both real-time systems. Yet, there remains a non-real-time T+1 or T+2 payment system, for low-level paper-based transactions. This is called the Bulk Electronic Payments System (BEPS).

The obvious question is whether China can supplant the BEPS system with digital currency to eliminate paper transactions. It is fair to say that in a country with digital real-time payment, and now a CBDC, T+1 and paper are anachronistic. It also seems fair to say the system will face reduced usage. Many other commercial cash transfer systems in China, including special networks for tax payment and even "in-city" payment networks, might also benefit from the CBDC's real-time nature. This may mean that the older systems lose their relevance and are closed, or updated to include the digital RMB. Whether this will be the case is challenging to predict. The system that carries tax payments, for example, is highly specialized and will most likely soldier on, but streamlined with new technology.

> *In a few years CBDC payment by state-owned enterprises (SOEs) will be the norm.*

I mentioned that the impact on B2B transactions would be minimal "at first." State-owned enterprises (SOEs) will eventually switch a large portion of payments to CBDC. Rumors already abound that large-scale supply contracts offered by SOEs are showing up with an option for the SOE to convert payment to CBDC. It is likely that in a number of years CBDC payment by

SOEs, even those of relatively high value, will be the norm. SOEs will be among the first to make this conversion due to the desire of the government to better account for their profligate spending, a process made much simpler with CBDCs. Close behind them will be small- and mid-tier businesses that can free themselves of the relatively small fees incurred using the payment platforms.

Once SOEs convert to CBDC payment it will drive other businesses to follow, if for no other reason than SOEs are so massive they can drive markets. B2B payments will convert to CBDC because the new systems will be cheaper to use than the payment platforms, and will support the government's policies to promote CBDC adoption. The tipping point will come in a few years when SOEs start paying salaries in CBDC, which will cement its place in society.

POTENTIAL CBDC MARKET SIZE

So how big a market is there for China's new CBDC? The starting point, of course, is the existing mobile payment market which in 2019 neared US$ 50 trillion. That CBDC payments will come at the expense of mobile payments and cash use is a given. CBDCs, however, are not just a mobile payment replacement. As we saw in the discussion above on B2B payment, CBDCs will attract new payment flows not currently captured by mobile. Estimating CBDC market size by the percentage of mobile capture alone would underestimate CBDC usage.

As an example of this, let's look at the market for paper checks currently carried by the aforementioned BEPS transfer systems. In 2018 the IMF reported that BEPS processing for 2014 had a total annual transfer value of RMB 22 trillion or roughly $US 3 trillion. If the CBDC were to displace the majority of anachronistic paper checks, as is likely, a large portion of this US$ 3 trillion would switch to CBDC. These figures serve as an example of new payment flows that are not included in mobile payment figures.

Similarly, despite mobile payment's expansion within the consumer payment category, some 90% of B2B payments are still processed by banks. This is a massive flow of money and it's hard to predict what percentage might be transferred to CBDC payment. Clearly large-denomination payments will remain with the banks for some time, but there will be a gray zone where companies and institutions that have large CBDC holdings may choose to use that currency for payment. The size and extent of this trend is difficult to predict, but even small percentages would make for large amounts.

In the attempt of landing on a round number on CBDC market size, let's fall back on CBDC's cannibalization of mobile payment, even if it results in an underestimate. Let's assume we're looking at CBDC use in China five years after launch. This would give the digital currency ample time to become embedded into the financial system.

The most likely users to switch to CBDC from mobile payments are those who are not tied directly to e-commerce. E-commerce platforms like Alibaba are likely to require users to continue to use their proprietary Alipay payment system. Likewise other platforms tied to WeChat or other payment systems. In 2019 China's ministry of commerce valued national e-commerce at roughly US$ 5 trillion. Subtracting the e-commerce market value from the total mobile payment market of US$ 50 trillion leaves US$ 45 trillion in payments that are not dependent on e-commerce platforms. These payments could potentially avoid the small (.1% to .6%) fee the payment platforms may charge for cash transfer by switching to CBDC. If 10% to 20% of this market were to make the switch, a CBDC payment market in the range of US$ 4.5 to $9 trillion could develop.

The biggest change for China will come when employees start receiving salary in CBDC. I would expect China's SOEs to take the lead in offering the entirety or at least some portion of salary in CBDC. This is already happening in cities where trials are underway. Employees are getting transit subsidies paid in CBDC. While this merely amounts to tens of RMB, in 2017 the State Statistics Bureau reported that there were 60 million state workers on an average salary of RMB 78,549. Even if these employees were given only RMB 100 in CBDC in their pay annually, for transit or other subsidies, it would pump RMB 6 billion of CBDC into the market.

Given these observations, I don't think that a CBDC market size of around US$ 10 trillion or RMB 70 trillion is out of the question within the next five years. We've already seen that enthusiasm to learn about the new CBDC is high. While the payment platforms are cheap to use, at least when compared to credit cards in the West, there are still small efficiencies to be gained by switching to CBDC for payment. What is difficult to predict is how long it will take CBDC to replace existing payments that are not already made by mobile. B2B use and salaries are the prime example, with more to come. An in-depth analysis of China's payment systems shows a hodgepodge of payment platforms far beyond those mentioned above. Many will modernize by converting payments to CBDC, which will add significantly to this total.

WHEN IS IT COMING?

Many believe China's CBDC will launch for domestic use at the Winter Olympic games in 2022. By that time, the system will have had more than a year and a half of testing in the original pilot cities and almost a year of testing in the additional six -to-eight cities more recently added. In August 2021, Sun Guofeng, head of the monetary policy department at the People's Bank of China, said that: "internal tests are being conducted in Shenzhen, Suzhou, Xiongan, and Chengdu, with plans for use at the 2022 Winter Olympic Games in Beijing, although there was no timetable for the rollout."

From a practical perspective, and China is always practical, the CBDC will need to launch CBDC trials for the Olympic region about a month before the start of the games. This month will allow participating banks to fully integrate CBDC into retail systems, showcasing the PBOC's new payment system in the best possible light. This launch of CBDC trials would then be followed by the announcement of a countrywide launch during the Olympic Games.

China is rightly proud of its efforts with the world's first CBDC, and launching the system at an event with global reach and significance would be a great way to capture the world's attention. It's not hard to imagine the international coverage that China's new CBDC would generate from sports commentators and others talking about China's astounding system of digital payment—a publicity coup on a global scale.

There is, however, another possibility that I think is looking increasingly probable. The PBOC may have trials at the Winter Olympics but choose to keep the CBDC in an extended national trial. A lengthy trial period would give the PBOC time to work its way methodically down the list of 27 trial cities, slowly increasing user numbers until a formal launch is a foregone conclusion. This has two potential benefits. First, it guarantees that any problems are confined to the "trial" period, ensuring a perfect launch. Second, it gives the PBOC time to deal with what I call the "TikTok effect" —the real possibility that foreign governments, the US in particular, will respond aggressively to China's CBDC when it launches as they did with TikTok. Additional time to ensure domestic success and to line up international support without taking flak might be foremost on the PBOC's mind. Rest assured, China's CBDC will be showcased at the Winter Olympics, even if it is just a trial.

13

CBDC IN INTERNATIONAL USE: ATTRACTING USERS WITH "THE VIRTUOUS CYCLE"

China on issuing its CBDC:

> *"We must build an independent and high-quality financial infrastructure … quicken the pace of research and development of the central bank digital currency…."*
>
> *Chen Yulu, deputy governor of the PBOC*

The West on issuing a CBDC:

> *"We do think it's more important to get it right than to be first, and getting it right means that we not only look at the potential benefits of a CBDC but also the potential risks."*
>
> *Jerome Powell, US Federal Reserve Chair*

China's CBDC will not disrupt the financial world with its launch in domestic markets. Disruption won't occur until its first use settling an international trade—that will be the day when the SWIFT messaging system and correspondent banking networks fall silent and the revolution begins. Even if just a single transaction, it will mark the end of one era and the beginning of another. For China, it will be a global step in what has already been a very long voyage.

Only when countries start to use China's CBDC in international trade will it be relevant to the West. Most just don't care what happens within China's borders. The best example of this was the Trump administration's executive order banning US companies from "transacting" with WeChat. It shows how little interest the US has in digital payment advances within China, even when they are critical to US business interests.

For a niche audience of finance specialists, China's CBDC launch will be front-page news, even amid disagreements over technology that are so divisive that they birthed the term "splinternet." Pundits will acknowledge China's technical sophistication and mourn the loss of privacy with China's CBDC (after using big-data equipped Apple Pay to buy their morning coffee). The accolades will be short-lived and likely half-hearted. A few will talk about domestic use of the RMB, and even fewer will give credit to Alipay and WeChat for their role in advancing digital payment.

> *"Can China's new digital RMB replace the dollar as a reserve currency?" It's certainly an interesting question, but frankly, it's the wrong one.*

A single burning question will preoccupy my peers at the outset, bearing on how the digital RMB will escape the confines of domestic use and impact the West, i.e.: "Can China's new digital RMB replace the dollar as a reserve currency?" It's certainly an interesting question, but frankly, to my mind, it's the wrong one.

With some 60% of the world's currency reserves and 80% of international trade denominated in US dollars, it's easy to presume the dollar will be the currency of choice for years to come. So the question of whether the digital yuan can replace the dollar is a "red herring" or, to put it a different way, akin to a magician's sleight of hand. The question distracts from the real issue, by refuting the possibility that the digital RMB will change the game by challenging the dollar.

Most pundits will confirm that the dollar's reign as the reserve currency is secure, and emphasize that RMB holdings in global central banks are only 2% of the worldwide total. The pundits will avow there is nothing to fear, the status quo will hold, and the digital RMB will not dethrone the dollar.

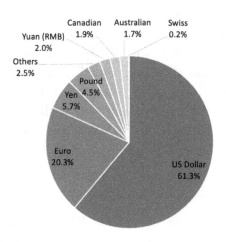

China's yuan is only 2% of global central bank's reserves.
Source: IMF, Q2 2020

This perspective may be a shortsighted. The digital RMB's intent is not to dethrone the dollar in global financial markets. There has *never* been a statement from a Chinese official stating this intent. However, the Chinese government has been unequivocal in stating its policy goal of decreasing dollar dependence, both internally and, by implication, externally. China Finance, a magazine published by the PBOC, said it best: "China needs and has the ability to build a new payment system network to break the monopoly of the US dollar, and a legitimate digital currency will be an important tool for the internationalization of the yuan." This is a clear signal that decoupling from the dollar and US-dominated financial sector is a strategic goal.

China's CBDC is now a pawn in a much larger geopolitical game than when conceived in a laboratory seven years ago—a time before tensions with the US over trade and technology peaked. The digital RMB launch date is still unknown. Its use in global trade will only come after it is fine-tuned in domestic markets. So the dollar's dominant position as global leader won't even be challenged for at least two years, maybe three. Good news for the dollar and pundits who predict maintenance of the status quo.

THE DIGITAL RMB AS AN ENTRY TOKEN

What pundits are missing regarding the digital RMB is that it's not a play to replace the dollar in international financial markets. Instead, it may be considered a digital entry token to a new kind of trade platform, specially designed to facilitate trade with China. The digital RMB is not intended to replace the dollar as a reserve currency. Instead, it's laser-focused on one goal: facilitating trade with China.

The digital RMB will give access to a new kind of digital trade platform that will provide users with a host of benefits, including preferential exchange rates and trade loans through digital logistics systems that speed shipments through customs. The digital RMB is not intended to replace the dollar in uses over which it has no control; rather, the focus is on the one area that it can control, which is the dollar's current dominance in China trade.

To achieve its goal of reducing dollar use in cross-border trade, the digital RMB will use a game plan lifted straight out of internet commerce: entice users with free services, convenience, and good value. Think of it as a digital platform like Alibaba, which offers multiple services bound together to form an ecosystem. This equates to Amazon's "flywheel" at a countrywide level. China's CBDC will give users large and small access to an ecosystem for global trade, making transacting with China as easy as buying on Amazon or Alibaba. This is a killer feature, a counterplay in a world that is actively looking at "decoupling" from China.

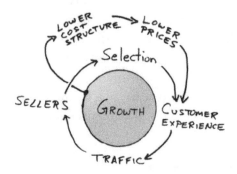

China's CBDC will allow access to a trade platform that models itself on Amazon's flywheel—a "virtuous cycle" where improvements anywhere on the flywheel cause it to accelerate.
Source: Amazon

Unlike internet companies, where the cost of supporting free services—whether email or bank accounts—is born by investors, the PBOC and trading companies will absorb the costs of these platforms' services. These costs, however, will be exceedingly low and hardly a burden relative to the benefits to China of increased use of the RMB and trade. As an example, preferential RMB foreign exchange rates and free money transfers are inexpensive to offer on a digital system that is closed to currency speculators. The digital RMB exchanged can be programmed to go directly back into China's factory system, and nowhere else, with calculable benefits. The digital RMB, to some extent, breaks the rules.

The digital RMB's pinpoint control panel makes it a powerful tool for China. Traditionally, world foreign exchange rates are fixed on global markets, and currency is converted at whatever rate your local bank offers. In China's new digital world, the rules are different. A digital currency with big data behind it can operate with many other criteria to determine the exchange rate. So China can, within reason, vary foreign exchange rates depending on the country, product bought, currency converted, or amount exchanged; the possibilities are endless. Most importantly, any differences in these digital rates do not affect global markets. What happens on the digital RMB platform stays on the platform.

This flexibility is an impossibility in traditional currency markets, where changes in exchange rates can be costly to nations because they impact buying power across the full spectrum of currency use. A country that deflates its currency to boost exports, for example, will pay for it with increased prices for oil or other commodities. In the digital currency world, however, where the digital RMB cannot be used for speculation on currency markets, the cost of foreign exchange "incentives" are relatively inexpensive. The marginal cost to the PBOC of any foreign exchange incentives can be calculated and directly offset with benefits to production, trade, employment, or other national interests.

> *While it may sound crass, imagine a system that can have a "sale" on loans worldwide if the money is spent in specific industrial sectors.*

Similarly, the cost of loans from China's big four state banks can be adjusted depending on the country of origin, product purchased, or political expediency. While it may sound crass, imagine a system that can have a "sale" on loans worldwide if the money is spent on specific industrial sectors in China, or is used by Chinese companies to purchase commodities from abroad. One may argue that underwriters at the big state banks can do this today without digital systems. This is true, but it is limited to high-value loans, and is labor intensive. The digital RMB will allow this level of customization for smaller counterparties on a fully digital platform. Customers can receive loan or finance decisions within minutes, combined with free and immediate transfer of funds, all without the use of SWIFT and the traditional banking system's costs and surveillance.

For China, the first international trade conducted on its digital trade platform that circumvents the SWIFT network will be a significant milestone. China's digital RMB reduces China's reliance on SWIFT and decreases its vulnerability to trade restrictions potentially imposed through the network. SWIFT (as noted previously, the Society for Worldwide Interbank Financial Telecommunication) is a central pillar of the global financial system. The SWIFT network enables its 11,000 member institutions to send 39 million cross-border money transfer transactions daily with a value of US$5 trillion.

China building an effective platform that provides financing and transfers funds without using SWIFT is considered a significant threat by foreign governments and banks. Funds transferred using digital RMB deprives banks of substantial fee income, while governments lose critical surveillance capabilities that are built into the network. SWIFT's monitoring and blocking of payments in accordance with US and international sanctions have led to charges that it has been "weaponized" and are at the root of China's desire for an alternative.

NEXT-GENERATION DIGITAL TRADE IN THE GREATER BAY

Evidence for these digital trade platforms and their potential benefits already exists, in China's blockchain-based digital trade finance systems. As of July 2020, the two largest systems—run by the China Construction Bank and a combined CITIC, Bank of China, PBOC initiative—have processed more than US$ 100 billion in trade finance transactions. A separate blockchain platform run by the PBOC, called the "Bay Area Trade Finance Platform," has over US$ 10 billion in transactions. Still another, the Guangfa Bank blockchain trade platform, has US$ 8 billion in transactions. Trade platforms also exist on the Hong Kong side of the border, with the Hong Kong Monetary Authority's eTradeConnect.

These digital trade platforms focus on trade within the "Guangdong-Hong Kong-Macau Greater Bay Area," also referred to as the "Pearl River Delta." In 2017, the Greater Bay Area contributed US$ 1.5 trillion, or roughly 12 percent of China's GDP, which should clarify why Beijing wants to turn it into a unified economic area. The massive opportunity that unification represents in GDP terms explains the proliferation of trade platforms in this region.

The challenge to unifying this area is that Hong Kong and Macau are special administrative areas and have separate currencies, taxes, customs, and financial controls. Trade within the zone is truly international, even if technically they are administrative areas within China. Blockchain is seen as the solution to integrating these different economies, while acknowledging their unique status.

What is relevant for the digital RMB is that these trade platforms are focused on SMEs rather than on big companies. By focusing on the "little guy's" ability to weather the cost of finance and cross over the Macau and Hong Kong borders, China hopes to boost its SMEs' productivity. While sizable transactions in oil and other commodities are just starting on these platforms, low-value business between these regions can be made viable by easing data-sharing burdens. Traditionally, SMEs' costs in time and money for transactions with Hong Kong and Macau have been an obstacle. Not anymore. China will use the same approach with international SMEs, to help them transact directly on the same platforms, which is something they would not have done before the advent of this technology.

> *SME financing dropped from 7%-8% to around 6% using blockchain trade finance platforms.*

The PBOCs digital research institute gives us a hint as to the platforms' effectiveness. It claims that its Bay Area Trade Finance platform reduces the time required to process trade financing applications for SMEs from over ten days to around twenty minutes. Participating in a separate project, Ping An Bank and the PBOC independently report that the cost of SME financing dropped from 7%-8% to around 6% when using the blockchain platform. This shows that right now, China's blockchain trade finance platforms are saving time and money for trade companies.

The PBOC is so pleased with the Bay Area Trade Finance platform's performance that they intend to connect more countries and international organizations to it to create a "global trade finance highway." Here we have a clear signal that it plans to use blockchain trade platforms to make China more competitive and convenient for international trade. The timing, coinciding with China signing the Regional Comprehensive Economic Partnership (RCEP), couldn't be better. All fourteen signatory Asia Pacific nations all looking to reduce tariffs and boost market access.

It should not be a surprise that the Greater Bay Area cities were chosen as the second batch of centers to test the new CBDC in August 2020. The RMB replaced the US dollar as the most-used currency for trade within the region in late 2020, making the transition to digital RMB a natural fit. Testing the digital RMB here is critical, as transactions with Macao and Hong Kong will model the international use of the digital RMB. Continuing trials with digital RMB are now underway, and these platforms will be among the first to send the digital RMB internationally.

INTERNATIONAL USE OF CHINA'S CBDC CONFIRMED

China's efforts to internationalize the digital RMB are not all focused on the south's Greater Bay Area. In a telling press release, the Xiong'an New Area in Hebei province recently released its plans to explore CBDC internationalization. Xiong'an New Area serves as a development hub for the Beijing-Tianjin-Hebei economic triangle, and as a "new area" is subject to special economic and development support. The "Cross-border E-commerce Comprehensive Trial Zone Development and Implementation Plan" calls for "encouraging the use of renminbi for the pricing and settlement of cross-border e-commerce activities," as well as the "exploration of digital renminbi for cross-border payments."

What is particularly interesting about this announcement is that unlike the PBOC, which has been relatively quiet about using digital RMB in cross-border activities, Xiong'an New Area proudly announced their objectives in helping the new currency go international. They claim they will "support bold innovation by relevant qualified financial institutions, payments organizations, and third-party cross-border e-commerce platforms." This is a virtual blueprint for digital RMB's global aspirations.

China's blockchain use doesn't stop with trade platforms and financial services. Alibaba-owned Ant Group is working with China Merchants Port, China's largest port operator, to build a blockchain-based platform to carry out completely digital import-export transactions. The platform will allow buyers, sellers, logistic companies, banks, customs, and tax officials to conduct contactless digital export and import transactions. The goal is to become the world's first blockchain-based digital port system.

When China's digital trade systems are complete, the preferential terms for digital RMB users and access to fast-track customs and delivery will make it hard for many to say no. The focus on ease of use for SMEs to increase their participation in China's export market is genuinely revolutionary. "Exports made easy" means that China will have a real advantage over other countries selling its products worldwide.

With all due respect, this is where traditional currency analysts are getting it wrong. They see the digital RMB as nothing more than a repackaging of the RMB, without recognizing the digital ecosystem's associated benefits. I agree completely with US Treasury Secretary Hank Paulson, who stated, "A central bank-backed digital currency does not alter the fundamental nature of the RMB."

> *Digital currencies don't follow the rules.*
> *They make new ones.*

At the same time, I can't blame him or other analysts for being shortsighted. Their view of currency is formed by years of experience within a predefined set of rules, and they only worked on the existing US-built financial system. The problem is that we all should have already learned from cryptocurrencies that digital currencies don't follow the rules. They make new ones.

With the digital RMB and blockchain-based trade systems, China will do for trade what Alibaba did with mobile payment and e-commerce sales in China. Meaning they'll put it on a platform that makes it irresistible to use, like Amazon's flywheel on a grand scale—enabling access to China's nearly unlimited supply of goods without the many difficulties associated with international trade. The focus will not be solely on large importers and exporters, who may already have the power to negotiate a better deal, but small- and mid-tier companies excluded from the market. China's CBDC ushers in not just a currency but an entirely new trade ecosystem.

14

CBDC IN INTERNATIONAL USE: DEATH OF THE DOLLAR?

China, on its dependence on the dollar:

> *"The US dollar could become a major risk issue that has us by the throat."*
> Zhou Li, former deputy director of the Communist Party's International Liaison Department

The West, on China's digital RMB:

> *"A digital RMB would still be a Chinese RMB. No one is reinventing money."*
> Henry M. Paulson, Jr., Chair of the Paulson Institute and former US Secretary of the Treasury

China's digital RMB will not explode on the scene and miraculously conquer currency markets. Instead, it is more of a ten-year project that will evolve in specific stages, and takes a long-term view. The first step (a baby step) is its testing within the Greater Bay Area, helping to expedite currency conversions between Hong Kong and Macau. For practical purposes, this can be considered internal to China, because of the close relations between its banks and these trade counterparties. This is a safe place to sort out the inevitable snags arising with such an ambitious undertaking.

Once the system is tested and refined in the Greater Bay Area, it will roll out one by one to Belt and Road Initiative (BRI) countries. The final launch, shortly after BRI countries, will be to importers on a global scale. China's position as the world's largest exporter gives it a tremendous advantage when promoting its new digital currency. It already has a large captive market, and even modest increases in its use within trade can bring about considerable changes in the digital RMB's international stature.

Rank	Exporter	Value US$ Billions	Global Share %
1	China	2499	13.2
2	USA	1647	8.7
3	Germany	1489	7.9
4	Netherlands	709	3.8
5	Japan	706	3.7
6	France	570	3.0

Leading Merchandise Exporters 2019
Source: WTO

BY THE NUMBERS, THE DC/EP IN TRADE

To better understand and calculate the DC/EP's potential impact, let's take a closer look at how it might affect trade alone. I will focus first on Belt and Road countries, then move on to China's remaining global exports. The intent is simple. Look at the current RMB usage in these two markets, and see what might be possible if China's DC/EP were to capture a larger percentage of this trade over the coming decade.

What is much less simple is that overseas markets are unlike China's domestic DC/EP market, where we can base our estimates off existing mobile payment usage. Frankly, there is no easy comparison to make, as China's CBDC is the first ever that will target cross-border trade. The best we can do is look at existing RMB use in these scenarios and estimate how much of the market China's DC/EP might capture. While the numbers will clearly be debatable, the objective is less an accurate prediction of future use than an illustration of its potential scale. For clarity's sake, in the coming calculations I will designate China's CBDC as DC/EP.

TRADE WITH "BELT AND ROAD" COUNTRIES

China's Belt and Road Initiative (BRI) program is the world's largest infrastructure development program. It encompasses seventy countries, impacting three billion people, and sees total costs in the US$ 1 trillion range. For perspective, the BRI is estimated to be about twelve times the size of the US's post-WWII Marshall plan.

While the BRI's main focus is on infrastructure, stated goals also include "unimpeded trade" and "currency circulation," making China's use of DC/EP compelling. Many BRI countries are already trading in RMB or have portions of their development loans denominated in RMB. This trade group is therefore incentivized to use DC/EP, and is a natural launching point. As most BRI countries are developing nations, more than a few may welcome the stability that the RMB brings as a currency in trade.

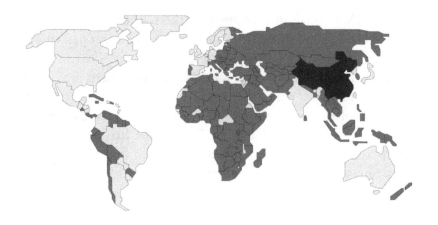

As of January 2021, 140 Belt and Road countries have signed
a Memo of Understanding with China.
Source: Max Senden

China's "General Administration of Customs" reports that trade with BRI partner countries totaled US$ 1.34 trillion or RMB 9.27 trillion in 2019, up 10.8 percent year on year, and showing a 10-year growth rate of 6.1 percent. Not surprisingly, most BRI total trade is still denominated in US dollars, with only 14% transacted in RMB in 2016. This has changed quickly in recent years due to China's effective promotion of the RMB.

SWIFT's RMB tracker data from 2019 provides compelling evidence of how quickly BRI countries are accommodating the Chinese currency. SWIFT reports that "there was a surge in payments traffic to and from China with some countries along the 'Silk Road Economic Belt' [BRI] between 2014 and 2018." The average increase for BRI countries in the survey during this period was an impressive 95%. Singapore, a global hub with extensive high-value transactions, likewise saw payment traffic with China grow by an astounding 231%. RMB payments from Africa into China have also increased by an impressive 123%. Most relevant for our calculations is that among China's top trading partners that are also BRI members, RMB usage increased by an astounding 144%. This is an annual gain of 20%, showing the positive impact of the BRI program on RMB adoption. These trade partners alone account for over 22% of China's total export sales, or 73% of total BRI trade.

Let's plug in the numbers. In ten years, we'll assume that the BRI market grows at its historical rate of 6%. This means a market size of US$ 2.26 trillion in 10 years. Next, let's take a stab at the amount of RMB that BRI countries could potentially hold in ten years. I will put my marker down and predict an increase from 14% of BRI trade currently valued in RMB, to 60% over the coming decade. A 14% annual increase may seem bold, but it falls far short of the 20% gains currently realized by leading BRI trade partners.

I don't propose that BRI countries will get much above 60% in RMB usage, but I do think that the SWIFT numbers are telling us that they will take the gifts China offers to get there quickly. They are incentivized to adopt the RMB and in the next decade, China's CBDC will drive this process further, allowing impressive gains. If the RMB were used on 60% of BRI trade in ten years, the total RMB market would be valued at US$ 1.37 trillion.

Now the question is, to what extent will the DC/EP take hold as a percentage of total RMB used? As we saw in the previous chapter, China's new digital trade platforms are specifically designed to target BRI countries as customers. They were purpose-built for the mid-tier traders throughout BRI countries who would benefit greatly from the convenience and savings of going digital. So the increase in RMB use will be driven by China's DC/EP.

Here I'm going to posit another big number and say that in ten years, the DC/EP may represent 60% of all RMB usage in BRI countries. Here alone this would make a market of US$ 0.82 trillion. Combine the DC/EP's cheaper and faster service with the Chinese government's push to de-dollarize trade, and the uptake will be nothing short of explosive.

> *BRI total trade valued in DC/EP would be more than Japan's **total** global exports.*

It would be helpful to put this number in context. The easiest way is to go back to our WTO trade table to see which country has similar values. According to the table, Japan's merchandise exports are US$ 0.70 trillion. So the BRI total trade valued in RMB would surpass Japan's **total** global exports. I use Japan as a measuring stick as a means of highlighting that China's exports are so massive that changes in export valuations can eclipse or match the output of entire industrialized nations. An impressive figure, and a game-changer, if the RMB can continue its high rate of adoption, and if the DC/EP proves to be as compelling to use in trade as I predict.

GLOBAL MERCHANDISE EXPORTS

Now, let's focus on the rest of the world, to explore how the DC/EP might do in terms of the 70% of China's trade apart from the BRI program. These partners are not incentivized to trade in RMB, so we will lower our expectations for DC/EP adoption. The following trade figures are from the World Trade Organization (WTO) and include data for both merchandise and services imports/exports. By including all of these categories, we will be tallying trade in a method similar to what was done for BRI countries.

The WTO reports total trade for China of US$ 5.30 trillion. According to the WTO, world merchandise exports totaled US$ 19 trillion in 2019. China's export contribution was US$ 2.49 trillion, making it the world's leader, holding roughly 13% of total. The WTO reports that China's merchandise imports account for an additional US$ 2 trillion in trade value. Service imports and exports as reported by the WTO are relatively small, with US$ .50 and US$ .28 respectively. Services are not the primary focus of China's DC/EP, which is designed to foster merchandise exports. Still, some portion of the cross-border transfers in the service sector will be in DC/EP. This is particularly true for China's service exporters that are state-owned, which will be inclined to use DC/EP.

Following along the same lines as our analysis of BRI data, we will use a ten-year market growth rate of 4.8% from WTO statistics. As we do not wish to double-count BRI trade (30% of China's global total), we will reduce this trade figure by 30%, to essentially remove BRI trade from the data. The result is that in ten years, the global market for RMB use will be approximately US$ 2.32 trillion.

According to Singapore-based DBS bank, about 20% of China's total trade settled in RMB in Q2 2020, a figure that is in line with SWIFT's most recent estimate of 18% for 2017. However, as we saw with BRI countries, RMB usage has increased significantly over recent years. PBOC data shows that from 2014 to 2019, China has almost tripled RMB use in cross-border trade of goods. This at a time when overall international RMB usage was down from its peak in 2015. (Much of this overall decline was due to the downturn in RMB-denominated investment products such as "Dim Sum" bonds.) The Chinese government has been making great efforts to increase RMB usage, and its gains in trade use are a bright spot in an otherwise mixed effort.

China Cross-Border RMB Settlement for Goods
RMB trillions

Cross-border RMB settlement for goods tripled in five years.
Source: PBOC

So how much of a gain can the RMB make in trade? Let's assume that in the coming decade, China can increase the use the RMB to lift the percentage of RMB-settled trade from 20% to 40%. This assumes annual growth of 7% over ten years. This is hardly an exaggeration when the tripling of RMB use over the past decade implies recent growth of RMB use of more than 24% per year. I am not claiming that *all* RMB use will increase 7% annually, just the component attributed to trade.

It is important to understand that trade is only one small part of currency use and I concur that RMB will continue to be hobbled in international currency markets. The use of RMB in finance and investment, for example, is limited and is an area where it continues to perform poorly. In fact, China's stock market crash of 2015 and the subsequent devaluation of the RMB helped to contribute to an overall decline in RMB use in this sector that continues to this day, even while RMB use in trade increases.

In trade, the driver for these gains in RMB and DC/EP use is clear. The government is pushing its strategic goal of revaluing as much trade as possible into RMB to better ensure its security. Examples of this include China's efforts to start importing iron, copper and trade oil futures, using RMB. China's efforts to promote the RMB in trade continue to be a singular bright spot, and it is reasonable to assume that when bolstered by the DC/EP, these positive results will likely accelerate.

In world markets, it is clear that China's incentives for use will be significantly diminished compared to their sway in the BRI countries. So rather than assuming that the DC/EP will be a strong driver for trade within this group, we will assume that a conservative adoption rate of 25% of total RMB trade will be revalued to DC/EP. This would result in a total DC/EP market value of US$ 0.58 trillion. It's smaller than the BRI market, but still significant.

Adding the results of both BRI and global DC/EP use together, we find that the combined market has a value of US$ 1.4 trillion. Or to use Japan once more as our measuring stick, twice the total exports of Japan. This shows the amazing potential of China's trade markets. Given the increases predicted in these scenarios, the overall RMB market, inclusive of DC/EP, would be US$3.69 trillion (of which the DC/EP represents 38% of the total). The DC/EP's contributions to China's future trade will be significant.

Even so, these numbers are far overshadowed by the ultimate yardstick, China's domestic DC/EP market, which I valued at roughly US$ 10 trillion in chapter 12. Why the disparity? Clearly China's massive population and love of mobile payment factors in, but there is a bigger issue. In this trade analysis we're only considering one-way transit of payments through the system, meaning that the value of goods entering or leaving China gets counted only once. In real markets, captured in the mobile payment data that the domestic estimates are based on, payments cycle through the system and get counted many times. As an example, take a payment for a coffee: I buy you a coffee, you repay me, the coffee shop transfers the money to a bank: one coffee was purchased but the value of the coffee was transferred three times. This also happens with global trade and the real numbers are likely to be significantly higher than those I am able to show in this limited analysis. Still, despite this methodology's limitations, I believe it achieves our goal of getting a *feel* for the numbers.

PUTTING THE RESULTS IN PERSPECTIVE

SWIFT data is the gold standard for understanding currency use in trade. The next step is to correlate the increase in RMB usage to a rise in ranking on the trade finance market's SWIFT table. China's DC/EP will of course not use SWIFT to transfer funds, but examining the current state of play using the SWIFT tables can give us an approximate idea of where it might sit if it did.

SWIFT commonly reports two different rankings for the use of currency. The one most familiar to readers is for "Global Payments." This is an expansive tally of all currency transferred on the system. Unfortunately for our purposes, it includes transfers to purchase investments like government bonds, which muddies the waters in regard to our trade-focused analysis. However, there is a second SWIFT compilation called the "Trade Finance" ranking. As its name suggests, it captures two specific SWIFT code groups, which are focused exclusively on trade. These trade-based figures offer a better and more conservative basis for our digital scenarios (though they admittedly have some drawbacks).

July 2020

1	USD	86.33%
2	EUR	7.00%
3	JPY	1.84%
4	CNY	1.84%
5	IDR	0.44%
6	SAR	0.42%
7	AED	0.39%
8	GBP	0.24%
9	AUD	0.16%
10	PKR	0.16%

RMB's share as a global currency
in trade finance markets based on value.
Source: SWIFT RMB Tracker

In the current rankings, Japan and China are tied in third place, having a 1.84% share in trade finance activity. This figure is paltry compared to the US's mammoth 86.3% market share. The dollar's outsized role is impressive, but it presents a problem. The huge number is in part driven by the oil and commodities markets, valued in dollars, these categories being distinct from the non-commodity cross-border goods trade. Unfortunately, there is no way to break out trade in goods from these overall figures. To clarify this distortion: around 50% of global trade contracts are quoted in US dollars, according to IMF research, yet the US accounts for only about 12% (IMF figures) of global trade. The dollar's insurmountable lead is so large and seemingly assured that it makes some oblivious to the potential for the DC/EP's impact. This is the dollar's "exorbitant privilege" as the global reserve currency. This term was first used by France's finance minister in the 1960s, and was later adopted by the PBOC.

The SWIFT table rankings are expressed as percentages; the raw value of transfers in each of the categories is not reported. In order to get a better understanding of the impact of the DC/EP, we are going to take the future trade values and map them back to the current SWIFT tables to get a feel for their impact. Clearly we can't know what the future holds, but we can at least use these relative ratios between currencies as a means of giving the DC/EP's potential contribution additional perspective.

China's 1.84% standing on the SWIFT table is a direct result of RMB-valued trade finance. As the DBS figures above show, only 20% of China's combined imports and exports are valued in RMB. This means that for China's current US$ 5.3 trillion trade market, only 20% or US$ 1.06 trillion is conducted in RMB, and it is the economic impact of this portion in the form of cash transfers that is recorded in the SWIFT rankings.

Our calculations above showed that the combined increase in RMB use in part attributed to the DC/EP would create an RMB market valued at US$ 3.69 trillion, of which US$ 1.4 trillion is in DC/EP. This larger RMB market represents an increase of 3.5 times when compared to the current trade market in RMB. If we were to increase China's 1.84% share on SWIFT by 3.5 times to match the increase in RMB use, we would get a value of 6.4%. This would put the RMB at about the same level of use on trade markets as the euro. Most importantly, the DC/EP would contribute 38% of this increase.

This means that the DC/EP would help lift RMB usage to about that of the euro. Still no match for the dollar, but if you were in the import-export business and requested euro value contracts, no one would think twice. The RMB's 6.4% share in global trade would still be small relative to the dollar, which would shrink to around 80% on the table, as gains in RMB use will come at its expense.

> *A 6.4% share in global trade finance puts the RMB at about the same level of use as the euro.*

THE DC/EP WILL BE A ROCK STAR

Many will dismiss this result, and say that the dollar is still in the lead by a wide margin, and that these paltry gains are immaterial. I would agree were it not for the fact that a digital currency is involved. While the predicted gains will in no way unseat the dollar, no one should ignore the potential. If the DC/EP is able to perform at levels approaching those I suggest in the early years following its international launch, naysayers will be in for quite a shock. The DC/EP could very well be the first currency to cause the dollar to lose *any* market share since the launch of the euro. Within global trade, the DC/EP could help the RMB achieve rock star status, even if it does not have the long track record typical for induction into the hall of fame.

China's export markets are tremendously powerful and give the DC/EP tremendous potential if successfully harnessed. The question is, can China entice trade partners to use it? I agree this is a big if, but given China's proven advances in digital trade systems, it would be unwise to discount this as folly. There is beyond dispute a clear trend for increased RMB use in trade with China's BRI trading partners and elsewhere. It remains to be seen how these trends develop in our post-COVID world, but recent trade data is encouraging. If the DC/EP can help propel the RMB to reach adoption levels in the 6%-8% range in global trade, its place in the history books is assured. It will be celebrated as the first digital currency extensively used in trade, and more importantly, the first to impact the dollar.

I do not profess that this outcome is preordained, but I hope that the reader finds the assumptions I've made, even if thought to be overly optimistic regarding the DC/EP's potential, are within the realm of possibility. What is beyond debate is that the DC/EP has an important role in RMB internationalization, and that the trend towards increasing RMB use is already well underway. Whether the DC/EP can attain these success levels is less important than the fact that it marks the beginning of a new chapter.

> *"A journey of a thousand miles begins with a single step."*
> From the Dao De Jing, ascribed to Laozi

TRADE IS ONLY PART OF THE EQUATION

My analysis, based on trade, considers only direct payment into and out of China. Given this, I am significantly underestimating the DC/EP's potential. I focused on trade because it allows the use of hard numbers to illustrate the DC/EP's prospective reach. What I have not done, due to lack of data, is show the great potential for the DC/EP in payments between counterparties outside of China. Many pundits claim the DC/EP will be a show-stopper for this use, but again, hard numbers aren't easy to find.

But let's consider some possible scenarios. Traders in BRI countries could opt to use DC/EP to settle trade among themselves. Favorable exchange and transfer costs between local currencies using the DC/EP may render it cheaper and faster than a dollar-based transfer on traditional banking networks. While some would say this is preposterous and that the dollar is the root of all value, the cost efficiencies and immediacy of digital cash transfer cannot be taken lightly. Amusingly, there is already a precedent.

Cryptocurrency markets have already captured significant cash transfer markets across the developing world. The most prominent are stablecoins, whose market capitalization has grown to some $20 billion in Q3 2020. The largest of the stablecoins is US dollar-based Tether, with a $16 billion market capitalization and a daily trading volume of approximately $1.6 billion. The high daily trading volume shows that Tether is being used in trade and money transfers across the globe and, on an annualized basis, would support a trade market of $0.5 trillion, which resemble Japan-sized volumes. Other indicators of cryptocurrency's popularity in the developing world can be seen in the premium that buyers are willing to pay above market price to gain access to these currencies.

A sovereign-backed DC/EP, with a value more stable than many cryptos, and a transfer mechanism approved by local governments, might be attractive enough to replace some of this cryptocurrency flow. The entry price would be complying with KYC requirements. A high bar for some, but it might just provide access to a better means of currency transfer and value store than cryptos or stablecoins, if their legality is in question. The deciding factor will be how China carries out KYC for international business users. To encourage use, China will need to innovatively integrate its DC/EP into a given local financial system, likely through mobile carriers as well as banks.

For many cryptocurrency fans, KYC is a deal-breaker, By the same token it could be a major attraction to others, if it allows trades to occur legally. Crypto users in many developing nations simply don't have other options, because local banks offer poor service, and the fees they charge are considered usurious. Many choose crypto because it is the best option available. Cost is also likely to be in the DC/EP's favor, as transferring into or out of cryptos for anything but the most popular fiat currencies can be very expensive. These are among the real draws that make the DC/EP preferable to crypto, at least for some. Add to this WeChat Pay and Alipay's increasing popularity on the African continent and it's not hard to see how DC/EP could very well trump crypto for convenience. Before dismissing this possibility, remember that developing nations were the primary target for the original incarnation of Facebook's Libra stablecoin. It is not outlandish to think that the DC/EP could fill this role.

INTERNATIONALIZATION WITHOUT CONVERTIBILITY

The DC/EP will allow China to advance RMB internationalization without full convertibility. This is a concept that most currency analysts struggle to get their heads around. I'm fond of saying digital currencies play by their own rules, and this certainly could be an example that can't be found in any textbook.

China's dilemma has always been the zero-or-one binary choice of convertibility. Hand over the RMB to the international banking community, float it on global markets, and receive the privilege of convertibility. Otherwise, remain forever isolated. China's choice was predictable: try to attain a solution between the binary options, the halfway point of limited convertibility, achieved through currency controls to limit RMB access. With DC/EP, there is a new, third choice. China can use the DC/EP in foreign markets without handing control of the RMB over to the Western financial system. This is something that no one has experienced, and many never considered possible before the advent of digital currency.

For China, the market risk for DC/EP is indeed much lower than floating the RMB on international currency markets. China owns the marketplace, controls the exchange rates, and there will be no currency speculation, eliminating many of the risks associated with convertibility. While the benefits of internationalization of the RMB by fully floating on world markets are clear, so are the risks. The Asian Financial Crisis is still ingrained in China's recent memory, as are the high costs to the PBOC of defending its currency from attack by speculators.

> *The DC/EP is not supplanting the dollar in traditional markets, but making an entirely new market of its own*

Suppose the DC/EP can allow China to transact international trade on global markets without convertibility (and there is every indication it can). In that case, China will have broken many rules of finance. Most importantly, it will succeed in increasing internationalization of the RMB without putting itself at the mercy of Western financial markets. The DC/EP is doing an impressive new trick. It is not supplanting the dollar in traditional markets, but making an entirely new market of its own.

THE "BIG 4": CONVERTIBILITY, VALUE, CAPITAL CONTROLS, AND LIQUIDITY

There are four critical questions about the DC/EP that come up so frequently that I call them the "Big 4." They are issues concerning convertibility, store of value, liquidity, and capital controls. These are all fundamental concepts in currency use, and users need to scrutinize them before blindly buying into China's new digital currency. Let's address these issues one by one, teasing out how the DC/EP has been inspired by the non-traditional cryptocurrency world.

CONVERTIBILITY

"The RMB must be fully convertible to be of use in trade." This is among the most frequent observations made about using the DC/EP. The currency will certainly be convertible, with the caveat that users will need to do it on the digital systems of PBOC- controlled state-owned banks or those of partner banks. Therefore it will lack "full" convertibility on the traditional financial system, and you cannot use the DC/EP in speculative currency trading.

Using the DC/EP will be much closer to the cryptocurrency model that uses digital exchanges.

In the world of digital currencies, full convertibility is less of an issue. Most of the major cryptocurrencies are not convertible within the traditional banking system. Bitcoin or Ethereum need local exchanges to transfer from fiat currency to digital. Exchanges are the on- and off-ramps to the digital currency world. For China's digital currency, local Chinese banks will provide the exchange function, and eventually, perhaps, so will their authorized local banking partners.

It's important to note here that the big four Chinese banks already boast a network of some 618 branches outside of mainland China, of which seventy-six are in BRI countries. Local branches of China's state-owned banks, and eventually local partners, will provide a spot rate for fiat currency conversion and place DC/EP into a customer's account. Once the customer has DC/EP, transferring the currency within the DC/EP network will be instantaneous and free. Currency conversion rates are likely to be a time-averaged RMB rate rather than the volatile spot price on currency markets. We do not yet know how the PBOC will handle digital wallet limits for international users, or manage KYC for smaller currency users.

VALUE

"Who wants the RMB anyway? The RMB and DC/EP do not represent a safe currency for storage of value." This is a real issue with traditional currencies. The cost of entering and exiting currency positions through foreign exchange markets is expensive, and users are likely to remain in a given currency for an extended time. This is particularly true in trade finance, where importers face significant exposure to foreign exchange risk if they convert local currency and then wait for the paperwork to be processed.

The DC/EP, however, borrows from cryptocurrencies, where the holding time may be very brief and accompanied by low entry and exit costs. For example, a trader in a BRI country might keep savings in a native currency or dollars and swap to DC/EP only when needed. There will be little risk of storing funds in RMB because the transactions will be digital and immediate. The digital currency only acts as a bridge. Transacting in DC/EP, as with cryptocurrencies, will not require the user to hold the currency if better alternatives are available.

There are also many BRI countries where the RMB is seen as a stable currency. Users might choose to remain in DC/EP as a hedge against local currency fluctuations. Many businesses in the developing world never had access to anything but dollar-value trade, because there were no alternatives to the dollar in their markets. The DC/EP represents the first opportunity of an alternative. The ability to store value is relative to what is available on local markets, transfer costs, and the holding period. For all of the RMB's shortcomings, there are certainly less attractive currencies.

CAPITAL CONTROLS

"But what about capital controls?" These are another frequent source of contention. The PBOC defends the RMB from foreign exchange speculation and capital flight by limiting currency export through capital controls. Their primary effect is to reduce the transfer of RMB into offshore markets, decreasing the PBOC's expense in managing offshore RMB against currency speculation.

The DC/EP gives the PBOC a perfect opportunity to experiment with granting exceptions to capital control rules. Offshore DC/EP holdings do not interact with the global banking system, making these safeguards less critical. The DC/EP's trackability makes it possible to know exactly where the currency is in use and enact exceptions with pinpoint control. The PBOC can also program the digital currency to follow the rules accompanying any exceptions granted. I would not expect these innovations to come soon after launch, but only after the PBOC becomes comfortable with international DC/EP use. I also suspect that when that time comes, selective lifting of capital controls will be a significant driver for DC/EP adoption.

> *Someday capital controls will be*
> *replaced by "programmed capital."*

It is also likely that the DC/EP will someday contribute to eliminating capital controls on digital markets. Capital controls are an old concept that suited banking markets. A new concept, more apropos in our digital world, will be "programmed capital" whereby capital can be deployed with embedded programming that controls its use and eliminates capital flight. This is an excellent example of how our new digital world will bring new policy tools with it. The reality is that the PBOC will have to learn how to use its new tools before deploying them, but digital currencies truly do make their own rules.

LIQUIDITY

"Yes, but how liquid is it?" Put another way, how easily can it be converted to cash? Liquidity is the final frequent question about the new DC/EP. The real question is, how liquid is China? The DC/EP marketplace is 100% owned and operated by the PBOC and other state-owned banks. As a consequence of not opening the market to speculators, all liquidity will be provided by a combination of the two, operating in local currency markets. The amount of interaction between the two in controlling foreign exchange rates is an unknown at this point, and it's likely that it will vary from country to country.

Whether this is cause for concern or not very much depends on one's perceptions of China and the PBOC. The facile answer is that the PBOC will provide liquidity to the market, and users should have little fear. The PBOC would not go to such extraordinary lengths to set up an international digital currency system and then abandon it. The wiser response is to explore three of the leading disaster scenarios among many that could cause liquidity events in the PBOC's new digital currency.

The first scenario, and arguably the most severe, would be a debilitating hack on the DC/EP system. China's digital RMB could potentially be subject to liquidity events if hacked, meaning either the system itself or the system's lines of communication are compromised. This is a disaster scenario that can't be discounted, and no systems are immune. Hacking the system, as unlikely as that sounds, is a real possibility. It's impossible to know the impact on liquidity for either of these events. Local connection issues would seem the easiest to repair. Still, in our new world where digital attacks are the province of nations, the Stuxnet virus being the most famous, these disruptions might be debilitating.

To manage the risk, the DC/EP might use China's new Blockchain Service Network for international transfers, as blockchain's multiple nodes make it more resistant to attack. Attacks on the system would be unlikely to impact heavily encrypted backups, but how long it would take to get one's transaction cleared in the event of this sort of disruption is unknown.

The next scenario that might create a liquidity event is the collapse or sudden impairment of a foreign currency traded on the system. DC/EP liquidity might be impacted if the PBOC was unwilling to accept any further additional risk from a specific currency. Of course, holders of DC/EP would be the lucky ones, but still subject to liquidity constraints that might make the transfer to the impaired currency impossible. The issue will become how the PBOC can best preserve DC/EP users' capital while minding its losses. During currency collapses or crises, traditional banking networks would also suffer from similar liquidity problems, so the DC/EP system would likely have plenty of company.

The final scenario is an attack on the value of the RMB in traditional currency markets that causes severe volatility on those markets and a liquidity event in digital markets. The RMB coming under attack is a reality, and in recent years, the PBOC has defended the RMB at a high cost. The PBOC has also willingly, and without notice, changed RMB trading bands, severely affecting the RMB exchange rates. Foreign exchange volatility is a two-way street. The DC/EP will not be immune from exchange rate volatility in primary RMB markets.

The critical question is, will the PBOC delay trading on digital markets and create liquidity events if bank markets go severely against it? Chances are, in this disaster scenario, the losses on digital markets will pale compared to traditional markets, and the PBOC will maintain some normalcy on digital markets. The PBOC is incentivized to do this because it would be protecting its trading relations, which are all the more critical during a financial crisis. For all of China's success in reducing its reliance on exports, her trading partners will always be considered lifelines worthy of protection.

THE IMPACT ON CRYPTOCURRENCY MARKETS

With the launch of China's DC/EP, two opposing camps are predicting very different impacts on cryptocurrencies. The first group maintains that China's DC/EP will help drive crypto even further into the mainstream. They believe that once CBDCs become commonplace, cryptocurrencies will greatly benefit from their association as distant digital cousins. I am inclined to believe that this is true, despite the cousins' enormous differences.

China's CBDC, and most others, are everything that cryptocurrency fans loathe. China's digital currency is central bank-issued, run on a state-controlled centralized network, not anonymous, and subject to pesky things like taxes, anti-money laundering, and KYC constraints. It's the antithesis of the money-is-free ethos that crypto fans promote. That said, CBDCs will be most people's first introduction to digital currencies, and it's more than likely that it will drive some to explore cryptocurrencies. The number could be significant given how many will be using CBDCs. That said, it's unlikely this will cause a flood of new crypto users, as many CBDC users will fixate on the idea that their money has to be "official" or "real."

The second, smaller group believes that CBDCs herald the demise of cryptocurrencies. CBDC users will be so enamored with the security and convenience of government-backed CBDCs they will reject cryptocurrencies en masse. This position is difficult to square with the KYC and anti-money laundering features built into China's and other countries' proposed new digital currencies. The ease of using crypto and its investment potential will undoubtedly continue to make it popular, though the increasing need to register its purchase and pay taxes on investment gains may reduce interest in using it as a cash replacement. While CBDCs will become popular especially when a "paper trail" is required, it is a bit harder to see how private citizens already enamored with cryptos would drop them for CBDCs.

What is evident is that despite the philosophical differences between CBDC and crypto fans, the market for cryptos seems to exhibit upticks with each positive CBDC announcement. At the very least, this appears to prove that the fate of these products is linked. Ironically, the most ardent detractors of CBDCs are often cryptocurrency fans. Many are vociferous in their dislike for CBDCs, yet offer no thanks to CBDCs for the potential boost they may bring to crypto markets. Simultaneously, CBDC fans often rail loudly against the lack of intrinsic value of cryptocurrencies, likening them to giant Ponzi schemes. At the same time, they give only the most begrudging credit to cryptocurrency's creators despite them having laid the foundations for CBDCs. Two camps, forever divided.

DEATH OF THE DOLLAR?

So is this death of the dollar? Yes, but not the way that most believe. The dollar has had a 75-year reign as the king of currencies, and the world's assets and trade won't revalue overnight. The notion that the dollar will succumb to a fast revaluing to DC/EP is patently absurd. In the prior chapter I stated that the question "Can the digital RMB replace the dollar?" was click-baity and wrongheaded. The better one is, "Can the digital RMB reduce the dollar's dominance?" My findings show that the answer is clearly yes. The DC/EP's most significant legacy will be the start of something new, and the end of the dollar's monopoly.

> *The better question to ask is*
> *"Can the digital RMB reduce*
> *the dollar's dominance?"*

If digital RMB can boost RMB to the stature of the euro and beyond when used for trade, it will have made a significant impact. Its value beyond trade will undoubtedly be much bigger, but we'll have to wait for hard numbers to know the exact extent. Where this will go over the next fifty years is unknown, but the West can ill-afford to be complacent that the dollar will continue to reign and that its financial system, based on technology from the 1980s, will continue unchallenged.

"But the dollar will still command 80% of global trade and is unassailable," some may protest. Inasmuch as commodities such as oil are dollar-valued, I fully agree this percentage will not change overnight. It is also a reason why, for now, China cannot fully separate itself from the dollar. As RMB markets grow and multiply, there will be a commensurate revaluing of commodities and supply chains in support of production. That's precisely what China is preparing for with its new oil and commodities trading centers in Shanghai. The DC/EP may not be designated as the default currency for trade in these markets, but its mere existence will likely help open minds to that possibility in the future.

DC/EP, used in trade, will support a steady increase of RMB activity in traditional banking systems, all at the dollar's expense. China prepared for this eventuality in 2015 by launching its "Cross-Border Interbank Payment System" (CIPS) for yuan payments. The system is now being used to handle trade between Asian and BRI countries and is expanding. CIPS now has one thousand participating banks in ninety-seven countries and processed 135.7 billion yuan (US$ 19.4 billion) a day in 2019 with 80% annual growth.

Promoting a currency's international use through a digital variant is entirely innovative. No one has ever tried this before. Doing so on a trading system, apart from the traditional banking system, is even more disruptive, and why so many do not see its potential. Even if the dollar maintains its dominant position in overall volume for some years to come, there is the real chance that China's digital currency will slowly erode dollar dominance. It will take away transaction after transaction until, at some point within some industry sectors or trade routes, the dollar simply becomes irrelevant, and the dollar's monopoly crumbles.

> *I was always told to*
> *"never bet against the dollar."*

The DC/EP's lasting legacy will be as the catalyst that ended the dollar's monopoly, beginning a transition away from the financial system that has reigned since the Second World War. SWIFT, correspondent banking, and a dollar-centric financial system served their purpose well through the post-war period. From my earliest days in banking, I was always told to "never bet against the dollar." This advice served me well but may no longer be sound. With investors from Ray Dalio to analysts at bulge bracket banks questioning the dollar's preeminence, the dollar may not be the safe bet it once was. While most concerns about the dollar focus on economic factors related to deficit spending, the rise of China's DC/EP is now an additional technological component to consider.

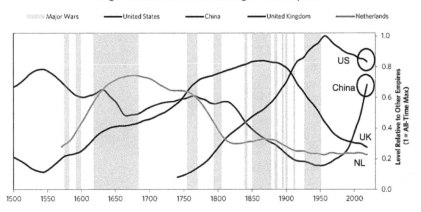

Rough Estimates of Relative Standing of Great Empires

"The United States is now the most powerful empire by not much, it is in relative decline, Chinese power is rapidly rising, and no other powers come close."
Source: Ray Dalio, "Principals"

The dollar's perceived unassailability contributed to complacency in the adoption of new technology across banking and financial systems. China is now using this complacency to its advantage and striking a blow to what it considers the dollar's Achilles heel: not its value, but its convenience. In this regard, China already succeeded, regardless of DC/EP's ability to capture trade in China's exports. In the wake of China's DC/EP development, central banks worldwide are now rapidly researching and prototyping CBDCs. It won't be only China using CBDCs to break the dollar's stronghold, but countries worldwide. All seek to give their citizens the immediacy and low costs in payment they've come to expect in our digital era. China's CBDC is the catalyst for this transition and has already earned an important place in history.

PART 3

CHANGING
RELATIONS

15

DIGITAL CURRENCY'S
AFTERMATH:
PLATFORMS AND DUMB PIPES

China on banking innovation:

> *"If the banks don't change, we will change the banks."*
>
> Jack Ma, 2008, Co-founder and former executive chairman of Alibaba Group

The West on banking innovation:

> *"It's all about the experience. Either banks remove friction or someone else will."*
>
> Brett King. 2019 Futurist, author of Bank 4.0: Banking Everywhere, Never at a Bank, and co-founder and CEO of Moven

W hen you go to your bank's website, odds are it's to check your balances or perhaps pay a few bills. Whether you did so on your computer or cell phone, I'll wager that while there you ignored the bank's latest advertisements touting their latest credit card or favorable rates. Like most users by now, you are comfortably numb to the bank's latest offers.

This experience is repeated billions of times globally every day. The utility of a bank's website is narrowly defined by immediate needs and how quickly one can accomplish these tasks. Banks enable this situation because your money is captive on their portal. You must use their system to access it. The reason, beyond legacy systems and ingrained behaviors, is that banks think of their portals as destinations with limited functionality. They are designed to do only two things: provide you with digital service and push product at you in the hope of making a sale. You go to their site or app not because you want to, but because you have to. There is no alternative. Until, that is, digital currency comes to town.

The system I described exists in the West today (at least in the banks most of us use); it also existed in China before the launch of payment giants like WeChat and Alipay in 2014. In the West, money is immobile, it belongs to you, but the means of transfer belongs to the bank. In practical terms, if your bank falls short of your needs, it is more than likely that you need to physically go to the bank, pay a fee for issuing a check to close your account, and march off to another bank. (To users of digital systems like Zelle in the US, note that for larger amounts you still need to wait for the "check to clear" even if the transfer is digital, so moving accounts digitally still has a lag time.) In China, instant digital payments through WeChat and Alipay broke that old system, and that country's new digital currency will further weaken the banks' control of how clients manage their money. It is a defining moment in banking services. Above all, it empowers the individual. Digital currencies will allow users almost complete freedom to move money wherever and whenever they want.

"STICKY" PLATFORMS REIGN SUPREME

Now compare any bank's website experience with a full platform tech service like Amazon. You go to Amazon not just to buy a book, but to read the candid reviews from other customers on millions of products, check out a few movies, see what's up with the latest music, and, if you're hungry, see what's available at the supermarket. Amazon is a platform that started with selling books, but went on to offer products and services that encompass virtually any lifestyle.

> *Platforms try to capture our time by providing us with as many diversions and as much utility as possible.*

What makes Amazon so special? It's a platform that aims to fulfill many of life's needs in one spot. It's the exact opposite of your bank's website, which offers one and only one siloed service. Platforms, whether built around social connections or e-commerce (the two most common core offerings), try to capture our time by providing us with as many diversions and as much utility as possible. We use them willingly because we get more out of them, and they harken us back because they satisfy our needs.

Platforms are built on two types of network effects. Both help define why more and more people flock to them. There are direct networks, where the more people participating on the platform, the more utility it has, and the more others will want to use it. Facebook, WeChat, and pandemic favorite Zoom all started life as direct platforms. As more people enrolled, the more valuable they became.

The other type are indirect networks, like Amazon. Here the customer base is augmented by increasing the numbers of sellers and complementary services, creating Amazon's flywheel and "virtuous cycle" (refer to diagram in chapter 13). Complementary parties are attracted for mutual benefit rather than direct connectivity. Currently, most successful platforms are combinations of the two, as almost all seek to recruit participants that complement the primary users. Regardless of the definition, you know you're on a platform (rather than, say, a website with limited functionality) because they are "sticky." You hang around and find yourself stuck because of the different things you can do, thanks to their creator's expansive view of the functionality their portal should provide.

Google constitutes a platform because it provides us with search, news, and email, among a plethora of other services. It is direct in that it uses your search results to make the search results better for the next person, and indirect in how it attracts third-party media to its news sites. Similarly, Facebook and Apple, the other two of the GAFA companies, also provide online services that cover a broad segment of our life needs. We don't buy an iPhone for the hardware, but for access to the ecosystem or platform of Apple's services. If we learned anything from the internet boom of the 1990s, it's that platforms reign supreme, and it was the GAFA companies' migration away from single services that allowed these once modest firms to become giants. Looking at the top ten world's most valuable brands in 2019, we see that seven of the ten are digital platforms.

Amazon	$315.5
Apple	$309.5
Google	$309
Microsoft	$251.2
Visa	$177.9
Facebook	$159
Alibaba	$131.2
Tencent	$130.9
McDonald's	$130.4
AT&T	$108.4

The world's most valuable brands. Seven of the world's top ten valuable brands (shaded in gray) are digital platforms. (2019, in US$ billions)

PAYMENT PLATFORMS AS SUPERAPPS

The banking experience in China, is, as you would expect, radically different. I no longer bank on either the bank's app or online; there is simply no need. My money is all accessed through WeChat Pay or Alipay platforms, which are aptly named "superapps" because of the number of services they perform. It's a remarkable experience that frees access to my savings and pushes banking to where it belongs, as the enabler of me doing something, instead of being the focus. It is a massive transformation in how we use banks and one that changes how users perceive banks as a necessity and money's place in our lives. "Seamless" is the best description. Money and technology coming together to form a seamless integration of using your money so you can live your life. Never a thought of how the money will move, where it will go, and the underlying mechanics. It simply all combines to help get stuff done. This is business as usual in China. Research shows that 93% of consumers with a bank account in China also use one or more of the digital payment companies. In practical terms, it means that banks have been driven off center stage by the superapps. It's so disruptive that it's no wonder banks in the West find it culturally challenging to adopt even the most basic of open banking techniques, like building open APIs, for fear that it will lead down a similar path of disenfranchisement.

Most of us don't wake up in the morning and say, "I want to visit my bank to see what's up." Instead, we use it to buy a house or send money. The bank is a means to an end, usually a vaguely unpleasant diversion required for us to get to our goal. Now imagine that the bank is no longer a necessary stop on the path to achieving a goal. Car sales showrooms' in-house financing programs realized this years ago with sign-now and drive away programs, which sought to reduce the effort of getting a car loan. The sellers realized that checking rates and going to the bank to sign the documents was likely to kill a sale, so they did an end-run around the process to keep customers onsite. Car companies took much of the auto financing business away from banks, so why banks remain blind to their own expendability is a mystery to me.

There have certainly been plenty of digital disrupters overturning other industries, like Uber, Airbnb, or Square. And it's not like the banks can't hire and nurture digital talent. It simply comes down to vision (or the lack thereof).

Imagine a world where your money is available on a mobile-based digital payment platform that addresses all of your life activities. Secure and convenient because it uses facial recognition to unlock payment, accepted nationally and used to pay bills large and small, all from a single platform. This isn't just buying a coffee using Apple or Google Pay, but a payment system that cuts across all of your life, including your internet presence, your local shops, rent, mortgage, insurance, investments, and personal cash transfers. Press a button on your phone, click buy, facial recognition confirms, and done. You never go to the bank, never go to your bank's website or app, meanwhile, you know that your money is secure. This dream was made real by the Version 1.0 digital payment systems, which turned China "cashless."

Ant Group (formerly Ant Financial) consumption scenarios show how the platform's ecosystem of services fits into all aspects of a user's life.
Source: Ant Group

This is the dream that Alibaba, the leading online retailer, nd WeChat, the leading social media platform, delivered in full. Each of these has its own payment system, and most Chinese users have accounts on both, connecting directly to their bank account. This enables payment virtually anywhere in the country and increasingly abroad. While I focus on these platforms because of their 94% market share, note that JD (Jingdong) Pay and Baidu Wallet are also competing with excellent products.

All of these systems were lethal to banks for a single reason: they were so easy to use. You activate your account by entering your debit card details, enter a few security details, then set up a passcode and facial recognition, and you're done, in about three minutes. Once you've got these systems up and running, you no longer deal with your banking portal but instead use the app, which takes money directly from your account. Note also that all of these systems have a wallet feature that allows you to store money on the app. So, for example, if you receive payment from someone, you can allow this balance to sit in your wallet, which is non-interest bearing, to be used for your outgoing payments, or if you choose, you can push it into your bank account.

These accounts are lethal in the real sense of the word. Consumer research shows that 42% of Chinese customers used digital banking services rather than their primary bank's offerings. Meaning that banks were not just fighting on the payment front, but battling over their ability to provide banking services, period, to their former customers. Speaking specifically of payment, Accenture predicts ongoing cumulative losses of $US 61 billion to China's incumbent banks between 2019 and 2025, due to the rival platforms.

BANKING AS A "DUMB PIPE"

With superapp payment systems in widespread use, the traditional bank has been relegated to the position of long-term money repository, losing the front-end business of being the default payment provider. It is a huge setback and an extreme blow to their formerly exalted position. They have lost control of the privilege of transacting customers' outgoings via online payment, debit, or credit card. For all but the most old-school of clients, they are now out of this equation. Even worse, customers who wish to go fully digital and ditch their traditional bank entirely, as many have, can bank with Ant Group's MYbank or WeChat's WeBank. Users who do this are essentially lost to the traditional system, which will have to work hard to win them back.

> A bank becomes a "dumb pipe" when it acts as a simple conduit through which money flows like water, with little added value.

Currently, it is mostly immaterial what bank you use in China, as the app does the work of connecting the payments. I continue to use a traditional bank as I need the foreign exchange services they provide, and as a foreigner living in Shanghai, still need to be physically present at a branch to receive or send foreign currency. For most of the population, however, the choice of bank is irrelevant, since all are equally connected to the apps, and are equally trusted for storing cash. There's the rub: you not only don't care what bank you use, your bank has no way to differentiate itself from others once you relegate them to the back seat. Among bankers, this fate is called becoming a "dumb pipe," a simple conduit through which money flows like water, with little added value. Which bank do you use? Who cares?

Why is this situation extraordinary? Can't I set up a "one-click" payment on Amazon, and have a similar experience there? Yes, and you can also use Apple or Google Pay in many ways to make payments without cash, on and offline. China's difference is twofold. First, WeChat or Alipay have connectivity with virtually every service and retailer available in the country. There's no question that a live cashier or an online shop will accept these services. Moreover, you can have both on your phone since they exist independently of which phone you buy. Whether it's an Apple or Android phone makes no difference.

The second distinction is that neither Apple Pay nor Google Pay are truly platforms, with an online ecosystem of services and users. Instead, they are a means of storing credit card details on a phone or computer and using these devices to pay elsewhere. You have to go—physically or online—to make an Apple or Google payment. With Alipay and WeChat Pay, the vendors are right there *on* the platform—obviously, a fundamental difference. Anything on the platform is yours for the taking, no questions asked. So while Apple and Google Pay are tremendously convenient, they don't harbor the platforms' comprehensive network of services to one-click you out of arrears, fulfill your daily needs, or otherwise tempt you away from your money.

BUILDING AN ECOSYSTEM

The "mini-programs" discussed in an earlier chapter were critical to the development of a rich on-app ecosystem for WeChat and Alipay, making them unstoppable. It's fair to say that they had already built a powerful presence before the launch of mini-programs, but it was this technology that made their utility explode. It enabled a "virtuous cycle" that made users and services converge, such that going off-platform simply became more bother than it was worth.

Mini-programs are essentially apps within WeChat or Alipay that allow users to add features to their accounts. Everything and anything one can imagine has been turned into a mini-program, because these apps are so cheap to build. Several large Chinese internet companies, most notably Pinduoduo, got their start as mini-programs. Since they use the security and payment systems provided by the parent app, the mini-programs are lightweight and easy to build. They are a developer's dream, likewise the dream of small business owners throughout China, who use them to extend their reach to a massive group of customers. As a result, each of the platforms has a vast ecosystem of services from third-party companies. It is Amazon's flywheel or indirect network effect on steroids. Mini-program designers working for small businesses add additional features to the platform, users find more reasons to use it, resulting in users becoming even more addicted to the platform's utility. It's a perpetual feedback loop.

So think for a moment about this humiliating example of how the traditional banks have lost ground. Because of the success of mini-programs and the stickiness of platforms, banks have countered with mini-programs built into WeChat or Alipay. While many of these mini-programs promote their latest credit cards, increasingly banks are building them to allow users to do most of their basic banking without downloading the bank's app to their cell phone. Banks found that they couldn't beat these apps, and rather than forcing account holders to download the bank's standalone app, they simply gave in and used WeChat and Alipay to reach their clients. This is the ultimate example of how platforms are forcing banks to become part of the "open banking" revolution, jettisoning the notion that clients have to come to their portal for service.

A search for "ICBC," China's largest bank, on WeChat revealed 30 mini-programs showing how extensively ICBC uses WeChat to reach clients. Services included in this small sampling include branch product sales, branch banking services, precious metal trading, and recruiting for recent graduates.

Staking a place on either of these platforms costs very little; mini-program technology's development costs are low, making them readily accessible to even smaller companies. The modest outlay offers significant potential gains by reaching new clients who are already shopping on the platform. It's the mall concept in digital form. Ali and WeChat have become the destination for the app development efforts of all companies in China, large and small. Meanwhile, Apple Pay or Google Pay have no platforms per se, and can claim only spotty integration, particularly among small- and medium-size enterprise websites.

PLATFORMS IN THE WEST, AND BANKS' BUSINESS TO LOSE

While the West is nowhere near WeChat Pay and Alipay-levels of payment and banking convenience, it's coming. No one can ignore Google's new "Plex" service providing current accounts, Facebook Pay's debut on everyone's favorite social network, Apple Cards, and even T-Mobile entering the financial space in the US. The goal of these companies isn't just to provide you with a credit card or quick payment, but to expand the capabilities and stickiness of their platforms. They've been watching China, and know that the mixture of a sticky digital platform and financial services is combustible. Their goal is nothing less than capturing your finances. But for now, they have to tiptoe around banking regulations that limit their ability to play in the financial space.

That's why each of the West's Big Tech platforms is tying up with a bank, or getting limited financial services licenses to launch these products. Unlike China, where the government issued WeChat and Alipay with banking licenses, regulations remain prohibitive for the West's platform players. Some will find, as I do, that China was prescient in allowing Big Tech into financial services to change banking for the better. Others will cite the potential for privacy abuses by Big Tech, and think that Western regulators are correct in protecting incumbent banks from Big Tech and segregating their functions.

Whatever your viewpoint, the reality in the West seems to be that this separation won't hold for long. The tech players are keen to add these services. They'll eventually crack this market, with or without regulators' help. Google, Amazon, and Facebook's WhatsApp are all initiating payment platforms in India. WhatsApp Pay already launched in Brazil. These efforts are a stark indication of how readily they will enter the payment space as soon as regulators allow it.

There is a warning to Western banks. They would do well to study the development of superapps in the China market, and in Southeast Asia, where Grab and Go-Jek car sharing are now leading platforms. In all of these cases, the platform didn't intend to be a bank, so much as try to relieve a pain point for their clients, which happened to involve banking. Alibaba launched its Alipay online payment service only after failing to find a bank that would partner with them to develop e-commerce payments. Rebuffed, Alibaba built Alipay by itself. Similarly, Grab and Go-Jek (now potentially merging) both found themselves co-opted into banking when they found that many of their drivers were unbanked, and ignored by incumbent banks. In the final analysis, it was the banks that denied consumers modern services; the platforms simply stepped in and filled the gap.

One can argue that these examples all come from the developing world, and that no such service gap exists in the West. The argument falls apart when digital payments are more easily made on Google platforms in India and on Facebook's WhatsApp in Brazil than they are in most of the US and EU. Uber Money in the US is another warning shot off the bow of incumbent banks, and it mirrors Grab and Go-Jek's experiences. Suffice it to say, digital payment is the bank's business to lose. It appears that their unwillingness to adapt or modify their business model to meet the new needs of the digital world may give Big Tech the opportunity they've been waiting for.

16

BANKING AS AN
AFTERTHOUGHT

China on open banking:

> *"In future, banks will be a type of service, not a type of location, and bank products must be seamlessly integrated into various settings and ecosystems."*
>
> "2018 China Direct Banking White Paper" China Minsheng Bank and China Financial Certification Authority

The West on open banking:

> *"Fintech's true promise springs from its potential to unbundle banking into its core functions of: settling payments, performing maturity transformation, sharing risk and allocating capital."*
>
> Mark Carney, Governor of the Bank of England, 2017

I n China's new cashless world, banking is broadly considered an afterthought. This displacement is profound for most retail bankers and frankly, makes them cringe. The formerly ubiquitous advertising that they are "your trusted life partner" now feels obsolete. Their constant claims of special offers and great rates are all rendered meaningless because offers and rates from 100 different competitors can be checked in a fraction of a second on your superapp, with money transferred to open or close accounts in seconds. Without a privileged role at the center of your financial life, what do the banks have left to offer?

This is the kind of soul searching that Western banks should undertake before digital disruption hits in earnest. Apple and Google pay have already begun to push plastic cards off center stage, but that has been delayed to an extent by users' familiarity with credit cards and their myriad loyalty schemes. How long before other sectors of banking are hit and how long will that loyalty last?

The Bank of International Settlements reports that "central banks representing a fifth of the world's population are likely to issue the first CBDCs in the next few years." The days are numbered for bank-issued cards for payment. In China, where there was no loyalty to cards, users abandoned bank payment in droves. Not only was mobile payment more convenient, but displacing the need to go to the bank made most Chinese jump for joy.

When I say joy, I'm not exaggerating. Going to the bank in China has long been a unique experience. Back in 2014, the average wait time at my local branch of ICBC was around an hour—if I caught it at just the right time. Accompanying every transaction was the mandatory stamping and processing of multiple sheets of paper, and in the end, no matter what type of transaction, I always had a thick wad of documents to file or fling after leaving the bank. I also had an actual bank book, something I found quaint.

> *Clients simply ran from the banks, ditched cash, cards, and never looked back.*

Around this time, banks did try to fight back by adding more automation and sophisticated cash-counting machines for deposits and transfers. These ATM-based transactions helped to reduce waiting, and allowed for some "digital" transactions, but you still had to visit the bank. While helpful, these services did nothing to solve the inherent problem of dealing with cash, still heavily used for payments. When finally presented with cashless, phone-based digital payments, and a platform for shopping at one's fingertips, clients ran from the banks, ditched their cash and cards, and never looked back.

This is a stark warning to banks in the West. They're already aggressively cutting branches, and relying on digital services to trim costs. If the credit card schemes are not enough to hold customers long-term (and I believe they won't be), then they too will become an afterthought. What else do they offer? As in China, the ability to check rates and the ease of shifting money will commoditize banking, making it an afterthought. And, if that time comes in the West, the launch of digital currency will only streamline the transfer of savings to whichever financial institution provides the best "deal du jour."

Any trip to the bank for me still takes quite a while. Do note that I am waiting with a group who all have grey hair and consider such a trip a social outing. There is a lot of chatting with the bank employees, and more than a few customers are getting lessons on how to use their phones to do banking with WeChat or Alipay. The irony of bank employees teaching their oldest and most loyal customers how to use their competitor's app never ceases to amuse me.

WHAT'S NEXT FOR CHINA'S BANKS?

So what are the Chinese banks doing to mitigate their situation, and what can we take away from this? If they've learned anything, it's that their role is not as secure as they once thought. While many Western banking C-level executives live in a state of denial, even with GAFA companies entering into finance, their counterparts in China have no such luxury. They know the impact of digital disruption intimately and do not doubt Big Tech's power to disrupt their market.

Their reaction was to not waste time and change their offerings, but to meet the digital threat head-on. According to the "2018 China Direct Banking White Paper," 135 new online direct digital banks have opened since 2014, showing how traditional banks rose to meet the challenge by jumping on the digital bandwagon. These direct digital banks were run in parallel with existing brick and mortar operations and were promoted as a sleek, easy, digital direct way to bank, manage wealth, buy insurance, and get a loan. Clearly, not all were so diligent. Among China's top six state-owned banks, only one, ICBC, was able to add a digital-only direct bank to their services during this period.

It's fair to say that all Chinese banks have improved their digital offerings following the explosion of alternative digital payments, but not all have followed through with the profound transformation required to compete effectively with digital players. Some have delayed by resting on old laurels, knowing that even with the kneecapping of their payment operations, their other profit centers are intact and still producing good returns. In theory, some state-owned entities could perpetuate this delay indefinitely, though none will. The government's push for nationwide digital transformation will not allow them to rest on bygone business practices.

The government's proactive policy is best for the traditional banks in the long run, because China's new digital banking sector is rapidly building out their services into new product areas. They are chasing down the incumbent banks' business lines, one by one. One example is in digital lending. Ant Group's MYbank and WeChat's WeBank originally entered the lending markets explicitly to target sectors of society not served by banks. It's now apparent that they have set their sights beyond the unbanked. The ease of the application process and the inevitable wooing of higher credit borrowers will slowly but surely impact the incumbent's retail loan books.

LESSONS FOR THE WEST'S NEOBANKS

A similar situation is developing in the West, where digital-only banks, called "neobanks" (or "challenger banks" in the UK market), have made inroads into retail banking in both Europe and the US. Observers debate their long-term impact, due to their current lack of profitability and their limited product portfolio relative to that of incumbents. But if China's digital banks have any lessons for the West, it's that incumbents should not be complacent. Digital challengers are masters of this format and will expand their offerings, in the same way China's digital banks continue their siege against incumbents in that country.

> *While clients do use digital payment and may have a digital-only bank account, the majority are still drawn to the safety of incumbents.*

The saving grace for incumbent banks everywhere is this: while clients may love the ease and nimbleness of digital payment systems, the security incumbents offer for savings remains absolute. Clients still retain the majority of their savings in traditional banks. According to China Banking News, China's largest digital banks, WeBank and MYbank, had total assets of RMB 82 and RMB 78 billion, respectively, at the end of October 2018. In comparison, ICBC, China's largest incumbent, had total assets of RMB 27 trillion, and personal deposits of RMB 8.2 trillion.

While clients do use digital payment and may have a digital-only bank account, the majority are still drawn to the safety of incumbents and there is no denying that the overwhelming amount of deposits are still firmly within the established banks.

What this boils down to is: banking roots go deep. China's incumbent banks are still holding on to the majority of the country's deposits even after a cashless revolution. This is a warning to the uphill battle faced by digital banking in the West. Pundits proclaim almost daily that GAFA companies will rout incumbents if allowed to fully enter banking markets, but I believe the disruption will be less severe than technophiles predict. China's banks have been shaken by Big Tech disruption, but they are not imperiled. The security offered by traditional savings accounts would be much harder to unseat.

There are several reasons for this. First and foremost is the issue of trust. While users enjoy the convenience of digital payments, it was never necessary to transfer funds in their entirety to the new digital bank, in order to use digital payment services. This was a stroke of genius, because it allowed the digital payment systems to prosper in parallel from the start, without uprooting longstanding banking relationships. Digital payment also didn't necessitate the hassle of closing an existing bank account. As bank accounts in China have low or no charges, leaving an account open costs little and is essentially a free avenue to use their services in the future. The ease of digital payments and the low impact of maintaining a traditional account creates a sense of comfort with the new status quo. However, most important of all is that most users recognize that it simply doesn't matter where you keep your account; banks are nothing more than a commodity and the relationship is at best ambivalent.

Neobanks in the West, keen to snare entire tranches of new business, are at an impasse with customers' inclination to maintain savings according to the old model. Neobank users may love the flashy and convenient app to make payments or other services easier, but they will continue to store most of their funds in an incumbent bank. Market research company Kantar reports that neobank customers globally use them for only 40% of their banking interactions. In the UK, a survey by finder.com showed that a full half of neobank users had GBP 1,000 or less in their digital accounts.

What this demonstrates is that users may like digital banks as a conduit for payment, but prefer to deprive them of the deposits they need to grow. Also, far more than their Chinese counterparts, neobanks in the West suffer from a deficit in trust. This is because they're all relatively new and, notably, not backed by household names. In China, most neobanks are sponsored by large tech companies or existing banks with strong name recognition. There is greater trust because of the sense that these corporate giants, or the government, would never allow these neobanks fail.

We all recognize that China is different. Especially regarding one particular feature of their internet and banking system, which simplifies the endeavor relative to innovation in the West. That feature is the digital national ID system. This assigns everyone an ID number, which is tied to biometric data and all mobile devices. This feature simplifies "know your customer" (KYC) requirements and helps to provide a smooth onboarding process for new clients. In essence, when you are on a digital banking platform in China, the bank knows who you are, because digital services are unambiguously tied to the user. The system isn't perfect: renting or stealing an ID number to hide bank accounts is not uncommon. That said, compared to the KYC procedures in the West that require wet signatures and in-person sign-up, this system is a clear advantage.

OPEN BANKING

Platforms in banking lead us to another trend in China that is a direct result of the success of Alipay and WeChat Pay. It's called "open banking." This is a cause célèbre in the West because it is a relatively new concept, brought by the "Second Payment Service Directives" (PSD2) regulations in the EU, which the UK has also enacted. The regulation essentially acknowledges that bank account and transaction data belong to the customer. Banks were forced to participate in open banking by providing a means for disclosing this customer account data to third parties. Banks must build a library of open APIs (application programming interface) that enable third-party developers to access data from the bank's systems, so that they can build applications and services catering to their clients. In the UK, these APIs must have a standard format for ease of use.

Without getting too technical here, APIs are gateways for data that a non-bank application can access to see your data on the bank's systems. All of this is password controlled, and each API documents what data it can deliver with prescribed levels of security. The functionality that APIs offer may differ slightly between banks. Still, most are developing libraries of APIs that will allow third-party fintech developers to access your basic account data and do simple transactions on their systems. If this sounds like a major cultural change for banks, I can assure you it is. Banks traditionally saw themselves as the guardians of your data, and the idea of allowing third-party access remains anathema to many.

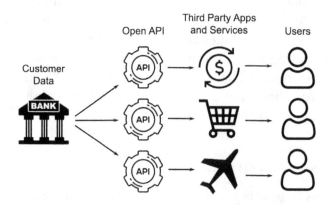

APIs are the foundation for "Open Banking," which allows bank data to be embedded in newly developed apps and services.

Here's an example of how it works. The most common use case of open banking APIs is in financial management apps.

These services ask you to input your bank account passwords. The API then allows them to access your balances on one or several of your accounts, monitor your spending, and aggregate this information into a comprehensive view of your financial health. More complicated apps might go so far as to input your data into multiple banks' or insurers' APIs to get a price comparison for a loan or insurance coverage. Soon they will allow direct payment from your bank account. For most in the West, this will mean that your online shopping can be deducted directly from your bank, reducing the hidden costs of routing the payment through a payment card.

The underlying concept is that once your data is shared, fintech companies can build new payment and other services that make the selection of financial products easier, cheaper, and fairer. Open APIs also have another exciting new use in allowing connected devices to access your bank. Soon, many internet of things (IoT) devices may also connect to your bank. For example, your car may pay for gas through a connection to a bank payment API. So open banking is, in broad terms, a major plus for the consumer, as it allows you to authorize other services and devices to access the account and use your banking data to provide you with better service.

OPEN BANKING BY DISRUPTION

China's experience with open banking was the exact opposite of the neat planning and organization used in the UK and EU. In China, open banking wasn't legislated into existence so much as forced upon incumbent banks by Alipay and WeChat. Both of these services used bank debit cards to provide a link between users' banks and the payment app. Once this link was forged, the banks were practically dragged into open banking by the amazing popularity of these payment apps.

It wasn't an amicable partnership as banks first viewed these superapps with well-deserved disdain. However, as the situation settled, banks realized that they had to do business with them and began opening a trickle of APIs to the payment apps. When it dawned that mobile was the future not just of payments, but of all banking services, the banks gave in. The platforms were so sticky that banks couldn't pry their users from them, and in the end, it became clear that advertising on the platforms, selling investments, and providing account management services on them was a necessity. In the UK experience, banks open their data to third parties, while in China the banks willingly became the third parties on the payment platforms, bringing their data with them.

China achieved open banking by disruption rather than legislation. Unlike in the UK, China's successes in open banking were not the result of a plan or concerted government effort. Instead, they were a survival strategy to combat Big Tech. It was a case of innovate or die. The irony is, the UK banks required government regulation to open, where China's state-owned banks opened themselves with no government prodding.

The two systems have one thing in common: banks had to change their organization and computer systems to enable the new required openness. Open banking necessitates a new team that understands both the tech itself and how it can be used to create profitable digital interactions. These new digital teams face outwardly to the marketplace, trying to entice new partners (and cajole senior bankers uncomfortable with the entire process).

OPEN BANKING AND PLATFORMS

Open banking requires that banks expose their services to the world, to free users from the hegemony of their proprietary websites and apps. What better place to do this than on a digital platform? Platforms are the natural place for open banking activities, and banks have two distinct choices on how to exploit them. The first, and simplest, is to station the bank on a platform built by others. This is precisely what China's banks did when they put themselves on WeChat or Alipay. Open banking API's enabled their customers to view their account details on mini-programs built for these superapps. This is the easiest way to proceed, guarantees a large potential user base, and is frankly the most intuitive. No wonder Citibank's new "Plex Account" on Google Pay follows a similar strategy, and even credits Ant Group with being the inspiration for the move.

The second alternative, also alive and well in China but not yet attempted in the West, is for the bank to build its own platform. This is a much more ambitious proposition and, in some instances, puts banks in direct competition with the digital platforms that are vying for their business. Impressively, some of China's banks have responded to the challenge with a vengeance.

ICBC Bank, for example, now operates an entirely new e-commerce site called "Rong E Gou" that sells consumer items throughout China. It is a massive effort with some 10,000 merchants reporting sales of RMB 1.27 trillion ($US184 billion) in 2016. It sells everything from automobiles to electronics, among them more than 100,000 iPhones said to be sold in 2015. Key to the platform's success was its innovative installment payment program that clients can use to build their credit rating. Having stormed the retail market, Rong E Gou opened a business-to-business site that, in roughly two years, sold some $US 218 billion in products to more than 225,000 business buyers. Here too users can get loans to help them buy, and improve their business's credit rating with repayment. Customers can also use ICBC points to help defray the cost of things acquired via ICBC services. Here a bank disrupted by an e-commerce giant responds by successfully entering e-commerce. It may sound amusing, but this is a deadly serious business for ICBC and is a cornerstone of their efforts to be something more than just a bank to their clients.

China Merchant Bank (CMB) is another institution challenging the "norms" of banking. It's noteworthy due to its professed strategy of becoming a digital bank. CMB has published and openly promoted its APIs to expand its business onto other platforms and, of course, to modernize its digital services. Like ICBC, CMB also operates an e-commerce site, but has gone a step further. It offers its business and retail clients travel management services, with the intent of challenging China's leading digital travel platform, Ctrip. CMB's goal is to provide business users with a "one-stop travel management system" to facilitate business travel bookings, scheduling, and expense reporting. This is another example of an open banking effort to provide more than just banking services.

Not to be outdone in the retail sector by its rivals, China Construction Bank (CCB) entered into an agreement with systems developer "Dmall," China's leading provider of digital transformation solutions for traditional retailers. Dmall works with nearly 10,000 shops and has 75 million registered users. According to China Banking News, CCB will provide banking services to develop an "online and offline full-channel ecosystem." What this means is CCB is entering into a retail agreement to put its services where they've never been before, directly on the web, and direct to the customer. While full details aren't out yet on this new partnership, you can assume that, like ICBC, CCB is going directly to the client and will provide their customers with a new retail presence.

Another solid player in open banking is Shanghai Pudong Development Bank, which has launched "API Bank." This is a technical marvel that allows third parties to access APIs across a broad suite of bank functions brought about by significant systems upgrades. Functions accessible by API include loan products, cross-border e-commerce, insurance and payments, and collection. Essentially a large portion of banking features once solely available through the bank's websites will now be made open to third parties. To make using these APIs even easier, the bank is also publishing WeChat applets so that coders building on the WeChat platform can access these functions more easily. The goal is to make services available to third parties who can embed them in their sites to put the bank wherever the client is—a significant change in strategy.

There is, however, one player in China that has mastered building platforms, and the APIs that fuel them, more so than any other: the insurance and banking giant Ping An. Ping An's mastery of building platforms is a model of how it can be done in the West. Moreover, Ping An did this starting not as a tech company but as a traditional financial service provider. They made a conscious decision to go digital, and instead transformed into a "finance + technology" and "finance + ecosystem" platform builder. If there was ever a role model for Western banks and insurers in building platforms, it's Ping An.

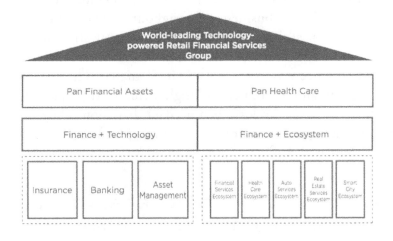

Ping An is a model for platform builders in the West. It is the only traditional financial services company that mastered digital technology to become the undisputed king of building platforms.
Source: Ping An

Their recognition of the "ecosystem" concept allowed them to have an expansive view of client needs that goes far beyond the constraints of traditional financial services companies. For example, health care patients don't only need coverage, but an independent way to select good doctors and get remote health care. In light of this, Ping An built and IPOed the "Good Doctor" platform. This ecosystem approach provides users with necessary services that are independent yet related to Ping An's financial business, all the while collecting massive amounts of user data.

Ping An's primary tech subsidiaries include Autohome, China's largest auto and home buying platform; HealthKonnect, a cloud service managing health insurance billing; Lufax, a leading asset manager and microloan provider; and OneConnect, a blockchain and core systems provider for banks and insurers. Ping An has so far IPOed three of these subsidiaries: Good Doctor, Lufax, and OneConnect, with a fourth planned for Autohome. The diversity along with the interconnected nature of these services is a model for platform builders everywhere. Ping An is embedded in the lives of people and businesses throughout China by providing indisputably useful services. While the company still advertises and pushes product the old-fashioned way, there's a lot less of it than there once was in the subway in Shanghai. There's simply no need, because customers willingly come to their platforms, use their services, and leave behind data that allows Ping An to embed itself into their unique customer journey. Who needs advertisements?

CHINA'S CBDC AND REVERSING THE TREND OF BECOMING A "DUMB PIPE"

Digital currency's disruption of the banking market is well underway. The new CBDC will only further upend banks. Digital payment through the superapps is already part of people's lives, making the revised status of banks as "dumb pipes"—simple conduits rather than revered institutional gatekeepers—a serious cause for concern in the industry. When CBDCs enter the marketplace, the banks' status may downgrade further. With CBDCs, you can make a payment without a bank account or a superapp, bestowing users with near-total control of how to send money. Banks still have a central role in issuing CBDC, but once issued, clients are free to use superapps or any other means to pass it around. It seems evident that eventually MYbank and WeBank, the related banking units of Alipay and WeChat, will be given leave to mint digital currency, further cementing the superapps' market dominance.

The big question is, can China's CBDC also help banks regain relevance and some of their lost status? Perhaps, but it's not going to be easy. Banks are going to have to win back clients and peal them off the sticky superapps. The easiest way to do that is "buy them back" with discounts that make using the bank an obvious choice. To do so, banks do not have to reinvent the wheel. Ridesharing is an excellent example of a service that everyone uses. If banks could make ridesharing cheaper than the superapps by negotiating a better deal for clients, they'd win back customers rather quickly. It's expensive and unsustainable, but it works and requires little effort.

The other way is by building the kinds of platforms that serve their clients' needs, a gambit which, as we have just seen with Ping An, can pay off in a major way. This path requires much greater strategic planning and is expensive, but has greater long-term value. This will require banks to do some soul-searching about how best to serve their clients and, more importantly, who they want to be in ten years. No matter which path China's banks take, it will be long, hard, and costly.

A research report by Goldman Sachs estimates that a 10% increase in bank mobile app users through CBDC will only lift revenues between 2% to 5%. So bankers looking to do nothing and wait for CBDCs to give them a windfall will be sorely disappointed. Digitally sophisticated banks like Ping An, ICBC, and CMB, which are active platform builders, are showing the way, and rising to the challenge. The vast majority will fall short with their fate as "dumb pipes" assured.

17

CREDIT AND INCLUSION

China on financial inclusion:

> *China will achieve the poverty alleviation goal set in the United Nations 2030 Agenda for Sustainable Development ten years ahead of schedule, which is of great significance to both China and the world, as no country in the world has ever lifted so many people out of poverty in such a short period of time,"*
>
> Xi Jinping, General Secretary of the Chinese Communist Party, and President of the People's Republic of China, speech to the 73rd session of the World Health Assembly

The West on financial inclusion:

> *The 2.5 billion adults [around the world] without access to financial services are disproportionately women and young people. There are at least 44 million unbanked or underbanked people in the United States, so clearly financial inclusion is needed in all markets.*
>
> Ajaypal Singh Banga, Chief Executive Officer of MasterCard

Credit is the holy grail of digital finance. It is the fuel that makes economies grow and is key to creating the lifestyles envisioned in either the American or Chinese Dream. There is no banker alive that wouldn't want to harness the power of big data to come up with the perfect algorithm to predict a customer's willingness and ability to repay. Bankers have dreamed about this since the dawn of the internet, and they're hard at work at it in the West. In China, it's already a reality.

The convergence of digital payment, high-tech payment platforms, a massive population without access to credit, and a recently failed P2P loan market all converged to make big-data based loans the next Big Thing. Where P2P crashed and burned, the results will be different this time around. The switch to digital cash transformed lending, which will only continue with the new CBDC.

We all know that currently in the West, banks rely on credit ratings developed by third-party companies as a critical component to assess a client's loan worthiness. Many obsess over this number daily. It impacts everything from how much we pay for a car loan to whether hospitals will admit us for care. While the exact process differs by company, your credit rating relies on data collected from your creditors, including card companies, banks, and anyone else who ever loaned you money. With this history the companies conjure a view of your ability to repay and manage credit. Banks take this raw credit score and add to it their proprietary methodologies, which quantitively define you as worthy or unworthy of credit under their lending criteria. Today the process is mostly digitized, and while a human may eventually review the results, you can bet that at most banks, there isn't a lot of room for in-person negotiation.

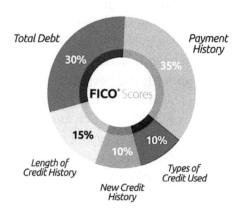

FICO score calculation.
Source: FICO

BIG DATA FOR A
MULTI-DIMENSIONAL VIEW

So far, there's nothing inherently wrong with the process, unless you are deemed "untouchable" because you have no credit history or, worse, a bad one. Credit scores are limited in what they consider; they do not paint a complete picture of who you are. They don't ask why you may have a problem that impacted your score now or in the past. A simplistic viewpoint limits the system, and even renders it inaccurate regarding your repayment ability. To fine-tune their understanding of potential clients, a laudable goal, banks are now adding "big data" to their evaluation toolkit.

If we were to design an ideal big-data loan underwriting procedure, we might include analysis of data concerning someone's history of Amazon purchases, all Facebook comments and Instagram posts, plus every digital payment he's ever made. This is the direction that banks in the West are going, and it's a safe bet that banks will come up with new and improved credit algorithms to more precisely calculate customers' creditworthiness with each new data stream they add.

While complete integration of someone's digital life into their credit evaluation isn't possible for banks in the West just yet, they're working on it. Giant improvements are being made to their analytical capabilities, particularly on their payment systems, to enable a more granular view of individual habits, by collating what, where, and when people buy things. As of yet, the mountains of data owned by Facebook, Google, and Amazon are not available for direct purchase. To access it, banks have started to reach out to third-party data brokers who harvest and collate massive amounts of information off the internet. Purchases from third parties may shield the major internet platforms from responsibility for selling such data, even when the data may have originated on their sites. With this arrangement, Facebook can truthfully say they didn't sell personal data. Rather, internet sleuths working for a third-party company, e.g., tasked by an insurer with finding brand-new parents, might dig up details of baby showers from users' social media posts, thereby absolving Facebook of responsibility.

Banks are also working with fintechs who provide "alternative credit scoring." This relies on their ability to find and analyze massive data footprints to assist in or create an alternative under-writing process. This is all new in the West, and hopefully will help address the over-reliance on credit scores, which exclude even deserving borrowers from the process. Opinions on this technology are mixed, however. Those with low scores see this technology as a significant advance that might help, while those well served by the current system, or those with privacy concerns, see this as another step on the road to digital perdition. The key holdup in rolling out these all-knowing systems is the separation of banking from big tech's enormous data collection engines. When these systems are widely connected, as they just were initially with the launch of Google's new savings and checking account "Plex by Google Pay," your bank's credit systems will look very different.

CHINA HAS NO BARRIER BETWEEN BIG TECH AND BANKING

Now let's leave the West and enter China, where the likes of Alibaba's Ant Group are hard at work mining the big-data stream generated by every transaction, like, and click-through on Alibaba's platform. Between Alibaba and its fintech affiliate Ant Group, there is no separation of tech from banking. WeChat's WeBank is doing the same thing. They're all mining not only the obvious bill payments and cash transfers, but everything you've bought, where you've sent it, how frequently you purchase, and tons of behavioral information like how many hours you work or sleep. All is captured via your interaction with the platform. Far more so than Amazon does in the west, these two Chinese giants know their customers and their habits, and can paint a surprisingly accurate picture of who they are. So much so that a purchase of a car baby seat or long working hours may have been the tipping factor on the granting of a loan. China's digital banks are going down a road that the banks in the West would very much like to travel. They've gotten there first due to a massive advantage in data. Their example will be the one to follow as they work their way through this new paradigm in lending.

FUEL FOR CHINA'S ECONOMY

It is essential to understand why credit is so important in China. Credit is a critical ingredient in the country's transformation from an economy that relies heavily on manufacturing to one that is service-based. China is "the world's factory," exporting cheaply made goods to the rest of the world, at prices that simply cannot be matched by local producers. This fostered enviable growth for the past two decades, and raised up such a large portion of the populace from economic hardship that the World Bank's poverty figures appear distorted by China's contribution. The manufacturing model, however, is challenging to sustain and prone to instability. By transitioning to a service economy, like those in the US and Europe, China can become more economically independent and reduce its reliance on heavy industry and exports. Nothing speaks louder than results. China's "exports of goods and services" as a percentage of GDP are down to 18% in 2019 from a peak of 36% in 2006.

To achieve this transition, China is focusing on high value-added services like finance and technology due to their fast growth rates and ability to spur internal consumption to offset soft industrial growth. The government's goal is to increase the service sector to 70%-80% of total GDP, on par with the US and Europe, from around 52% in 2018. To achieve this, the government must provide economic stimulus in the form of credit to both companies and individuals. China's ability to reach out to state-owned and larger private companies through the banking system is well established and relatively efficient. Personal and small business credit, however, is still relatively inefficient, as credit cards have relatively low adoption rates and banking services have long overlooked China's poor and/or rural population. The promise of an efficient credit system via digital technology not only fits with China's love of all things new and digital, but fulfills long-term goals of creating a service economy.

BIG DATA, CHINA'S SECOND ATTEMPT AT DIGITAL CREDIT

As discussed in earlier chapters, P2P lending was an unmitigated disaster that led to personal tragedy. Understanding why credit is so important in China helps us understand why that nation undertook a second attempt to digitize credit before the dust from the P2P crisis had even settled. The hope is that, despite a trade war and a pandemic-shaken economy, big-data based personal credit can help China continue its trajectory of growth and transformation. The stakes are high, because without ready credit, China's transition will be slower and even more vulnerable to the effects of both a prolonged trade war and the US's efforts to decouple from China's economy.

Timing is everything. Both WeChat and Ant Group were working on big-data based credit even before the P2P markets crashed in 2017-18. These credit products were a natural progression of their banking activities and would have eventuated even if P2P lending had been successful. There is little documentation but it seems likely that the P2P woes even hastened their development. Big data-based lending is like a scalpel compared to P2P's meat cleaver. While both get the job done, one does it with far more finesse. Had P2P lending survived, it is interesting to contemplate how these two forms of lending would have competed for market share.

NO CHANCE OF A P2P REPEAT PERFORMANCE

As we saw with Ant's now "paused" IPO, there is a big difference between China's low-touch regulatory stance with P2P and the kind of regulatory scrutiny big data-based credit attracts. The first attempt having gone so badly, the new version of credit markets is far more regulated. From the start, each company required a banking license to provide credit services. In theory these licenses would constrain lenders' behaviors, and allow regulators to monitor how each manages credit exposure. This was easier said than done as regulators accustomed to counting cash reserves were challenged to count complex non-cash reserves. Ant's regulatory imbroglio shows how regulators remain vigilant over the possibility of a second credit bubble on their watch, and are willing to go to extremes to avoid another fiasco. (More on this topic in chapter 18 on Ant.) Regulators, still traumatized by shell-shocked P2P, remain steadfast that there will be no repeat of the scandal and are unafraid to act.

Credit markets have two sides: providers, subject to regulatory oversight, and borrowers, with a cultural view of repayment obligation. On the borrower's side there are also significant changes to ensure there will be no repeat of the P2P market's excesses. The rollout, however troubled, of Baihang Credit in 2018 changes the stakes for borrowers. Baihang is a nationwide credit rating system squarely aimed at detecting individuals who would seek to defraud the system as some did with P2P loans. Any inducement of taking out a loan with the intent not to repay it is now gone.

China's new digital banks have enormous confidence in the ability of technology to diminish defaults on a massive scale. While their reserving practices have come under attack by regulators, their credit methodologies work so well that these have escaped critique. They are miles ahead of incumbent banks, who have a lot of work to do to catch up. China Construction Bank (CCB), one of China's Big Four, recently did a deal with FICO, the famous US-based credit score company, to onboard their systems to help with big-data analysis of their clients. This will allow them to analyze data to try to expand and improve their loan performance. It is every bit a credit arms race with their opponents to reach China's would-be borrowers.

CREDIT WITH A SOCIAL PURPOSE: FINANCIAL INCLUSION

Credit arms race aside, there is something far more important going on with these digital lenders, with a profound societal benefit. Digital lending is a tool for bringing greater financial inclusion to China's large unbanked population. More than just the latest toy for bankers, it elevates the endeavor to the level of national priority. Ant Group's mission statement makes this crystal clear: "to bring inclusive financial services to the world." Tencent's (parent of WeChat Pay) mission is a bit broader, to match its social media and gaming outreach: "Value for Users, Tech for Good."

While we may marvel at modern cities like Beijing, Shanghai, and Shenzhen, rural China is a vast and very different world. There are a multitude of small villages that simply cannot support a brick-and-mortar bank. China services this with an active "rural commercial" and "rural credit" banking system, which is separate from the large state banks. The system does a lot to bring banking into rural communities, but because of the low incomes and great distances involved, there are limits to what it can achieve.

Another issue is that the low educational levels in rural communities work against the loan application, fees, and lengthy review process; these act as a deterrent to many. Digital payment, and the new-found opportunity for credit it brings, is a powerful development tool to bring credit to China's rural communities, while at the same time elevating the reputations of the companies that provide it.

In a 2018 joint report by the World Bank and PBOC, researchers found that only 14% of China's small businesses had access to loans or credit. Meanwhile, in G-20 countries, 27% had access to loans. China's is a startlingly low figure considering that SME's, of which small businesses are a part, contribute 60% to China's current GDP. Bringing small loans to these ignored businesses will provide a significant boost to China's economy, and directly impact the standard of living in the more remote provinces.

That is precisely why Ant Group's MYbank and WeChat's WeBank are focusing on this critical and wide-open market. The report also helps illustrate the size of China's rural population, which accounts for 43% of its almost 1.4 billion residents, while for G20 countries, only 18% of the population is classified as rural. These statistics show that there remains much work to be done in bringing loans to small businesses, but China's digital payment companies have made breathtaking progress as regards financial inclusion.

China's progress indeed is nothing short of remarkable, and is receiving great praise from no less than the World Bank. This organization's Universal Financial Access 2020 program illustrates China's impressive efforts in bringing financial inclusion to its people. In the six years between 2011 and 2017, the country increased the number of adults with basic banking services by an impressive 16%.

Percent of adults with bank accounts and transacting electronically

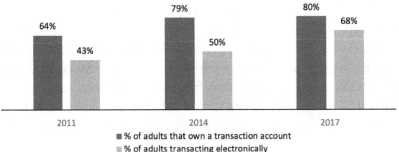

China's impressive progress in providing electronic banking services played a role in attaining its poverty alleviation goals ahead of schedule.
Source: The World Bank, Universal Financial Access 2020

Much of this increase is attributable to digital banking. While its exact impact on the unbanked cannot be gleaned from this data, it's clear that there is a strong correlation at work. China's banked population increased by 16%, while the number of people using digital payment increased by 25% over the same period. Digital payment has done much to improve the financial life of China's rural population, and these companies are now taking the technology abroad.

China's fintech has done such a fabulous job at bringing banking to the unbanked that Ant Group is now working with the United Nations Economic Commission for Africa and the International Finance Corporation to promote digital inclusion throughout the continent, through investment and technical assistance. This is a great example of how China's tech companies use the technology and, perhaps more importantly, the mindset that has been so successful at tackling the nation's unbanked to help beyond its own borders. Ant recently inked deals with the Government of Ethiopia, Flutterwave, a Nigerian e-commerce favorite, and the pan-African Ecobank where it set up an instant payment link between Alipay.

266 | RICH TURRIN

Even if it lacks the UN's stamp of approval, WeChat is not far behind. They set up "WeChat Africa" in South Africa with a local telecom partner, and are also providing technical assistance to others throughout the continent. Most recently, they scored a major deal connecting Kenya's dominant mobile payment system, M-Pesa, as well as SimbaPay, with the WeChat network, allowing the free flow of trade payments from small businesses transacting directly between Kenya and China. China happens to be Kenya's largest trading partner, with some $US 4 billion in trade annually

CREDIT FOR ALL, WITH AMAZING RESULTS

As usual, it is Alibaba subsidiary's Ant Group that has taken the technology lead in lending. Ant Group owns 30% of the lender MYbank with partner Fosun International Ltd, a Chinese international conglomerate and investment company headquartered in Shanghai. Founded in 2015, it has aspirations that are nothing short of breathtaking. After a brief five years in business, MYbank stated after the pandemic hit that it planned to extend credit lines to 70% of small and micro businesses in China in 2020, up from 50% in 2019. This success put it squarely in regulators' crosshairs.

As of year-end 2019, the bank reported a total lending balance of RMB 2.1 trillion with 21 million small companies served. According to Ant, some 80% of these entities had never borrowed from a bank before. In 2019, the average outstanding loan balance was approximately RMB 31,000 ($US 4.3K), and the 2019 default rate on loans was less than 1%. For perspective, according to the China Banking and Insurance Regulatory Commission the 2019 industry average non-performing loan ratio was 3.22%. So, in a robustly sourced comparison with their peers, MYbank's results are awe-inspiring. They are testimony to the company's digital underwriting prowess. Coronavirus is, of course, testing Ant's (and everyone else's) predictive powers. While ninety-day overdue accounts have risen to 2% of portfolio balance (from around 1%), delinquency rates are already improving, and are not indicative of major disruption due to the pandemic.

If these figures aren't sufficiently staggering, here is one of the best illustrations of digital efficiency I have ever seen. Ant reports that the operating cost of each loan made by MYbank is RMB 3 ($US 0.50), compared with an estimated RMB 2,000 ($US 290) for incumbent banks.

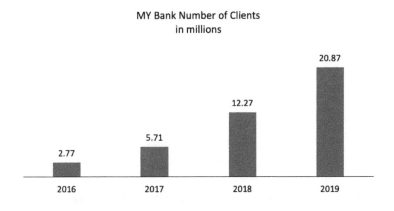

**MY Bank Number of Clients
in millions**

MYbank's explosive growth in lending.
Source: Ant Group

MYbank built its systems around the "310" lending model for loans, which means that every loan should take no longer than three minutes for the application process, with approval in less than one second, and zero human intervention in the loan process. It is a heady goal and it highlights Ant's digital strengths in both the sign-up process and in servicing the gears that make up the machine. The bank's loan approval rate is four times that of incumbent lenders in China. Incumbents reject some 80% of small business loan applications and take at least thirty days to make the decision. So there you have it, thirty days or one minute. Take your pick.

MYbank's "310" lending model.
Source MYbank

MYbank won't talk about the specifics of how its technology determines creditworthiness. It does say that its system is AI-based and analyzes some 3,000 separate data points with each loan. What is not a secret is that the most potent component of its system is MYbank's access to Alipay and Alibaba's data on each new client. Access to this data gives MYbank a detailed picture of the borrower's life that helps them determine creditworthiness.

The easiest way to think of what is inside Alipay and Alibaba's data is to imagine that it contains all of your historical data on Amazon, eBay, and your bank records. But even that is just part of the story. Since Alibaba deals with SME's, they are more than likely selling on the Alibaba platform, because who in China doesn't? So MYbank will also know the applicant firm's sales figures and, to a certain extent, the cost of its goods.

To be fair, the records will have gaps where the user may be using WeChat Pay or cash in a local account. This doesn't mean that MYbank is flying blind, because it can access all the balances of accounts connected to the Alipay app, including the local bank where the cash resides. One can't escape its analytics, and frankly, because it represents a real breakthrough in credit for China's SME, users don't want to.

There's one big reason users don't want to escape from Ant's big-data ecosystem. While loans based on big data are not necessarily cheaper, at least they are available. Recent filings for Ant Group's IPO reveal that the average unsecured loan carries a rate of about 15% a year, while its twenty million SME borrowers pay around 11%. In theory, these rates are higher than bank rates, but in practice, banks rarely lend in these sectors, so it's not a question of rate so much as availability. Another advantage of Ant's loans is that they eliminate the weighty cost of collateral required in traditional lending.

The Bank for International Settlements (BIS) studied two million Chinese firms that received credit from both Ant Group, using big data, and commercial banks. BIS found that "greater use of big tech credit—granted on the basis of machine learning and big data—could reduce the importance of collateral in credit markets." In times of market volatility, like during coronavirus, changes in collateral value make traditional lending more expensive, and shut out smaller businesses, which in turn exacerbates market swings. A big data-based loan, relying on immediately available data on the applicant's consumer behavior, transaction volume, and drawing in competitor intelligence, reduces the impact of market volatility and allows for lesser disruption to lending. Big data-based lending permits a fundamental change in the nature of loans: away from traditional collateral-based exchanges and with a much lower entry price for small businesses.

WEBANK'S DIFFERENT APPROACH

In December 2014, WeChat launched WeBank to provide digital loans to platform users, with the brand name Weilidai (microloan). While its competitor MYBank also provides microloans to China's underserved rural communities, WeBank does it with a decided emphasis on small personal loans to the country's humblest residents. This plays to WeChat's advantage in that its data stream focuses on personal social content and payments, while MYbank's data stream has a small-business focus.

Boosted by huge numbers of small personal loans, WeBank boasts an incredible 200 million customers served by the end of 2019. WeBank's lending portfolio size in 2019 was RMB 162 billion, compared with MYbank's RMB 2 trillion. Portfolio size, however, does not fully account for WeBank's total lending, given its short loan duration that averages fifty-two days. The astonishing size of WeBank's total lending can be found in figures for total lifetime lending from 2017 of RMB 870 billion, which dwarfs the already impressive MYbank's RMB 446 billion for the same year. As another indicator of relative size, WeBank's net income for 2019 was RMB 3.95 billion compared to MYbank's RMB 1.25 billion. All of this is accomplished with a non-performing loan ratio of 1.23% for 2019. More impressive still is that 80% of WeBank's borrowers have no higher academic qualification than high school, and most are ineligible for a bank loan. Given that the World Bank reports that some 225 million adults, or 15% of the Chinese population, are unbanked, these statistics, while staggering, are entirely believable.

WeBank boasts an average loan size of RMB 8,000 (US$ 1.2K) for an individual borrower, with an operational cost of around RMB 3 (US$ 0.50) for each account. Users of the system get notification of approval within five seconds, and receive the loan in their WeChat account within one minute. WeBank also has an SME-based lending unit, "WeiYeDai," with an average loan size of RMB 210k ($US 30K) On average, each borrowing company has ten employees, and 66% have never borrowed from a bank before. For the year ending 2019, the platform served 230,000 small businesses, with total lending of RMB 180 billion.

ASSET-LIGHT LENDING

In contrast to China's massive state-owned banks that hold loans on their books for the long-term, the newer digital banks do not. Some, like Ant, securitize the loans that they originate and sell them in the asset-backed security markets, or sell them to local banks. Securitization keeps their balance sheets small by continuously selling off their positions to reduce their capitalization requirements. In 2017, according to Reuters, Ant Group was China's largest issuer of consumer loan asset-backed securities (ABS), accounting for 60% of a market that they virtually invented. The size of these issues and the inexperience with this new asset class has drawn some concerns from regulators. Ant shelved plans to issue a number of these securities in 2018 over regulators' concerns, though has since returned to ABS markets. In the interim, Ant augmented ABS issuance with loan facilitation arrangements with banks, in a manner pioneered by WeBank.

WeBank's strategy for selling off the loans it originates took a different approach than MYbank's, which emphasized ABS issuance. From the onset WeBank had a more open stance regarding working with local banks. A full 20% of the loans it extends went onto its balance sheet, with the remaining 80% being sold to local mid-tier and smaller banks. These banks were always local to the borrowers, which meant their servicing teams could be called in if necessary. By taking this partnership strategy early on, WeBank was able to assist local banks, which lacked the ability to issue these digital loans, and position itself as a valued partner. It is a successful system that Ant adopted only after its access to ABS markets was restricted.

Ant adopted the practice, but instead of reserving for loan losses at 20%, kept a more aggressive 2% of loan value on its books in reserves. WeBank's more cooperative approach may have been critical to the long-term health of its lending book and overall profitability of its parent Tencent. Its higher level of reserving helped it avoid the calamity that befell Ant just before its IPO in November 2020. Regulators mandated that microlenders hold a full 30% of loan value in reserve, forcing changes to Ant's business plan and disruption to its future profitability. This meant a manageable 10% increase in reserves for Tencent, but a 28% boost for Ant, which doomed its IPO. Ant clearly has the funds to cover the change in reserve ratio, but its long-term profitability will be materially reduced, which caused a significant modification to its business plans and the cancellation of its heralded IPO.

BANKS FIGHT NEW COMPETITORS AND PARTNER FOR DATA

The major banks didn't take this assault on their lending business sitting down. In 2017 the China CITIC Bank and Baidu combined to form aiBank, and in 2019, JD.com teamed with giant China Merchant Bank to develop a digital lending operation. Both will have big data-driven digital lending capabilities similar to those of MYbank and WeBank.

What is interesting about these partnerships is that they show China's leading banks partnering with the local equivalent of Google (Baidu), and China's largest retailer (JD.com), to acquire the skills and the data required to be competitive in this new world of lending. Without these partnerships, incumbent banks would be at a severe disadvantage. When digital payment from WeChat and Alipay limited their access to payment data, there was very little they could do to fight back. The bigger problem, however, was systemic: the banks never foresaw that they would have to digitize their loan process in the first place. They were left in the dust as clients moved en masse to the digital payment platforms, without looking back.

The problem for incumbents isn't only that they are competing against the digital payment giants. It is that the success of MYbank and WeBank went on to inspire a new crop of banks, established on the fly by other players in China's tech realm. The diversity of these new banks demonstrates that lending isn't the exclusive domain of traditional institutions anymore, but is instead wide open to any company with access to data. Food delivery companies, electronics giants, ride-hailing, and cell phone manufacturers have all joined in consumer credit, new competitors that the old-line banks could not have imagined a few short years ago.

Meituan Dianping is famous in China for food delivery. In 2017, it created Yilian bank to provide private banking and small loans. While the parent company focuses on food delivery, it also has operations in consumer products, hotels, and group buying, which gives it an advantage in understanding the viability of the small businesses to which it lends. What makes this example particularly noteworthy is that it shows how the boundaries of financial services are being pushed further and further in China. Meituan Dianping's ambitions in banking became even clearer when they obtained an insurance license to support its users with a full range of services. The tie-in to its client base in the restaurant business is indisputable, because Meituan is a critical service for most restaurants. With delivery volume data, it has its fingers directly on the pulse of restaurants throughout China. Ingraining into their finances is a logical next step. Loan balances in 2018 were RMB 1.4 billion, with an average value per merchant of RMB 70,000 and an average loan term of one year.

Xiaomi is famous for manufacturing smartphones and other devices. As you may have guessed, it also has a banking license, operating under the name Sichuan XW Bank. Xiaomi's strategy is to harvest data from its 300 million active users to build a credit profile based on their device usage. China Banking News reported that Sichuan XW Bank was serving more than 25 million consumers as of mid-2018, making a total of 84.7 million loans worth over RMB 270 billion (US$ 38 billion).

Suning.com is one of China's largest retailers, with more than 1,600 stores in over 700 cities. It formed Suning Bank in 2017. Famed for its sales of electronics and home appliances, it used its dominance in this market as the lynchpin of its strategy as an online to offline (O2O) lender. Suning.com reports a total of 25 million customers, including 2.89 million loans in 2019.

Finally, there is ride-sharing company DiDi Chuxing which, in 2019, launched a complete suite of financial services aimed at its drivers, including car insurance, personal loans, and crowdfunded medical insurance. All are available on its ride-sharing app, and a separate DiDi Finance app. As the services are new, there are no reports of loan value or number of users. Didi is following in the footsteps of Singapore-based Grab, which pioneered offering financial services to its drivers. This is a rare case where a Chinese company wasn't first to market. Uber can only dream.

BANK DISRUPTION AND THE HOPE OF CBDC RE-EMPOWERMENT

If big data-based lending predicated on digital payment algorithms sounds like a disruptive product, it is—in the true sense of the word. In only a few years, MYbank, WeBank, and others have been able to change the very foundation of lending in China. To put those loan amounts into perspective, the "2018 Consumer Credit Market Research Report" (2018中国消费信贷市场研究) released by Tsinghua University indicates that consumer credit in China hit RMB 8.45 trillion in October 2018 and RMB 5.81 trillion for 2017. The total credit on the books of WeBank and MYbank alone at the end of 2017 was RMB 1.3 trillion, or 22% of all of China's consumer credit. Granted that this is not an exact comparison since digital lenders span both SME and consumer sectors, but it helps put the loan amounts in context. Ant's total lending of RMB 2.1 trillion in 2019 compares to RMB 13 trillion in short-term consumer loans issued by all Chinese banks.

Making the same comparison with small- and micro-enterprise ventures, this time using figures from "China MSME Finance Report 2018," shows that China's top five major commercial banks lent RMB 7.42 trillion to small- and micro-enterprises. MYbank and WeBank loan books would be roughly 18% of this total. China's largest lender, ICBC, lent a total of RMB 2.22 trillion to small- and-micro enterprises in 2017 (annual report), meaning that these two new banks alone were responsible for roughly half of ICBC's lending. All of these are impressive figures for companies that started business in earnest only five years ago. China's payment platforms, once viewed as outside the financial system, *became* the system. It also shows why incumbent banks raced to partner with tech companies to build their online lending platforms. If the digital upstarts could command such a large market share in only a few years, it was clear that they too needed this technology to remain relevant.

Banks are down but not out when it comes to digital lending, and China's new CBDC offers them a glimmer of hope for a way back to dominance. The CBDC gives banks an opportunity to regain their grip on data, lost with the advent of cashless payments. People might go back to their bank's apps and directly spend from these wallets, which would enable banks to get a better understanding of their spending habits. Such a transition isn't guaranteed, and much depends on people's level of addiction to the WeChat and Alipay platforms. If banks can make inroads and entice people to use their payment systems, they'll regain access to both spending data and other lifestyle data captured from cellphones—a necessity if they are going to compete with WeChat and Alipay. How to entice clients to switch is the question. Chinese banks already have points and awards programs, and they will likely have to buy clients back through heavy use of such initiatives. It won't be cheap, but their digital future hangs in the balance.

CONSUMER CREDIT ON THE RISE

As one would expect, online lending provided through myriad digital platforms and advertised on every mobile phone screen is causing a significant increase in the use of consumer credit. Figures from the Bank of International Settlement (BIS) show that credit to households in China has increased some 65% since 2014, which was China's year zero for digital banking activities. It remains a concern for government officials, who first put the plan to increase credit use in motion. Nonetheless, China still lags: according to BIS data, the country's total household credit to GDP ratio of 54% pales in comparison to the US's 75%; it's worth noting that China maintains one of the world's highest savings rates.

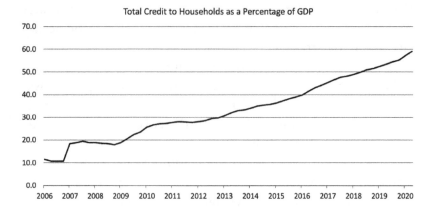

China's credit to households as a percentage of GDP increased by 65% since 2014 when online credit operations started.
Source: Federal Reserve Bank of St. Louis

The government's newest concern is that China's digital banks will fuel irresponsible credit use, a fear that largely spurred the regulatory changes on Ant and its more than 7,000 microlender rivals. Fresh from putting an end to the undisciplined lending in P2P markets, it's easy to see how this is a nagging issue for regulators. In November 2019, the People's Bank of China's annual financial responsibility report stated, "The debt risks of the household sector and some low-income households in some regions are relatively prominent and should be paid attention to." The report called for more stringent policies to "guard against household sector debt." Similar warnings, in 2017 and 2018, met with inaction.

It's important to understand that credit is a new phenomenon in China, particularly for young people. It is not something they will likely learn about from Mom and Dad. Not surprisingly, advertisements of happy youth enjoying new cell phones bought on credit vastly outnumber public service advertisements warning against irresponsible credit use. Young people in the West are similarly inculcated, but with greater awareness of the risks, or at least the importance, of credit score management. In using fintech to carry out its long-term policy goals of increasing personal credit, China is experimenting on a massive scale with unpredictable results.

I HOPE THIS IS COMING TO A LENDER NEAR YOU

Contrary to the common view that big data will ruin everything, this is a use case where big data is ushering in great societal benefit; China is showing the way forward. Big data has the potential to allow members of society who are currently marginalized or even invisible to be recognized. The problem is not unique to China; it is every bit as relevant for the West. Western credit markets have a real problem when applicants don't fit the mold used by the credit check companies. For example, Experian estimates that in 2019, 62 million adults in the US do not have enough information to generate a credit score. Our most humble members of society find themselves cut off from the credit process, because they lack data that would make them worthy of a loan, as is the case with China's rural population.

For its part, the Federal Reserve estimated in 2017 that there were some 63 million unbanked or underbanked Americans, representing 25% of households. A similar situation exists in Europe. A 2016 report from the World and European Savings and Retail Banking Group found that some 8.6% of Europe's population were financially excluded. These figures show that there is room for improvement in our banking and systems, which might benefit from a China-like digital approach.

If you analyze the data and technical requirements for these China-based credit products, you'll see that we in the West already have all the essential ingredients to build them. The difference is that in China, much of the data is already centralized and owned by the platform granting the loan. WeBank and MYbank already have user IDs tied to cellphones, a requirement in China, and ample records of payment history. WeBank has records of texts and calls made on WeChat, while MYbank has records of e-commerce transactions. There is another critical difference: these lending apps don't have to ask permission to use data because it's already theirs.

Data of similar quality to China's exists for users in the West, but it is more difficult to access because it is dispersed across multiple platforms. Aggregating it into a large enough data set to analyze behavior is challenging, but not impossible. One easy way to gain access is by simply asking users for access to their social media accounts, in exchange for a reward. US lender Kabbage (recently closed due to the impact of the pandemic on its SME clients), offered discounts to borrowers who linked their Facebook and Twitter accounts to the site. Kabbage's "social climbing" technology could better calculate the users' "Kabbage Score" using big data, thereby offering better rates. Decisions took seven minutes in a digital process, only six minutes slower than MYbank's "310" approach. Singapore's Lenddo is another example of a lender using alternative data to expand financial inclusion. The company works in developing countries across Southeast Asia, Africa, and South America, where large swaths of the populace have no credit history.

Digital credit underwriting is coming. The largest credit companies, like FICO and Experian, are aware of this and are already at work on "alternative data" sources. Experian recently purchased "Clarity Services," which aggregates data from telecom companies, auto finance providers, and rental payments to supplement the data traditionally used to calculate credit scores. This is in addition to its partnership with TransUnion and Equifax on "VantageScore," which provides alternative credit ratings for those with no credit data. In 2016, FICO launched "FICO Score XD," an alternative score for borrowers with little credit history based on public records, property data, and bills from utility, cable, and cell phone providers. So while Score XD is in use for borrowers at the bottom of the credit spectrum, expect these techniques to work their way up to more creditworthy borrowers very soon.

The big question is if and when the GAFA companies (Google, Apple, Facebook, or Amazon) will get into the business of banking or at least start providing big data directly to their banking partners to assist in the credit process. So far, they haven't crossed the Rubicon. For example, Apple does not yet appear to provide Goldman Sachs, issuer of the Apple Card, with data gleaned from your Apple device usage to assist in the credit evaluation process. Whether this will change remains to be seen. Amazon's credit card offerings also appear not to use Amazon data in determining credit limits.

The most likely candidate among the GAFA companies seems to be Google, which is now providing checking account services through its Plex digital checking and savings accounts in partnership with Citibank and several other banks. Whether Google can provide platform partner banks with big-data analysis that assists them in the credit evaluation or client selection process remains to be seen, but it would not at all surprise me.

US bank laws require that the GAFA companies work with bank partners and not own the bank themselves, so a direct copy of WeChat or Ant at least for now is out of the question. That said, Google appears to be coming very close to copying China's model. Facebook's best efforts to copy WeChat Pay through its Diem (Libra) stablecoin are ongoing, but significantly scaled back due to controversy with government regulators.

BAIHANG CREDIT, CHINA'S STATE-RUN CREDIT RATING AGENCY

Miraculously, China is still without a data-rich public credit rating agency. That does not mean that China's population doesn't have credit; as MYbank and WeBank have shown, there is an abundance of credit and credit scoring available. What it does mean is that in a country famed for its digital prowess, there is still no central authority monitoring who has credit and how much. While private credit companies like Alibaba and WeChat cover the majority of the population, making another P2P crisis unthinkable, the lack of a central system is noteworthy.

China's PBOC-backed personal credit rating platform Baihang Credit (百行征信) is a work in progress, and stands as a great example of how fintech success in China isn't preordained by the government. The PBOC approved Baihang in February 2018 and put it under the National Internet Finance Association of China (NIFA) to create a big data-based national credit system. To put this timing in context, this was only about six months after protests rocked Beijing and Shanghai following the costly US\$ 7.6 billion collapse of P2P lender Ezubao. Baihang was, in part, created to ensure that there would be no repeat of P2P lending and to bring order to personal credit.

China has never had an independent or government-backed large-scale personal credit rating service like FICO or Experian to centralize loan data. Unlike the West, where credit histories are so well-established that they now may start before adulthood, in China credit is a relatively recent phenomenon. Cards have mostly been the province of the wealthy. Kapron Asia reports that in 2015, the PBOC had data on only 25% of the Chinese population. In 2019, after a year of operation, Baihang reported that it had credit data on only 150 million residents, showing the limits of public credit system data.

Prior to P2P, most of China's population had not had the opportunity to borrow. Perhaps if more circuit breakers had been in place before the launch of P2P, the results would have been different—mitigating situations such as borrowers applying for loans from several different platforms, which rendered lenders unable to discern the scale of indebtedness. Given that crisis, a government system of monitoring and sharing personal credit data became a clear priority.

Baihang's story in particular is noteworthy because it shows how deep the conflict between public and private interests can be in China. In 2015, the PBOC authorized eight online lenders to collect and analyze data on private credit, and to conduct pilot programs on credit scoring using big data. This was a significant undertaking, and important because it was the predecessor to the digital credit systems used by both MYbank and WeBank. The government's plan was for each of the participants to build a system based on data shared among them, with each entity's product then being evaluated.

National Internet Finance Association of China (中国互联网金融协会) (NIFA)
Sesame Credit (芝麻信用) subsidiary of Ant Group,
Tencent Credit (腾讯征信),
Qianhai Credit (前海征信) subsidiary of Ping An Group,
Kaola Credit (考拉征信),
Pengyuan Credit (鹏元征信),
CCX Credit Technology (中诚信征信),
Intellicredit (中智诚征信),
Sinoway Credit (华道征信).

Baihang Credit Shareholders and the participants in the
PBOC Pilot Program
Source: China Banking News

The eight online lenders built prototype systems, but much to the government's chagrin, they didn't share data. Not surprisingly, only one of the eight systems was deemed worthy. Alibaba's Sesame (aka Zhima Credit) emerged from this effort and was permitted to launch online in 2015. The government was displeased with the results, with the PBOC announcing in early 2017, "The preparation the eight companies have made for running the personal credit rating business is far below market demand and regulatory standards."

If this sounds like a failed project with uncooperative partners, it was. So imagine creating Baihang Credit out of a partnership of the same eight participants. To this day, Baihang is in limbo. Founding a company on a public-private partnership where the private partners don't wish to contribute is hardly a recipe for success. Of Baihang's eight participants, data sharing agreements were in place with only three of the partner companies as of late 2019. The issue of the public-private partnership came to a boil in September 2019, when in a rare display of defiance to the government, both Alibaba and Tencent refused to make their loan data available to Baihang Credit. From the perspective of the two market leaders, the flow of information and benefits are asymmetric: they provide the data, and their partners—who are also competitors—use it against them. Resolution to this impass appears to have arrived in early 2021 through new anti-trust regulations which forced both of the superapps back to the negotiating table.

So interestingly, credit rating in China is mainly in the hands of private companies like Alibaba and WeChat, among many others. Alibaba's Sesame Credit amassed some 520 million users by 2017, a great success, and had a virtual monopoly on credit rating until recently. WeChat's credit rating system had a difficult start. "Tencent Credit" launched a pilot in January 2018 only to find it forcibly removed by the government the very next day. A rare event and a major embarrassment for Tencent's WeChat, which finally launched its credit system "WeChat Pay Score" in June 2020. Credit scores in China are not used only for loans; they help reduce deposits on rental or shared items like portable mobile power banks, computers, and apartment rental. These are small benefits that pop up on digital apps that generally make people happy.

There is an essential distinction between credit systems and China's "social credit system," which is confusing to many. Credit systems like Sesame Credit or WeChat Pay Score are not part of China's "social credit system" even if they contain big-data analysis beyond the scope of Western credit rating. It is common to hear these systems erroneously referred to as "social credit," even if they are not. The "social credit system" is an effort independent of the PBOC, with coronavirus delaying its 2020 rollout, probably for several years.

CREDIT, THE DOUBLE-EDGED SWORD

The reaction by ordinary Chinese to their new credit-scored lives is almost overwhelmingly positive. Most perceive the perks they gain for having a high credit score as a treat, a reward for honesty. Those that receive loans via digital platforms are generally pleased with their experience. Most, though not all, use credit responsibly and the ability to access credit during coronavirus lockdown was critical to many. A major increase in credit defaults was not recorded by either of the big lenders during this period, as the Chinese economy opened within a few months following lockdown—a severe enough event, but less damaging in China than the prolonged impact in the West.

For most Chinese users, there is little sense that the credit scoring systems have exceeded their mandate by including personal data. This goes straight to two critical factors. First, the systems never existed at scale without access to big data. So there is no before-and-after comparison to be made by the majority of the population. Second, credit scoring is for most of the population a byproduct of using the major payment apps. No one can envision life without the apps, so the fact that they are acquiring behavior-based credit data doesn't merit consideration. From a user perspective, post-P2P, the big data-based systems have performed admirably even if regulators have nagging concerns that they are creating another bubble.

That credit has become so easily available is of course a double-edged sword. It's a boon in a post-COVID society that is trying to stoke domestic demand for goods and services, while the rest of the world is in lockdown. At the same time, it is also a runaway train, with regulators fearing a repeat performance of the P2P crisis. It threatens to move so quickly that it could exceed regulators' ability to monitor and manage the rapid expansion of credit in society, which is nothing to be trifled with. While the major lenders told regulators that "this time would be different," overseers still burning from the P2P crisis were not convinced, and the recently mandated increase to microlender's reserving requirements speaks volumes about their level of concern. This was a fateful move for Ant Group and led at least in part to the cancellation of its IPO. We will cover this in greater depth in chapter 18; for now suffice it to say that the fiasco had at its core a regulator still shell-shocked from the last credit boom.

18

ANT: FROM FIRE TO PHOENIX

Ant Group on its "paused" IPO:

> *"Just like looking into the mirror, finding out our shortcomings, and conducting a body check-up, we have been actively following regulatory guidance and complying with requirements."*
>
> Eric Jing, Executive Chairman of Ant Group

The West on Ant Group:

> *"Citigroup spent years watching Asian consumers flock to outside apps [Ant] for their payments and lending needs, and the bank now believes the same will happen for deposits."*
>
> Jane Fraser,
> Citigroup Chief Executive Officer

The message in Ant Group's now-foiled "world's largest" IPO isn't merely one of massive valuations, iron-fisted regulators, or outspoken visionary founders. It also remains one of hope. In 2008, when Jack Ma said "If the banks don't change, we'll change the banks," no one believed he could do it. At the time, this was viewed as nothing more than the arrogant boast of a visionary founder, akin to those of his Western counterpart, Elon Musk. The amazing thing is that, as with Musk, it wasn't just a rant. Ma did it. In laying out a path for the digital transformation of financial services, Ant secured a place in history and in the record books. The company demonstrated how fintech can help foster financial inclusion and make our lives better—not just domestically, but worldwide.

BREAKING BARRIERS TO INNOVATION

Ant helped establish China as the global leader in digital payment, and was instrumental in China going cashless. It also gave entrepreneurs and consumers far greater access to loans, changed the way people manage their money, and brought the concept of a tightly knit financial platform to life. It changed not only how we pay, but how we consume financial services and relate to money. Probably most important of all, Ant made people across the world ask, "Why not here?"

For most, the greatest barrier to innovation is simply not understanding what is possible. Envisioning an abstract digital future is hard, especially when that future conflicts with years of well-established notions of how things are done. Ant showed the world what fintech or—as Jack Ma branded it, "techfin"—could achieve. His company illustrated the advances that technology could bring to finance, and in so doing, demystified our future. The whole world was invited to watch as new marvels revealing the future of finance were unveiled on a seemingly weekly basis.

At the core of this vision was an ideal that was far more revolutionary than mobile payment. Banking's paradigm of focusing on the wealthy had to be broken, with digital the key to reaching the poor. This, above all, is Ant's greatest achievement, giving the developing world hope that they can harness digital to fully engage in the future. This message resonates well beyond China to the financially marginalized around the world.

If that sounds idealistic (particularly from an author who prides himself on pragmatism developed over a career in banking and training as an engineer), it is. Ant is worthy of its own book, especially regarding its contributions to inclusion, a dedication held within the company's culture with religious fervor. Yet, in the aftermath of its paused IPO, Ant is also emblematic of the delicate balance between China's regulators and fintech innovation. For our purposes, Ant's greatest lessons come from its dramatic and rare defeat.

ANT GROUP'S "WORLD'S LARGEST" IPO

Reviewing Ant's abruptly halted US$ 34.5 billion IPO is essential, not just because of the cloak-and-dagger interaction with regulators, or because of its vast scope, but primarily because it shows that China's great fintech experiment is still evolving. While other countries rightly tout their construction of "fintech regulatory sandboxes" as a means of advancing fintech, China is one giant sandbox, on an unparalleled scale. Ant's paused IPO reveals that China is struggling to come to terms with the massive changes brought about by fintech development in the country.

Prior to its demise, Ant Group's IPO was so big that it erupted into a global frenzy for shares. At its peak, I was fielding several messages a day from my LinkedIn network asking how to buy Ant shares. The listing was split in half on two separate stock markets, one on Shanghai's newfound STAR Market (a NASDAQ equivalent specializing in science and technology shares) and the other on the Hong Kong Exchange. In Shanghai, its listing was oversubscribed by 872 times, and it received a record breaking RMB 19.05 trillion (US$ 2.85 trillion) of bids. On the Hong Kong Exchange, it was 389 times oversubscribed, drawing bids valued at HK$ 1.3 trillion (US$ 167.7 billion). Its listing was removed a full day ahead of schedule due to demand, which included bids from an astounding twenty percent of Hong Kong's population. Ant represented about 40% of Shanghai's STAR Market total capitalization and 5.5% of Hong Kong's.

So much money poured into Hong Kong that the central bank had to intervene eighty-five times to weaken the Hong Kong dollar against appreciation. The funds remaining in Hong Kong months after the paused IPO continue to bolster the stock market. Before the Shanghai IPO, Ant would amaze the world by selling US$ 9 billion of STAR Market-based mutual funds on Alipay—reaching ten million small investors within about 72 hours, some investing as little as one RMB. The transaction enraged bankers and fund managers throughout the country as it cut them out of fee income from retail sales. Ant, as always, was just looking out for the little guy.

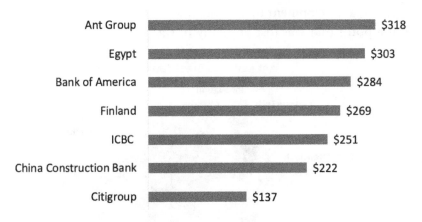

Ant IPO valuation compared with GDP and total market capitalization in US$ billions

Ant Group	$318
Egypt	$303
Bank of America	$284
Finland	$269
ICBC	$251
China Construction Bank	$222
Citigroup	$137

Ant Group's IPO valuation eventually climbed to the level of national GDPs, far higher than the market capitalization of China's largest banks.

As the fear of missing out took over, Ant's IPO valuations started to climb into unforeseen territory. When it first filed its listing in late August, Ant's original valuation may have seemed immense yet justifiable at its target of a mere US$ 200 billion.

However, over about two months, the hype surrounding the IPO became white-hot, and valuations climbed into the stratosphere. Peak valuations put Ant's value at US$ 318.5 billion, making it worth more than the world's largest bank, JP Morgan Chase, or the economies of the United Kingdom, Egypt, Finland, or South Africa. These sky-high valuations were certainly unsettling to regulators watching on the sidelines, frightened by the implied level of growth for Ant's business.

Ant is many things to many different people. To most, it's a payment company; to many others, a superapp. To me, it's the company that cracked the code for AI-enabled online lending. Ant's half-year results, released in the IPO prospectus, showed something surprising to those who may not have been following the company closely. Ant broke down its business by revenue sectors, and CreditTech, which includes lending in its many forms, led the way with 39% of revenue, just ahead of payment revenue at 36%. Ant had become more reliant on lending than payment services, a development that regulators had been following closely, but a point that was lost on many in the industry.

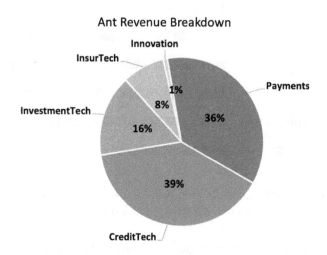

While many think of Ant as a payment company, its credit operations now provide its largest single revenue source.
Source: Ant Group

Ant's stratospheric valuations were predictive of high future growth, meaning that investors were betting that Ant's blazing performance would continue. The problem with this is that much of Ant's recent growth came from expanding its CreditTech operations, which grew by 58%, from 24.8% of revenue in 2017 to 39% in its half-year 2019 results. To match the expectations implicit in these massive valuations, Ant would presumably have to unleash a torrent of fresh credit in the marketplace.

While Ant earmarked money toward international expansion and other domestic growth sectors, credit remained the most profitable and easiest place to generate revenue. Regulators were already concerned about the company's credit growth, though there was no indication that there was a bubble per se. Their concerns focused primarily on the amount of leverage Ant was using to generate its loans, giving it an unfair advantage over bank lenders to dominate the market. Ant's use of leverage allowed it to hold a mere 2% of its credit portfolio of RMB 1.7 trillion in reserve, a portfolio roughly twice the size of those held by any of the major banks. A breakdown of its CreditTech operations showed that 88% of its consumer loans went through their banking partners, 10% were securitized (a process halted in 2018), and 2% only held on its balance sheet.

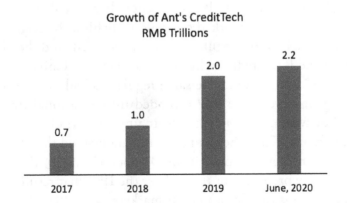

Growth of Ant's CreditTech business,
more than tripling in the past three years.
Source: Ant Group

Banks lent through Ant because of their demonstrable underwriting prowess, something no one disputes. But to regulators, Ant's growth seemed without bounds. The normal capital constraints that would limit individual banks' lending didn't apply to Ant or any of the other online lenders, and there was no way to put on the brakes. An Ant Group flush with IPO cash and a need to show investors returns was a red flag to the regulator, and was too alarming to be allowed to grow unchecked.

> *"Ant Group sincerely apologizes to you for any inconvenience caused by this development."*

A NEW BREED OF REGULATORS

To many who watched the cancellation of the Ant IPO on the evening of November 3, 2020, it seemed like vengeful banking regulators smote Ant from on high, in retaliation for any number of imagined failings, most of them having nothing to do with credit. I was certainly surprised, as this is not how things are supposed to happen in China. China's concept of "losing face" is as old as the culture itself and is generally avoided at all costs. Internal disputes are worked out quietly, behind the scenes.

But these banking regulators are a new breed, and they were fresh off the P2P credit meltdown that had cost China an estimated US$ 120 billion. The same regulators had been accused of being inactive while P2P exploded into a national tragedy. Now they were on the sidelines watching Ant's IPO turn into a feeding frenzy. While they had certainly understood that it would be big when they approved it on October 19, 2020, they were not remotely prepared for the scale of the IPO that resulted and its implications for China's credit markets.

Frankly, they were so unnerved by what they saw that they knowingly sacrificed China's dream of outdoing US capital markets by bringing the world's largest IPO to their country. This was a hefty price to pay in Chinese national pride—one that went far beyond Ant's IPO and cut to the very bone of China's desire to open markets and attract foreign investment. They also knew that blocking the world's largest IPO dead in its tracks two days before launch would reverberate in financial markets for years, and open China to scathing criticism. All of that was worth it compared to going down in history as sitting idly by while Ant's credit book grew unchecked.

That regulators chose this time to publish regulatory changes with a material impact on Ant's IPO makes the adage "better late than never" truer than ever. They stopped the IPO in its tracks by changing the rules that define Ant's CreditTech operations, forcing a reevaluation of the company's profitability, which led to pulling the IPO from the marketplace. In addition, they issued a regulatory warning to Ant, summoning its senior executives to Beijing for admonishment. Most telling of all, in official publications, the regulator criticized Ant for straying from its core payment business while "misleading users to consume beyond their means." By changing the rules surrounding Ant's biggest profit center, they shut down Ant's IPO on the eve of what would have been a crowning achievement. Let's examine what the regulator did.

MEET CHINA'S NEW MICROLOAN REGULATIONS

The new regulations proposed by the People's Bank of China (PBOC) and the China Banking and Insurance Regulatory Commission (CBIRC) are called "Online Microloan Operations Provisional Administrative Measures." While not yet finalized at the time of this writing, they go a long way to reeling in China's overheated online lending community just as the same regulator belatedly did with the P2P market.

The regulations impact Ant along with all the other microlenders in China. As of September 2019, there were 7,200 domestic microlenders with outstanding loans of RMB 902 billion. That these numbers roughly matched the P2P market's peak of 6,000 lenders with outstanding balances of RMB 1 billion certainly was not lost on officials who decided to act before allowing further credit expansion to hit bubble territory.

Here's what the proposed regulations do and how they effectively limit Ant's CreditTech operations, the source of its greatest growth:

1. Require reserving: Microlenders must fund at least 30% of any joint loan with a financial institution.

   This rule, above all of the others, is what halted the Ant IPO in its tracks. The change requires that Ant hold reserves against all loans it facilitates, even those under loan facilitation agreements with the many banks it serves. From Ant's prospectus: "Approximately 98% of the consumer and SMB credit balances enabled through our platform as of June 30, 2020, were underwritten by our partner financial institutions or securitized." Meaning that Ant's loan book contains a mere 2% of the outstanding credit it underwrote, and its reserves only for this 2%. This is an amount of leverage that banks, who had had reserve requirements on their total outstanding credit balances closer to the new regulation's 30%, could not match. Analysts estimate that to reserve at 30% for all of its outstanding loans, up from 2%, Ant would have to triple net assets at its microlending subsidiaries by some US$ 16-20 billion. This massive cash influx would account for roughly half of its IPO proceeds.

   Ant's participation in its loans is through a 2.5% fee for setting up the loan and a cut of between 30-40% of the interest on the loans it facilitates. From Ant's prospectus: "We generate 'technology service fees' from our partner financial institutions as a percentage of the interest income they earn on credit balance enabled through our platform." The problem is that these service fees do not guarantee equal participation in portfolio gains and losses. The asymmetry in Ant's payout enabled it to loan enormous sums without limits, which is what scared the regulators.

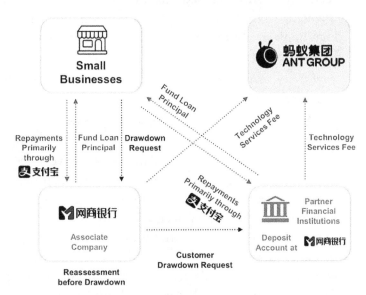

Credit Line Drawdown Process
(MYbank Joint Lending with Partner Financial Institutions)

Ant Group receives payment through "Technology Service Fees."
It participates in the portfolios it selects but through fees rather than direct profit or loss on the loan portfolio.
Source: Ant Group

2. Reduce leverage: Loans financed by banks or shareholders must not exceed the microlender's net assets. Second, funds obtained from the issuance of bonds, asset-backed securitization products, or other debt instruments should not exceed four times the company's net assets.

    Ant facilitates bank lending by using its technology to underwrite loans that sit on the books of banks, which provide the capital for the loans. Ant had no limit on the amount of these loans because it did not have any participation in them beyond service fees. With this rule, the amount of loans it can now facilitate is limited by its net assets, crimping its loan volume with banks. This is an additional restriction on top of the first rule (above), requiring Ant to carry reserves for all of its loans. The rule also limits the amount of money raised by asset-backed securities, which closed another potential avenue for financing its new reserve requirements. Ant can increase its loan book size but only with a corresponding increase in its net assets, fundamentally changing its business model.

3. *Tighter surveillance:* Microlenders can operate only in a province in which they are registered.

Ant's Huabei and Jiebei are its largest owned lending operations; they provide loans throughout China through banks licensed in Chongqing. Ant will now have to register and operate lending operations in each of the provinces. This is similar to the US's requirement that banks and insurers have state-level licenses. China had similar laws for banks that were essentially unenforced throughout Ant's lending history. In essence, the bank regulators were willing to overlook this breach in the past, but no longer. As we saw with the P2P crisis, pushing regulation to the provinces is by no means a recipe for success, as some provinces are relatively unsophisticated.

4. *Limit borrowing:* New limits are either the lower of RMB 300,000 or one-third of the borrower's average income over the past three years, with institutional loans not exceeding one million yuan.

The limits on loan amounts are consumer-facing and will likely have a limited impact on Ant's operations. The average balance of personal loans on its Huabei platform is below RMB 2,000, with a maximum of RMB 30,000. JieBei has an average balance of RMB 700, with a maximum of RMB 50,000. Still, these restrictions may be meaningful for other microloan companies. Tencent's WeBank announced it is reducing the maximum loan size on its "Weli" loan platform, from RMB 300,000 to RMB 200,000 (US$ 30,500).

5. *Raise capitalization:* Microloan companies must now have registered capital of RMB 1 billion, with those engaging in cross-border operations requiring RMB 5 billion.

These limits impact smaller microloan companies and have minimal impact on Ant. The irony is that these rules may shutter the smaller upstarts that could someday challenge Ant's market dominance.

"THIS TIME WILL BE DIFFERENT"

Why China's banking regulators passed these new restrictions is relatively straightforward. They simply couldn't believe that "this time will be different." There is no question that online lending is no longer subject to the crude fraud seen in the P2P markets, and regulators acknowledge that big data-based lending is successful. The sticking point is that they are rightly unwilling to concede that unsupervised and unconstrained credit issuance will miraculously work itself out and not create another bubble, regardless of how high-tech its underpinnings.

From our earlier chapter on P2P loans, it is clear that credit bubbles in both East and West shared several similarities. In both the P2P crisis in China and the mortgage-fueled 2008 financial crisis, the arrangers of loans did not participate in the lending they facilitated. While there were undoubtedly other factors at work, the lack of "skin in the game" meant that the arrangers did not share in the losses if the loan went unpaid.

> *Skin in the game means "having personal monetary risk associated with any deal you make."*
>
> N.N. Taleb

"Skin in the Game" is the title of N. N. Taleb's important book discussing the benefits of a moral imperative in which one is "harmed by an error that harms others." For example, chefs most certainly need to "eat what they serve others" as a means of ensuring quality. In financial matters, it means "having personal monetary risk associate with any deal you make."

This brings us back to Ant and the regulators. Ant, for all its digital prowess and unquestionable mastery of digital lending, is asking regulators to believe "it will be different this time." Ant is a transformational company and has no more ardent supporter than me. That said, its brand of tech-based lending has a problem, not with the technology, but with its negligible participation in the loans, and lack of skin in the game.

> *Participating means taking on losses, which is at the core of the new 30% funding requirement in the draft regulations.*

Ant justly deserves credit for "cracking the code" for digital online lending, a skill it has raised to the level of art. Yet even with Ant's documented prowess in digital lending, its model of arranging loans with low capital commitment means that it has little skin in the game. Ant's use of "tech service fees" gives it some participation in the deals it creates, but in fact positions it as a tech company and not a bank. In the regulator's eyes, it wasn't "eating what it served others." Participating means taking on losses, which is at the core of the new 30% funding requirement in the draft regulations.

> *Regulators faced a dilemma. Remaining silent on the regulation changes would create a global outcry by investors.*

This is the fundamental reason regulators pulled the plug on the Ant deal. Regulators undoubtedly faced a dilemma. Remaining silent on their new microloan regulations until after the IPO would have created a global outcry by investors accusing them of changing the rules of the game after taking their money. Changing the rules before the IPO, even at the 11th hour, would cause investors to protest but not leave them financially impaired.

JACK MA AND "THE SPEECH"

On October 24, 2020 Jack Ma made an impassioned speech in front of "The Shanghai Forum" that raised more than a few eyebrows. Jack likened the current banking system to "mortgage pawnshop thinking" and stated, "The Basel Accord is more like a club for the elderly. It wants to solve the problems of an aging financial system." Along with metaphorical references that were not particularly kind to regulators was this one that in retrospect seems prophetic: "When innovation is far ahead of the regulation, when the richness and depth of innovation far exceed the imagination of regulation, it is abnormal and society and the world will fall into chaos." How true, but his audience—including China's vice president, current and former central bank heads, and China's most senior bank regulator—was likely not amused.

The facile answer for the timing of Ant IPO's cancellation is that with this speech, Jack Ma provoked the regulators, who immediately took retribution by canceling the IPO. With this narrative, Jack Ma is turned into a tragic Greek hero, slain by regulators' actions reduced to a vendetta against an innovator of mythical proportions who had grown too full of himself. It's a simple answer that works for many as it plays into the existing stereotypes for China—i.e., China rules with an iron fist, brooks no dissent, and punishes those who do—which must be true because it feels right. The more likely scenario is that Jack Ma's speech was the result of his already knowing that the regulations, soon to be released, were toxic to his coming IPO. His was a last-ditch plea laced with metaphors asking regulators to understand that "this time will be different." It is inconceivable that Jack Ma, with his many connections in the worlds of financial regulation and politics, was unaware of the train crash in the making when he approached the podium.

While we can never know definitively, I do not believe that the "pause" in Ant's IPO represented a personal vendetta against Jack Ma due to thin-skinned regulators. Jack Ma and Elon Musk share the trait of being outspoken and raising regulators' ire. While this characteristic may not win them friends, it also does not spur regulators to carry out personal vendettas. What prompts them to act is fear. In China, regulators are still consumed with anxiety that another P2P crisis might be brought on by loan arrangers who would not be as careful or skilled as Ant. The regulations that serve one also serve all, including out-of-nowhere low-quality microlenders who do not have Ant's discipline and ethos.

While definitive proof is hard to come by, the lead-up to the IPO gave us more than a few glimpses of regulatory discontent. In August, China's Supreme People's Court slashed the maximum private lending rate. The new rate of 15.4% is now fixed at four times that of the country's loan prime rate. Previously, the top rate ranged between 24% and 36%. While the law didn't target Ant specifically and covered all lenders in the country, as the leading online consumer lender, Ant was jolted. Sadly, this step may very well cut off access to loans for the most vulnerable.

Earlier in July, the PBOC urged the State Council to conduct an antitrust investigation into Alipay and WeChat Pay. The PBOC argued that the payment giants used their 94% market share to elbow out the competition. Clearly, the regulators were serious. After Ant's IPO pause, China's State Administration for Market Regulation issued draft anti-monopoly rules against China's internet platforms, which sent shares across the country into a tailspin.

Finally, in mid-September, a mere seven weeks before the IPO, the PBOC announced that companies operating more than two financial businesses in the country would be classified as financial-holding companies. This requirement would oblige the companies to have a minimum of RMB 5 billion (US\$ 731 million) in paid-up capital. Ant quickly set up a subsidiary to deal with the regulations, which presented them little financial hardship. The financial-holding company rules had first been proposed back in 2018. Perhaps everyone, myself included, should have sounded an alarm when they were finalized just before the IPO. While regulators didn't exactly telegraph their move on Ant, it's evident that there had been discontent beyond the usual push and pull with regulators for which Ant is famous. For Ant watchers, like me, this all seemed perfectly normal; Ant and the regulators have long been like oil and water.

THE AFTERMATH

If you are expecting smoking-gun evidence as to why China's regulators waited so long to pull the trigger on Ant, I must disappoint you. So far, none has surfaced. The reason probably has more to do with why the regulators were late to control P2P loans. Analog speed regulators that are spread across diffuse departments, all with limited regulatory responsibility, can't keep up with digital speed. The nascent "new breed" of emboldened regulator did, however, make the right call. I support the micro-loan rule changes and believe they will avert a credit bubble in the microloan sector. I also agree with Jack Ma that the Basel regulations are a "club for the elderly" as they did nothing to prevent the 2008 global financial crisis.

Regulators acted boldly to avert a crisis, which is praiseworthy, but they took far too long to do it. China's regulators surely had the new microlending regulations in the works for many months. It's unthinkable that they would draft and drop them on such short notice in response to Jack Ma's speech. That they were held up in committee and shuttled between officials in a bureaucratic tug-of-war wouldn't surprise me in the least. I also think that the delay will be career-ending for some regulators, because creating this level of discord is rarely rewarded.

> *Regulators assumed Ant's US$ 400 million
> in capital would take months to deploy, not
> days.*

The former mayor of Chongqing, Huang Qifan, who approved the banking licenses for Ant in his city in 2014, appears to support the idea that regulators were indeed moving at analog speed on Ant's lending activities. Huang commented that he approved Ant's banking license and those of other banks because he disliked P2P lending, and that the financial regulators under his charge in Chongqing had been unable to keep up with Ant. His regulators assumed that when granting Ant's license, the approved US$ 400 million in capital would take months to deploy in lending markets, not days. Huang also stated that they did not envision Ant leveraging its capital in ABS markets.

In the West, the regulators' pause of Ant's IPO met with howls. China could not be trusted, would never develop meaningful capital markets, was incompetent, had never done anything like this before, and didn't know what it was doing. To ensure conformity with stereotypes, most of the news coverage was accompanied by the accusation that China was under the blind control of the Communist Party, which could not brook a national giant of Ant's stature. I may have missed a few, but I think that sums it up. Few, aside from some skilled China financial journalists, noted that credit markets were unsustainable or that the PBOC had already closed down another major industry when it shuttered P2P markets. Ironically, the last P2P lender closed its doors the same month that many reported that China had never done anything like this before.

Wall Street banks took the news in stride and coolly marked down their estimated losses of $400 million in fees to regulatory risks. Simply another day doing business in China. Predictions that Ant's paused IPO would cause long-term damage to China's capital markets are demonstrably ill-founded. Wall Street is still pursuing its modern-day China goldrush by buying wholly-owned

Chinese securities subsidiaries with a vengeance, showing that Wall Street still views China's long-term prospects in a positive light.

In December 2019, Goldman Sachs became the first to buy out its China partner and claim 100% ownership of its China operations. The long list of Wall Street's top firms joining in China's opening of its securities markets includes JP Morgan Asset Management, JP Morgan Chase, HSBC, Morgan Stanley, Credit Suisse, Citigroup, Vanguard, and Blackrock. All are setting up wholly-owned, or majority-owned, financial operations to get in on China's ongoing capital market reforms and liberalization of the financial sector.

The fallout in China was interesting and diametrically opposed to that in the West. Many netizens saw that regulators acted in the public interest, and even if belated, thought they were to be congratulated. While some were sympathetic to Ant, microlenders are not always viewed with affection in China. The ubiquity of microloans has even made them fodder for comedians, who are less than charitable to lenders.

To many in China, the frenzy over Ant shares was reminiscent of the boom-and-bust cycles they recently experienced in the stock market, the P2P market, and even the $US 1 billion collectible sneaker market. All of these markets required intervention by the PBOC to protect the public from harm. Ant was viewed as simply one more to be managed and reined in, even if you loved the company, used their services, and disliked your local bank. The regulators were doing their job, and Ant should do its by going back to the drawing board—no hard feelings.

ANT RETURNING TO ITS IPO AND ANTITRUST

Ant is coming back for an IPO. The regulations will change, Ant will adapt and still be tremendously profitable, successful, and most of all, innovative. It is important to remember that 61% of its revenue was unaffected by the new regulations. Anyone counting Ant out does not know the talent and dedication of the people working there as I do. They are back at it and retooling their operations to meet the new requirements imposed by regulators.

It won't be easy, and the days where Ant can reserve 2% of loans outstanding are ending, signaling a change in how much capital Ant needs and a rethinking of their business model. That Ant will look a bit more like a bank when it's done reorganizing is a given. Liang Tao, the vice-chairman of China's banking regulator, stated in his first public statement following the IPO pause, "Fintech companies, which use technology to enhance financial services, should be regulated like banks and must observe the same risk and compliance requirement as financial institutions on main street." Jack Ma's comments about Basel regulations being a "club for the elderly" did not sway regulators who will require at least some modified form of risk control from Ant.

> *Anyone counting Ant out does not know the talent and dedication of the people working there as I do.*

Practically speaking, Ant has until October 2021 to complete its IPO under its listing agreements in Hong Kong and Shanghai. Ant has a lot of restructuring to accomplish during this period to make the deadline. If the restructuring were based solely on the microlending regulations, I'd be confident that Ant could make the listing requirements. Ant's valuation would need to be adjusted downward to match the new regulatory environment—estimates range between 30% to 50%—and then Ant could potentially come to market. While its IPO might no longer qualify as "world's largest," it would undoubtedly be massive and cause for celebration in China.

The problem is that in conjunction with the microlending regulations, all of China's tech industry is now facing antitrust issues, as are the GAFA companies in the West. It would seem that regulators in the US, EU, and China, who rarely agree, do indeed agree when it comes to the outsized impact of big tech on society.

Antitrust regulations will also require that Ant change its operations. China's State Administration of Market Regulation recently reported that it would fine Alibaba and a Tencent backed company the maximum of RMB 500,00 (US$ 76,464) for failing to report deals for antitrust review. The penalties are modest, but the regulator's strong statement, "The internet industry is not outside the oversight of anti-monopoly law," was not taken lightly.

That Ant will deal with antitrust issues is a given; what is unknown is what the new regulations will mandate. As former finance minister Lou Jiwei recently stated, "China could restrict the number of banks a single fintech platform can partner with, to prevent any platform from gaining too much market share and becoming 'winner takes all and too big to fail.'" Another official stated that Beijing could be considering a digital tax on the massive amount of user data big tech holds in China. Neither of these proposals, among many others in circulation, would be fatal to Ant, but they do surround it with an air of uncertainty that makes an IPO impossible. Clearly, regulators in China realize this, and I expect their moves to be swift.

For Ant's part, executive chairman Eric Jing, in his first public comments since the paused IPO, stated that Ant would be more "transparent and predictable," a good thing that will keep it in better stead with regulators and the IPO to come. He also made it very clear that Ant will reorganize and conduct a "body check-up" to come out of this as an even better company. The three initiatives he announced include:

1. *Deepening understanding of security and development.* "There cannot be innovation and development without ensuring security, and without the security of the national financial system and the entire financial sector."

2. *Improve corporate governance.* "We will further enhance information disclosure to make it more transparent and

predictable to the public, as we believe sunlight is the best of disinfectants."

3. *Risk management.* "Comprehensive risk management will be implemented at every individual business."

Jing's comments are exactly what the market needs to hear, and they will guide Ant Group in getting its IPO back on track following its reorganization.

ANT'S NEW STRUCTURE

In late December 2020, the PBOC issued a communique designed as a public rebuke of Ant that put forward five concrete issues for resolution. While the notice's tone and timing were noteworthy and provoked gasps from foreign media, all five of the items were issues of which Ant was already well aware. It showed that the regulator's bark is worse than its bite. Had the regulator wanted to break-up Ant or inflict irrevocable damage, as suggested by many pundits, it could have easily invented newer, more damaging items. The five issues were:

1. A return to the origin of payment, enhance transaction transparency, and strictly prohibit unfair competition.

2. Operate personal credit investigation services in accordance with the law and to protect the privacy of personal data.

3. Establish a financial holding company.

4. Improve corporate governance and strictly rectify financial activities such as illegal credit, insurance, and wealth management in accordance with the requirements of prudential supervision.

5. The securities fund business must be carried out in accordance with the law, governance of securities institutions strengthened, and all asset securitizations must be compliant.

While no doubt serious, all of these issues were items that Ant was in the process of remedying. So from Ant's perspective, the public humiliation was worse than the actual issues to be resolved.

To resolve many of these issues Ant reached an agreement with regulators to set up a new consumer finance unit that will reside within its new financial holding company. The new unit will house its Jibei and Huabei lending groups and allow Ant to continue lending on a pan-China basis. The new lending activities will require greater capitalization than its prior activities, but will be compliant with the regulations and no longer deemed illegal. Ant's other financial activities in wealth management and insurance will also gain legality within the financial holding company. Without the structure, Ant would need to license individual loan companies in each of the provinces, as required by the microloan regulations. It will also give Ant a platform from which it can issue asset securitizations in a manner that should be acceptable to the regulators. In one restructuring, Ant will effectively resolve issues number three, four and five on the PBOC's list.

The financial holding company will also house all of Ant's other units, including Alipay and Ele.me (Are you hungry?) food delivery. While Ant's food delivery service may at first seem unrelated to financial activities, on the platform they are all interconnected. Food delivery can create a credit event, or have special financial incentives associated with Alipay. Teasing apart a platform where all of the pieces are by design interconnected led the regulator to keep them all together in the holding company.

This structure allows Ant to sidestep the first and most feared item on the PBOC's list, that Ant return to its roots in payments. Ant will retain the ability to continue operating its credit business securely within the consumer finance unit. Pundits who feared that Ant would have to forgo all lending activities should be appeased. For all of the regulator's concern over Ant, they have no intention of breaking up or otherwise crushing the company.

> *A strong case can be made that Ant will play an even greater role in China's consumer finance market.*

Item two on the regulator's list regarding personal data also appears to have found resolution with the formation of a new credit data operations group held outside of the financial holding company. There appear to be two sides to the issue with personal data. First is Ant's relationship with clients. Ant will have to better communicate with customers what data it is collecting and how it will be used. This may require that Ant stop collecting certain data streams if the client desires to opt out. This potential blow will likely be softened by many clients opting to continue sharing data, given their reliance on Ant's services.

The second issue concerning personal data is data sharing with the government. The regulator is requesting Ant to provide credit data to Baihang, China's national consumer credit company, discussed in chapter 17. Ant and Tencent both famously refused to share credit data with Baihang. Ant, and perhaps Tencent, will segregate credit data in a dedicated unit separate from their credit evaluation technology. This will allow both to develop some form of basic credit rating that satisfies Baihang's reporting requirement while keeping their precious credit rating methodologies within the financial holding company. A win for all parties.

For all of the regulatory changes, a strong case can be made that Ant will play an even greater role in China's consumer finance market now that it will be compliant with regulations and have more skin in the game. The new financial holding structure makes it very difficult for new smaller challengers to enter the market. Several weaker microlenders already announced that they would exit the market or reassess participation after assessing the new regulations. Ant and other larger companies will be unchallenged given the capital required of new entrants. In addition, with the new financial holding company, Ant will now have a clear regulatory standing and the ability to launch a greater range of banking products. Banks may find that Ant is a bigger competitor after it reorganizes than before.

Ant's reorganization, of course, comes with one significant drawback: slower growth. Ant will have to adapt to this new structure and will undoubtedly need several years of operating experience to prove to investors the levels of profitability its new operations can attain. I will not make light of the significance of these changes. They are massive and will require Ant to trade fast growth for long-term stability. Prior to the IPO, Ant would never have made that trade, but forced by regulators, Ant will not just comply but excel. I will also make another prediction, which some will find amusing. During the next IPO that follows its reorganization, the regulator will be effusive (as much as any regulator can be) in its support of Ant's new model.

FINTECH IN CHINA IS ALIVE AND WELL

For many, the pause of Ant's IPO was nothing short of heartbreaking, and this is not just a sentiment held among Ant's employees. Ant is a global symbol of financial inclusion and the good that fintech can bring to the world, and many now see it as a fallen angel. Some have even gone so far as to speculate that fintech in China is a spent force and that Ant itself will no longer be fighting for the little guy as it historically has.

To the greater issue of fintech in China, I can only say that the country's regulatory sandbox is still open for business. The rules are changing, and expecting China's fintech giants—now bigger than the West's "too big to fail banks"—to roam free of regulation is unrealistic. The concept that fintech innovation in China is coming to an end, or has been diminished, is impossible for me to square in a country on the cusp of launching the world's first large-scale CBDC. The fintech innovation that China's CBDC will generate will be stunning, and you can expect fintech leaders like Ant to be in the middle of it, if not more prominent than ever. As discussed in chapter 12 covering the domestic use of the DC/EP, the PBOC will need Ant's platform if it wants to succeed.

As far as Ant goes, its aspiration to help the little guy continues unabated; any thought that Ant will simply roll over and stop being innovative are exaggerated at best. Ant continues to make the news, most recently with its newly awarded Singapore wholesale banking license. A Chinese fintech will now own a Singapore bank with all relevant connections to the Western financial system. I could not imagine a better platform for innovation or launching China's DC/EP for international use.

In the run-up to the IPO prospectus, executive chairman Eric Jing wrote something that left an indelible impression on me: "The financial system of the past 200 years was designed for the industrial era and served only 20% of the population and organizations. As we enter the digital age, we must better serve the remaining 80%." Statements like that are not the superficial rhetoric of a founder on the cusp of a major deal. They are the words of a true believer, and the entire organization is hellbent on making finance work for everyone. You will have to see it to believe it.

19

THE CASE AGAINST CBDCS: THE ILLUSION OF PRIVACY

China on CBDCs and privacy:

> *"We know the demand from the general public is to keep anonymity by using paper money and coins ... we will give those... But at the same time, we will keep the balance between the 'controllable anonymity' and anti-money laundering.... We are not seeking full control of the information of the general public."*
>
> Mu Changchun, Head of the Chinese Central Bank's Digital Currency Research Institute

The West on CBDCs and privacy:

> *"The idea of having a ledger with everybody's payment details might be acceptable in China, but would not be attractive in the US."*
>
> Jerome Powell, Chair of the Federal Reserve

The most common attack against CBDCs focuses squarely on the lack of privacy that digital currencies impose on their users. I won't make light of this feature of CBDCs. The real-time insights that governments find compelling for fine-tuning economic policy, tax collection, and anti-money laundering represent a real change in how they access and interpret our payment data. Or at least so it seems.

When examining CBDC privacy, many compare it unfavorably with the anonymity and privacy provided by cash, then decry that with CBDCs, privacy is stripped away. The problem with this comparison is that it doesn't represent most people's actual spending habits. Even before coronavirus accelerated the trend, most of our payments shifted from cash to credit cards or mobile. The real correlate of CBDC privacy is not with cash, but with the levels we can expect from our current digital transactions. This makes the discussion much more complicated, as we must compare privacy in two distinctly different digital worlds.

CBDC PRIVACY

At the time of this writing, there is only one CBDC in circulation, and two large scale pilots underway. With these we can begin to benchmark CBDC privacy. It's clear that the Chinese government has a full view of all transactions made with its new CBDC. Without question, this is the level of CBDC trackability that privacy advocates fear most, a system that vacuums up all data and gives the state complete access. As discussed earlier, for the Chinese people this is nothing new: the same kind of exposure is status quo on China's data-scraping payment platforms. Indeed, relative to them, China's CBDC users potentially gain more anonymity, thanks to the currency's "controllable anonymity" feature, whereby the payor can be made anonymous to the payee.

> *"Digital payments are usually traceable,*
> *unlike cash payments, as they leave digital*
> *footprints that enable a transaction to be*
> *followed."*

Sweden is currently running a pilot of the e-krona. While the technical platform is in trial stages, the Riksbank makes it clear in "The Riksbank's e-krona Project Report 2" that there is no obligation to supply value-based e-krona anonymously. However, its pilot system does give us hope that a CBDC future could include a degree of privacy. The pilot uses the now-familiar two-tier architecture (for China's, see chapter 11) but uses a system of accounts and a decentralized network. While the Central Bank authorizes transactions, it does not tally user details, only the account balances and payments. This is a win for privacy advocates, but perhaps a pyrrhic victory at best. The Riksbank also makes it plain that "digital transactions with e-krona will be traceable," shattering any thoughts of cash-like privacy. The bigger question this raises is, if Sweden can't make transactions private with decentralized networks, who can? Here the Riksbank has an answer, stating ominously, though factually as we will soon see, that "digital payments are usually traceable, unlike cash payments, as they leave digital footprints that enable a transaction to be followed."

The first and only CBDC in operation in Q4 2020 is the Bahamas' "Sand Dollar." While a small project compared with those in China and Sweden, it is noteworthy because it showcases the use of CBDCs in promoting financial inclusion. The Bahamas consist of 7,000 small islands, many of which lack banking infrastructure. The Sand Dollar is providing these residents banking services, without the need for banks. Privacy, however, is not guaranteed. The Central Bank of the Bahamas states clearly that "the anonymity of cash is not being replicated," and that "all transactions are linked to an anti-money laundering/counter financing of terrorism engine to safeguard regulatory compliance and governance." So while the Sand Dollar provides clear benefits in financial inclusion, its privacy is similar to China's, with all transactions available to authorities.

So far, the first three CBDCs in pilot and production stages do not give much hope to privacy advocates. The trend is clear: allow governments to access users' payment data, and they'll use it. Sweden's e-krona does give us some hope in its design, which at least keeps private user details away from the government. The problem is that the Riksbank's statements about digital transactions leaving "footprints" are prophetic, and best be heeded.

Can CBDCs be built with true privacy safeguards? Yes, fully decentralized CBDCs akin to cryptocurrencies could be programmed, but it is inconceivable that any government will go this route. The issuing government would lose the ability to monitor the use of its currency, presenting real issues of tax evasion and money laundering. While cash use is generally considered the "gold standard" of privacy, in most cases it ends up in the banking system where the government can discern some macro perspective of its use, and control its movement once deposited. A genuinely private CBDC would disable even this tenuous degree of control.

When governments design a CBDC, they are left with a sliding scale of privacy settings and need to determine where their CBDC should reside on that scale. That the first examples of CBDCs tend toward a general lack of privacy should not be surprising, as the standards are based, at least in part, off the privacy modes currently used for digital payments. This leaves us with an unpleasant but necessary question: how much privacy are we giving up using CBDCs, compared to what we're already using?

THE ILLUSION OF PRIVACY

In the West, most of us are already using credit cards and either Apple or Google Pay to make payments. Our lives are at least in part cashless, even if not yet to the extent experienced in China. If we take Apple's privacy policy at face value, our privacy is secure: "Apple Pay allows you to make easy, secure, and private transactions in stores, in apps, and on the web." The problem is, Apple's concept of privacy does not extend beyond the data being held "privately" on the iPhone. The moment we open the app to pay, our activity and data is an open book.

Credit card transaction data is the "holy grail" for marketers, who use it to infer our preferences and habits in ways that are right out of WeChat and Alipay's playbook. Privacy critics regularly pummel China's payment apps for their data collection ability, while in the West, similar analysis techniques have long been in use. The scraping is obscured through a system of using intermediaries to do much of the processing. Apple Pay and credit card companies' privacy policies may seem reassuring, but they do not reflect the tracking of the path your transaction data takes after you make an electronic payment.

Typically, using a credit card or mobile payment device at a retail or online purchase will involve as many as six different companies, all of whom have access to your data and can in turn sell it:

1. Retailer: confirmed store visits or internet purchases are commonly sold to data brokers. (See picture below.)

2. Merchant processor: The credit card processing software or machine used to relay the card info to the card network. Examples would be Square, Stripe, or any of your local bank systems.

3. Card network: Visa, Mastercard, and American Express eventually process your payment but also collect data that they sell to marketers for customer insights.

4. Issuing Bank: Your local bank issuing the card may also monetize its clients' data with sales to brokers.

5. Fintech Apps: Some popular apps like Venmo, Chime, or even Bank of America use fintech service providers like "Plaid" or "Yodlee" who specialize in collecting and selling user data.

6. Merchant Bank: The retailer's bank may also collect and monetize its payment data.

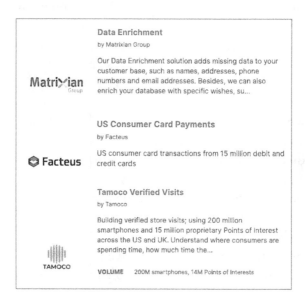

Data sets available on the internet include personal data, card payment data, and verified store visits. Combinations of these same data sets can be used to de-anonymize or re-identify most "anonymous" digital payment data.

In most cases, digital transaction data contains the place, the amount, and the time but excludes the buyer's name. It can, depending on retailer, also include product codes, item description, price, quantity, store details and shipping postal code. The problem is that your data isn't anonymous because data brokers can de-anonymize or re-identify this data by connecting the purchase data with other data sets. Researchers found that the credit card metadata from four purchases including date, location and price are sufficient to re-identify 90% of shoppers as unique individuals. Similar results have been reported by researchers and data analysts worldwide, making it clear that "anonymous" is a misnomer.

As if to add to the illusion that digital privacy exists, the same researchers found that companies don't even hide the practice of de-anonymizing data. The credit monitoring company, Experian, once done assessing your credit score, sells the transaction data it receives on your payment history in its ConsumerView customer insights product. This is a perfect example of how intermediaries sell your data (it's a sound business for Experian, which can sell the data twice). Ironically, on the same internet site where it sells transaction data, Experian sells access to a de-identified data set of 120 million Americans from a third-party company. The researchers found that the two data sets combined were sufficient to re-identify users in the Experian data set. So Apple's privacy policy may give you the assurance that "Apple" is not selling your data, but every other party involved in the transaction enabled on its app will, and does.

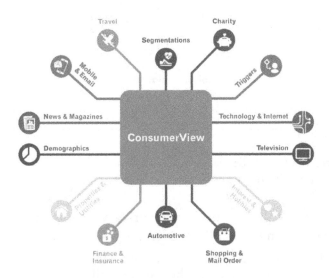

Experian repurposes data acquired through its credit scoring business to sell "ConsumerView" customer insights. Experian is one of many intermediaries repurposing and selling financial transaction data.

Finally, to ensure that the "panopticon" of credit card tracking is complete, there is Google. In 2017 Google announced that it tracked 70% of US credit and debit card transactions, a number that is undoubtedly higher today. The data is used to prove the efficacy of its online advertisements by showing advertisers their actual sales. Given most citizen's massive data footprint on Google systems through email, browser, and maps, de-anonymizing credit card data is a breeze. In addition to credit cards, Google is now offering its new "Plex" checking account service, which will give them complete access to users' payments. Google touts that it will not sell users' "transaction history" to its advertising arm, but this assurance ring hollow.

Mastercard's Data & Services division sells "actionable insights" through the collection of real-time anonymized transaction data.

We live with the "illusion of privacy," believing that our financial exchanges are private when, in reality, they are not. Not surprisingly, this illusion is also promoted by the big tech and financial companies even as they openly sell our data—assuring us on one hand that our data is secure, while profiting from its sale on the other. It's an eye-opening situation that is slow to be divulged because it shakes to the very foundations our notions of trust and fairness in the new digital world. Antitrust allegations against big tech brought in the EU, US, and China are perhaps a way of acknowledging our collective concern.

YES, BUT THE GOVERNMENT DOESN'T HAVE MY DATA

Some will argue that while our digital payments may be an open book to marketers and big tech, at least the information is not in the government's hands, as it would be with CBDCs. Reasonable, but in the US, credit card transaction data for some 600 million cards and personal data from mortgage loans and car payments are sent to the Consumer Finance Protection Bureau (CFPB). The data is not all anonymous. It's clear that with this data in its hands, the US government has unfettered access to your digital payment data. Any data it doesn't have it readily buys from data brokers, as recent admissions from the Defense Intelligence Agency and Homeland Security testify.

The CFPB's mission is "to protect consumers from unfair, deceptive, or abusive practices and take action against companies that break the law." This is indeed a laudable goal, one it has carried out with great success. But does accomplishing the mission require an entire nation's digital transaction data? This seems a question worth asking. Interestingly, few did when the bureau was founded. The CFPB did come under fire during the Trump administration for its management structure and for being a thorn in banks' sides, but its data acquisition policies seem to fly beneath the radar.

The crowning example of government surveillance of financial transactions came from Edward Snowden, now living in exile in Russia. In 2013 Snowden became famous for unveiling the US National Security Administration's (NSA) techniques in surveilling US and global internet traffic. In September 2020, a US court of appeals found that the NSA programs Snowden revealed were, in fact, unlawful—a small victory for privacy rights. According to Snowden's revelations, the NSA's now-infamous "PRISM" program routinely surveilled some 75% of the US's internet traffic, along with vast quantities of email and telephone calls. Less well-known is that the NSA also had a program appropriately called "Follow The Money" (FTM).

According to articles published in Germany's *Der Spiegel*, FTM gained access to the databases of major credit card companies, including Visa. The program also penetrated SWIFT on multiple levels, including "printer traffic (transfer amounts) from numerous banks." It is important to note that FTM access to SWIFT is in addition to the US Treasury's sanctioned scrutiny through the Terrorist Finance Tracking Program. So the same organization that can listen to German Prime Minister Angela Merkel's private cellphone calls (to the amusement of Huawei whose 5G systems are banned in Germany over fears of such snooping), more than likely still retains the ability to follow your digital payments down to the penny.

So far, my examples have focused on the US, but the EU is not appreciably different. While the General Data Protection Regulation (GDPR) is a great advancement in privacy, its policy on anonymized data is clear: "The principles of data protection should therefore not apply to anonymous information." So the techniques used in the US to de-anonymize data are also widely used in the EU. The EU also has programs like Passenger Name Record (PNR), allowing for the government collection of air travelers' credit card details and other personal identifiers. So a government's mass collection of credit card data is undoubtedly not limited to the US.

CBDC OR EXISTING DIGITAL PAYMENT SYSTEMS? TAKE YOUR PICK.

Our financial privacy discussion is sobering and will make many readers long for a large wad of cash. We've seen that the perceived gap in privacy between CBDCs and your existing digital payment systems is smaller than you might at first think. Under closer scrutiny, the facile argument that CBDC privacy is bad and the privacy offered by credit cards or Apple Pay privacy is good doesn't hold water. With CBDCs, our privacy is handed to governments, while with our existing payment systems, our data is handed both to the government and anyone who pays for it. How do we choose?

There is a strong case to be made that our current digital payment systems deliver the worst of all possible outcomes. Credit cards, the foundation of the West's digital payment system, charge roughly 3% for use, provide no privacy, and severely limit the role of transferring money to specialized intermediaries. While many don't think of it this way, it's a system with inherent flaws, one that up-to-date technology has surpassed. While CBDCs are far from perfect, at least they will deliver free cash transfer, a greater degree of financial inclusion, and vastly improved convenience, with little real cost in privacy. CBDCs potentially may also offer a path to taking our data off the major payment and big tech platforms. With CBDCs, we can make direct digital payments without our data passing through a long chain of financial intermediaries. This most likely won't end the sale of our data, but may give us additional control and clarity over exactly who has access to it.

From a privacy perspective, compared to existing digital payment systems, the benefits of CBDCs far outweigh the disadvantages. Those who say that CBDCs have privacy shortcomings aren't necessarily wrong. But complaining that privacy is lost with CBDCs implies that you had more privacy with the systems they replace, which is clearly not the case. Hopefully, some of the new crop of CBDCs can do better. However, my fear, which I think is well-founded, is that the Swedish Riksbank's comments about "digital footprints and traceability" will prove prophetic. My evidence comes from the cryptocurrency world, where the police routinely arrest particularly nefarious users of popular crypto coins that claim to protect privacy.

A LICENSE TO PRINT MORE DEBT

Another criticism of CBDCs is that they provide a potentially unchecked way for governments to print currency and increase debt without limit. This is particularly relevant during the pandemic, as governments worldwide are attempting to stave off economic crisis through direct government stimulus payments to both corporates and individuals.

While the broader argument against government deficit spending may have merits, the concept that CBDCs will allow governments to spend even more than without them is difficult to support. Governments have engaged in what some call a "debt tsunami" since the onset of the pandemic. The US deficit, for example, tripled to US$ 3 trillion for the fiscal year ending in September 2020. Clearly, governments do not need CBDCs to go into debt when faced with disaster. That CBDCs will open a Pandora's box that somehow leads governments into greater debt is an exaggeration, given the massive amounts of money governments can access through debt markets.

The real issue for CBDCs is less one of debt creation than of accountability. China's CBDC ties directly into the government's figures for the M0 money supply, so any creation of CBDC is offset by removing cash from circulation. This system is by design anti-inflationary, as additional money is not being created. The fear is that governments could open the floodgates and issue CBDCs that vastly increase money in circulation, and cause widespread inflation. To do this, an unscrupulous government would have to fail to report or underreport CBDC issuance to avoid devaluing their currency. This is a real issue, but in a two-tier CBDC system it would prove tricky, as the banks would have to report incoming CBDC and would have to be complicit in the scheme to underreport issuance. Frankly, it's easier for a government to achieve the same results by issuing checks or cash, without the additional burden of the CBDCs' complexity. In conclusion, CBDCs aren't the problem. A government intentionally misreporting and miscounting can do that more easily in analog than digital.

The US's stimulus payments create the same deficit, whether paid by CBDC, direct deposit, or debit card. That CBDCs have lower overhead costs and are more efficient at transferring money should make them a welcome addition to government payment capabilities. This is not in the least academic. As of November 2020, twelve million Americans had still not received their stimulus payments, more than eight months after the start of distribution. Sadly, most of these twelve million are low-wage workers whose income was below the minimum required for filing a tax return. CBDCs certainly would not resolve all issues in identifying these workers, but might have made a difference. CBDCs would free government resources that are currently busy replacing lost checks and cash cards to help mount a more determined search. CBDCs make it cheaper and easier to distribute Universal Basic Income, disaster relief, or other forms of stimulus payments, and would be a welcome upgrade to government payment systems that should not be feared.

DESTABILIZING BANK RUNS

Some critics of CBDCs point to the potential shocks that digital currency might deliver to the banking system, particularly through "a run on the bank." A bank run occurs when depositors rapidly transfer cash out in a flight to safety, which compromises the bank. The fear is that the ease of transferring CBDC or moving money into the relative safety of CBDCs could make these runs more frequent or more devastating. Bank runs are a real thing, particularly in developing countries where they may be sparked by rumors as easily as by a genuine problem with a bank's stability.

China's strict limits on converting bank account balances into CBDC give us a glimpse of how governments can reduce the potential for CBDC runs on banks. The inability to convert substantial sums to CBDC makes it impossible for China's retail CBDC users to create a "run on the bank." In addition, banks will likely have an "off-switch" for CBDC transfers to activate in times of cyberattack or other crisis. That CBDC critics lament the computerized efficiency with which CBDCs could potentially empty a bank yet cannot envision the computer having an "off-switch" amuses me to no end.

China will not be the only country to employ limits on CBDC movement. Most CBDCs will be structured with limits that allow users reasonable access to CBDCs for payment convenience while limiting the transfer size that the system can move. This isn't new. Credit cards and checking accounts all have limits on cash transfer. These limits protect both the bank and the general public from digital fraud. The thought that governments would purposefully allow CBDC transfers without limits and/or fail to protect banks and citizens is frankly disingenuous.

A variant of this concern is the interest-bearing ability of CBDCs and the potential for CBDCs to compete with banks if their CBDCs pay interest. Here again, one has to consider the unlikelihood of governments willfully competing with banks or putting them at a disadvantage. While it is technically possible for China's and most other CBDCs to bear interest, using this feature to banks' detriment is inconceivable. What would be gained? I can think of one exception: governments could use negative rates to dissuade the use of CBDCs and force conversion back to cash if they felt CBDCs were somehow destabilizing the financial system.

What is of concern, and a more realistic threat, is the potentially destabilizing effects of CBDCs to banks in the developing world, an issue flagged in the initial version of Facebook's Libra coin. If retail customers in developing economies are allowed ready access to CBDCs from other countries with more desirable currencies, that could significantly affect the local banking system.

China felt this pressure firsthand with Facebook's Libra, even if Libra is not strictly speaking a CBDC. PBOC vice governor Chen Yulu commented that Libra could potentially "curb the Chinese yuan's international development, weaken capital controls, and lead to volatile asset prices which could impact financial stability." The potential for foreign CBDCs weakening or destabilizing local institutions that are already in precarious condition is real. As CBDCs are so new, and their impact not fully understood, it will require close coordination between central banks to ensure they not become a destabilizing influence. No doubt China is pondering this, given its aspirations for an international digital-RMB.

THE CASE FOR KEEPING CASH

As the strong proponent of CBDCs and a "cashless" lifestyle that I am, it may come as a surprise to learn that tucked away in a back drawer in my home are envelopes containing cash in euro, dollars, and RMB. While I quite enjoy my cashless lifestyle, I am in no way in favor of eliminating cash. Cash simply works, and ridding myself of it entirely would be folly. The opportunity to use cashless payment more frequently, with CBDCs as one payment option, does not preclude the maintenance and use of cash in the financial system. China is an excellent example of this philosophy. For all its advances in going cash-free, no one at the PBOC talks about removing cash from circulation.

What became evident with coronavirus is that many citizens also have envelopes with cash hidden away in a drawer or closet. While the reports of massive hoarding of toilet paper made front-page news, Americans also quietly hoarded cash. The Federal Reserve Bank of San Francisco reported that the average amount of cash people kept at home nearly doubled from $257 to $483 between October 2019 and May 2020. The Bank of International Settlements reported that pandemic-related cash hoarding also took place in the UK, Japan, and Italy. Holding onto cash makes us feel good and provides some small amount of comfort in the event of a catastrophe. Anyone living in hurricane- or typhoon-prone areas, where storms can send society back to the Stone Age, understand this better than most.

The Swedish Civil Contingencies Agency went so far as to advise all residents to keep "cash in small denominations" at home in case of emergencies. The idea that a power cut, cyberattack, or major technology disruption would cripple the nation because of residents' reliance on digital payment is a real concern. Anyone in the UK who had a credit card attached to WireCard payment systems experienced this firsthand when the company failed, and cards went offline for forty-eight hours. Saying that digital system failures can't happen or will never happen seems foolish.

But when citizens hoard too much cash, there will be questions. In the UK, the Bank of England received a strong rebuke from a parliamentary committee which found that about GBP 50 billion is missing from the country's GBP 70 billion cash supply. The committee is convinced that a majority of these missing funds are being used for money laundering, among other illegal activities. For its part the BoE claims that "members of the public do not have to explain to the bank why they wish to hold bank notes." Unimpressed with the BoE's response and "lack of curiosity," the committee is demanding that the bank find the money. What is clear is that even "untraceable" cash use is scrutinized by government, if too much goes missing. Whether in digital form or cash, there's no way to escape scrutiny.

So for the record, cash will be with us for some time to come. It provides a simple analog solution to payment in an increasingly digital world. To say that it has no place in our future is to deny the fragility of our digital systems, which, time and time again, fail spectacularly. Their failures are reminders of how new we are to this digital revolution and that cash, which has been around for millennia, will still be an integral part of our modernized financial system. I would go as far as to say that hearing the call to eliminate cash should make readers, even the most "cashless," become wary.

20

OUR SHARED CBDC FUTURE

China on the future impact of CBDCs:

> "*The G20 also needs to discuss developing the standards and principles for central bank digital currencies with an open and accommodating attitude, and properly handle all types of risks and challenges while pushing collectively for the development of the international monetary system.*"
>
> Xi Jinping, General Secretary of the Chinese Communist Party and President of the People's Republic of China

The West on the future impact of CBDCs:

> "*Our job is not to protect bank business models [from digital currencies.] Banks will have to adjust. Our job is to ensure that if bank business models change, we manage the financial and macro-economic consequences of that.*"
>
> John Cunliffe, Deputy Governor, Bank of England

With the Bahamas' launch of the "Sand Dollar," the tiny island nation captured the title for the world's first live CBDC. Its size may be small, but at its heart are the same desires to digitize and simplify the movement of cash that underlie China's massive program. The Bahamas is just the first. With CBDC launches announced for Saudi Arabia, United Arab Emirates, Brazil, Lebanon, and Cambodia, it's clear that a CBDC future is upon us. Pilot programs in Sweden, Japan, Hong Kong, Thailand, Switzerland, and Lithuania further dispel any notion that CBDCs are just a fad that was restricted to China and a few early adopters. Finally, the European Central Bank and Bank of England's talk of a digital euro and pound further push the boundaries on what seemed a faraway future just a few years ago. We will see many CBDCs at work carrying both domestic and cross-border payments in the next five years. It's no longer if, but when.

As China has already proven with digital currency, CBDCs have many clear advantages in increasing both the mobility of cash and financial inclusion, while subtly changing our relationship with our financial institutions and money itself.

That said, CBDCs are not a panacea. They will bring new issues that may be just as difficult to deal with as some of the problems they replace. In short, they are a disruptive technology that will make the world a better place, but as with all disruptive technologies, they will be a lightning rod for trouble. The good they can do and their impact will undoubtedly be profound. Still, the digital CBDC future of our dreams—where our money miraculously transfers freely anywhere on the globe in the blink of an eye—will be hard-earned and will require considerable effort to implement and sustain.

WHAT TO EXPECT WHEN CHINA'S AND OTHER CBDCS HIT THE MARKET

I will certainly greet each new CBDC that hits the market with enthusiasm, but do not expect this reaction to be universal. The movement of money is highly politicized, and assuming that governments will all be thrilled when political or trade rivals (or even outright enemies) launch CBDCs is to live in denial. These launches will be hard fought, and you can expect pushback from rival governments on their use.

China's General Secretary and President Xi said it best while addressing the G20 Leaders' Summit in November 2020. He said that he hoped that China's CBDC would be met with an "open and accommodating attitude." That is about the best any country can hope for when launching its CBDC. Replumbing the financial system and rebuilding global trade to accept digital currency is a long and slow process that speaks to Xi's later comments about "risks and challenges." Working at both a country and institutional level takes time.

With every new CBDC launched, there will be a flurry of news coverage with pictures of happy people using the CBDC on their phones, just like the ones we will see in China. It's only after the party is over that the hard work begins. Getting a substantial portion of the population to use CBDC for simple domestic payments may be hard enough if psychological barriers to change are high (though this is not an issue in China). Harder still will be getting regional trade partners on board to accept CBDC in cross-border trade, which may require considerable diplomatic finesse—all the while knowing that certain countries are just going to say no.

China is preparing for this future. The signing of the Regional Comprehensive Economic Partnership (RCEP) with fourteen other nations is an example of the kind of partnership required to gain cross-border acceptance of CBDCs. The RCEP is a game-changer for Asia that unites trade for 30% of the world's population, and a like percentage of GDP. Notably, the agreement excludes the US. The idea behind RCEP is to slash tariffs and increase market access, a boon for the entire region, but especially for China, given its status as the region's leading exporter.

While the RCEP is at its core a trade agreement, fintech and the CBDC will be a major part of this effort. China is already announcing that most RCEP countries, many of which are included in the BRI, will be trialing China's blockchain trade and shipping platforms to streamline the flow of goods under RCEP. Indonesia and China have already announced their desire to revalue trade in their local currencies, the Rupiah and RMB. Once the partners are on these trade platforms, the adoption of China's CBDC will not be far behind.

While China's CBDC may be welcomed by some of its neighbors and BRI trading partners, it's clear that the US, and potentially the UK, will not receive it with open arms. Indeed China's CBDC will likely meet the cold shoulder shown to Huawei's 5G service. The analogy is almost exact. Both are tech products, and both are considered a way for China to spread its infrastructure and influence worldwide. US foreign policy seems to dictate that the threat be stopped at all costs. Whether the US chooses to actively dissuade countries from using China's CBDC (as it does Huawei's 5G technology) remains to be seen, but to expect a warm welcome would be unwise.

POTENTIAL GOVERNMENT RESPONSES

Pondering the US's likely response to China's CBDC, whether "open and accommodating" or overtly hostile as with Huawei, brings up a significant issue. What is the range of policy options governments can use to restrict or outright ban the use of another country's CBDC? While this topic may seem a bit dour, recent blocks and bans on TikTok and WeChat in the US and even more extensive blocks of China's apps in India show that we need to be prepared for this eventuality. It is likely that China's new CBDC, or someone else's, will cause a country to feel threatened and it will potentially lash out despite the potential good that CBDC technology can do.

Bans

The most benign act against a foreign CBDC would be a ban, meaning a restriction in use within the objecting country, making it illegal to use the CBDC to conduct transactions locally. Two ready examples of this serve as guidance. China bans the use of cryptocurrency as a means of payment within its borders. The ownership of cryptocurrency is permitted, but its use in payment and avoiding currency export controls is prohibited. Despite the ban, some US$ 50 billion is reported to have been transferred out of China via cryptocurrency in 2019. This is a perfect illustration of how difficult banning a digital currency or service can be.

The US also attempted to ban WeChat in the US, with no less than two bans, the first blocked in the courts as a violation of free speech. The first Trump executive order banning WeChat "prohibits any transaction by any person, or with respect to any property, subject to the jurisdiction of the United States, with WeChat's parent Tencent Holdings Ltd." Interestingly, buried in the executive order was a reference to instantaneous payments, that shows the kind of language that will inevitably be used against CBDCs: "I find that because of the ability to transfer funds or other assets instantaneously, prior notice to such persons of measures to be taken pursuant to this order would render those measures ineffectual."

So the ban gives no notice to WeChat users that the payment service will become illegal, because of the instantaneous nature of money transfer. It is likely that someday we will see a CBDC receive the same treatment. The US's first WeChat ban was blocked in the courts, and the second, on both WeChat Pay and Alipay, is in limbo given the change in presidents in the US. Still, the concept that a US company operating in China could be potentially banned from accepting Alipay and WeChat payments in China is sobering. It is not impossible to imagine a US or other company being similarly ordered not to take China's CBDC in trade payments. This would be relatively quickly confirmed with standard auditing and could represent a path for dissuading CBDC usage.

Blocks

Blocks are the next step up the ladder for governments to restrict access to CBDCs. As we saw with China's inability to curtail cryptocurrency, blocking a digital service can represent a real technological challenge. For blockchain-based decentralized networks like those used in cryptocurrencies, it's unclear exactly what or where to block to disable the decentralized service. Many users will turn to virtual private networks (VPNs) to tunnel out of the country and access another's internet. For example, a resident of China may watch US-based Netflix by using a VPN. (Not that I have had such experience.) This makes the transfer of CBDCs by blockchain networks relatively resilient to blocking. Given this, China may see the advantages of routing international transfers of its CBDC through its "blockchain service network."

In contrast, blocking centralized services like TikTok is potentially feasible and was examined in detail during the US's TikTok ban. The government could prohibit the downloading of the apps, followed by a mandatory block on internet service providers and hosting services from transmitting the content. Of course China itself provides the best example of how effectively centralized services like Facebook or Google can be blocked. This still leaves VPNs to tunnel out of the country for access, but, by and large, a CBDC run on a centralized network could be disabled using these techniques.

Sanctions

Leaving the digital realm, we can also imagine governments potentially using traditional sanctions to take revenge on a country for the purported damage arising from use of a CBDC. Punishing perceived digital infractions via non-digital means will probably become the norm given the challenges in applying digital blocks and bans. Sanctions aren't new; the US has used them liberally throughout the years, including noteworthy examples against Cuba, in place since 1962, or more recently against Russia for the occupation of Crimea in 2014. While sanctions' efficacy may be debated, at least they represent a response that can be graduated from light to heavy depending on the level of infraction. This is well-worn territory, and all governments understand the rules. China, whose companies were placed on various US blacklists during the Trump administration, knows their impact better than most.

Not without irony, the most likely reason a sanction might be placed on a country for CBDC use is for active violations of existing sanctions enforced by the US, EU, or the UN. CBDCs can be used as sanction busters, and the very thought of the imposition of further, stricter sanctions may dissuade some from using them in this manner. Sanction enforcement is an integral part of SWIFT and the international banking system, which maintain impressively long lists of individuals and organizations with limitations on their banking access. CBDCs represent a way for money to flow in and out of these countries which would evade detection and reduce the efficacy of sanctions. This is a real hot-button issue and of great concern for the US and others. As a new tool against sanctions, CBDCs will be pawns in the great geopolitical game and the first fintech product to achieve such stature.

All this said, I believe the fear that China and its new CBDC will go to work busting sanctions soon after launch is highly exaggerated. China has too much invested in its CBDC to draw international ire by positioning it as a sanction buster. China wants to use its digital RMB to reduce its reliance on US dollar-based trade. To do this, China will have to keep the digital RMB's image clean to attract international users. To raise the US's wrath by using its CBDC to bust sanctions, China would be reducing the number of potential users for its new currency and defeat the very purpose of its existence. The US's global response to Huawei gives some idea of what they might do. In addition, China's trade deals and bartering with sanctioned countries haven't gone unnoticed by the US. To drag the digital RMB into that quagmire would be a public relations disaster and stifle global uptake of its new currency.

The existence of CBDCs will raise levels of suspicion to new heights, and may prompt hair-trigger responses. The unintended consequences of sanctions can be onerous. In September 2019, the clients of China's COSCO shipping company, the world's largest shipowner, found out the hard way. Two of COSCO's subsidiaries were targeted for evading sanctions, causing clients to panic and to stop transporting oil on *all* COSCO tankers globally. This caused a massive increase in oil transport costs throughout Asia, which inadvertently penalized countries that had nothing to do with the sanctions. CBDCs may make such events more likely, which presents an entirely new problem generated by digital currency.

Cut banking access and digital attack

The next two levels of attack are what some might refer to as "nuclear options." We should all hope that neither is ever used by a country, but I would be remiss in not mentioning them. The first would be to retaliate against CBDC use by cutting access to traditional bank networks. While China's CBDC was designed to reduce dependence on the dollar and potentially deal with this eventuality, it would be a tremendous blow if it happened before gestation was full. China's CBDC or account-based RMB CIPS systems would take years to recover from this type of shock, given China's dependence on the dollar.

When dealing with recent sanctions, Russia made it clear that it would consider curbing its banks' activities on international networks "an act of economic war." China undoubtedly would react similarly to such a move and draw a similar line in the sand. It is beyond the scope of this book to speculate on what would cause such an act. Suffice it to say that this would certainly be front page news, and CBDCs would probably not be our primary concern given the dramatic events required for such a conflict to unfold.

Slightly less nuclear but equally aggressive would be sovereign digital attacks on China's or other CBDC networks. Cyberwarfare is an increasing reality, and it would be naïve to think that governments will not consider aggressions on CBDC systems. Perhaps this might be viewed as a lesser strike than cutting off countries from the banking system because it involves subterfuge rather than a call to arms, but it would nonetheless be a significant attack that would draw a harsh response. All CBDC networks, including China's, are vulnerable.

One need only look at the regular attacks on cryptocurrency exchanges and networks to see their vulnerabilities. One occurred in January 2019, when a sophisticated 51% attack was launched against digital currency exchange Coinbase's Ethereum blockchain network. A hacker gained access to more than half of the network's computing power to rewrite the transaction history (by controlling more than 50% of the processing network) and double-spent digital coins to the tune of US$ 1.1 million. Coinbase claims no currency was stolen, but blockchain's air of unhackability was quickly shattered. In 2019, some US$ 292 million was stolen in twelve major hacks on various exchanges. Ascribing such events to inadequacies that CBDCs can easily avoid is wishful thinking. While China's CBDC is immune to 51% attacks, if a hostile nation's collective digital expertise is focused on disrupting a CBDC network, they'll likely find a way.

IMPACT ON BANKS

CBDC's greatest legacy will be in removing the friction associated with cash movement. China's CBDC will continue the work already started by the mobile payment platforms in freeing money from banks' payment systems; once enacted in the West, CBDCs will provide citizens with their first real taste of free cash movement. I do not exaggerate in saying that will be transformational, but at the same time it will be less disruptive than many make it out to be.

For payment executives, compression on payment margins is not a new phenomenon. Digital upgrades, regulatory pressure, and new fintech competitors all take their toll on payment revenue streams. The pressure is so great that in a survey of banker and payment executives conducted by Accenture, 71% said that payments were on their way to becoming free. The advanced schedule of CBDC development brought on by the pandemic will only accelerate this trend.

China's banks will have a projected loss of US$ 61 billion in payment revenue, attributable to the mobile payment platforms, over the six years starting in 2019, according to Accenture research. While a big number at US$ 10 billion per year, this is on a 2019 total revenue stream of US$ 292 billion, showing that it is not a disaster so much as a slow bleed. While the accuracy of these estimates can be debated, given the opaque nature of China's banks, it's evident that no banks failed or were put in a disadvantaged position because of mobile payment. While it is difficult to calculate the additional cost to banks' payment business with the launch of China's CBDC, it too will not overly imperil the banks' bottom lines.

China's use of a two-tier CBDC structure strives to reduce the impact of the CBDC on the banking system. This tactic is not unique. Many countries will employ the same architecture to minimize the impact of their new CBDCs. The frequent claims that we are all hear—i.e., that CBDCs will disrupt banks—are grossly overstated and dependent on the notion that the government will unthinkingly adopt a CBDC architecture that is overtly hostile to banks. That is an unlikely scenario and a scare tactic designed to be alarmist.

What governments, including China's, cannot do is return lost revenue to banks' payment business. CBDCs will make payment free, and this is revenue that will be forever lost to the banking system. While CBDCs may give China's banks a chance to regain customers through their ability to provide instant payment, their ability to charge for this service, as they did with credit cards, is gone. This will not be unique to China but a trend that will go worldwide. As customers, we should all cheer, but bankers may have a different perspective.

Working off Accenture's estimates and assuming that CBDC uptake reaches half of mobile payments in the next few years, an unlikely large market share, China's banks could see the loss of an additional US$ 5 billion off of payment revenue. Not a disaster, as payments are but one of many revenue streams for banks, but all Chinese banks have begun to adjust downward their payment revenue estimates over the next decade to account for the new reality.

Accenture predicts revenue for the global payments industry of approximately US$ 2 trillion by 2025, with as much as 15% of banks' total global payment revenue of US$ 280 billion likely to be displaced by digital payments and non-bank competitors. These are big numbers that do not factor in to the introduction of CBDC, which will make them even bigger.

IMPACT ON CREDIT CARDS

Credit card companies are perhaps the most vulnerable to disruption by CBDCs. How can credit card companies justify service charges in the range of two or three percent when CBDCs will do the job for free? Undoubtedly, governments will seek to maintain credit card companies' relevance just as they will with banks. They have no interest in disrupting them out of business, but there is no way to guarantee their payment revenue stream. If cash transfers are free using CBDCs, the card companies will inevitably feel the pain of lost revenue.

The most likely outcome for the West's card companies will be similar to the PBOC's solution for its digital payment platforms. In China, the PBOC declared that Alipay and WeChat Pay are the wallets while CBDC is the currency in the wallet. Visa and Mastercard will most likely also become wallet providers whose networks and cards will carry either CBDC transactions or traditional credit card transactions, depending on users' needs. This guarantees their continued existence but offers no guarantee of maintaining their rich revenue streams.

Card companies will have an additional drag on revenue with increased resistance to the credit cards' high rates. With the advent of big data-based lending and CBDCs in the West, consumers seeking credit will have options that are just as immediate. This will cause broad-based rate compression for these companies as consumer credit rates normalize downwards. With CBDCs, the ability to get a digital loan from another source just as users in China get "310" loans (three minutes to apply, one second to be approved, and zero human involvement) from Alipay will be the norm. Credit card companies will have to work harder to keep people on credit card debt when better offers with equal or improved convenience become the norm.

On the positive side for card companies, they are masters of putting together loyalty programs through points, discounts, memberships, or other amenities that keep users locked into their cards. Also, they consider their cardholders members of a platform, an inherent advantage in a digital world. I would argue that they are better at this than banks and have a more intuitive understanding of keeping clients happy. Perhaps because they are used to an environment where users are free to switch cards, client retention has been an important metric and priority. The credit card companies will have to put their client-centric skills to work as we head into a new era of CBDCs. If they don't, the impact will be significant.

Card companies like MasterCard are already looking to ensure their survival in a CBDC-dominated future. They have gone to great effort to build significant portfolios of blockchain patents and even published open testing environments for government CBDC efforts. They are working to be part of the CBDC eco-system, not disrupted by it.

CROSS-BORDER INTEROPERABILITY

In its most basic sense, interoperability is the ability of one CBDC system to "talk" to another so that CBDC can be transferred smoothly from one system to another. It is at the root of the utopian dream for a global payment network where digital payments flow smoothly from one country to another without bank charges and punishing foreign exchange rates. There is no known, specific method to achieve interoperability, so it is more of a concept than a unique technology that can be quickly built into a new CBDC design. Utopian dreams aside, interoperability is a worthy goal as it holds the potential to simplify cross-border payments greatly.

As far as China is concerned, the dream of CBDC interoperability is akin to sitting around the campfire holding hands and singing "Kumbaya." It's a nice dream, but it isn't going to happen. China's CBDC was designed to extricate it from what it considers the constraints imposed by the Western, US-dominated financial system. Interoperability, the ability to connect China's CBDC with other countries' systems, would mean surrendering the independence of its CBDC to the Western financial system all over again. So plug-and-play interoperability with other CBDCs is not high on the list of priorities for China's CBDC.

This is not to say that China's CBDC won't someday "play nice" with other digital currencies; it certainly will. The PBOC's participation in the Multiple CBDC (m-CBDC) Bridge project with the Hong Kong Monetary Authority, Central Bank of the United Arab Emirates, Bank of Thailand and BIS Innovation Hub is an example of how China is willing to work with Belt and Road Initiative countries to make their CBDCs potentially interoperable. This project is also a good example of how China will tightly control access to *its* CBDC network through a very clearly defined and limited gateway. It will likely be considered a low-level interoperability that falls short of the goals of many in the blockchain community to have one blockchain connect directly to all others and automatically transfer assets. I'm sorry to disappoint fans of interoperability, but this feature also inevitably brings rules, sanctions, and blacklists that are by no means universally acknowledged or welcomed.

Another technical problem with interoperability is that CBDCs do not have common design standards. So far, each

CBDC in pilot phase or production is custom-built to the unique design specifications that suit each country. The Bahamas' Sand Dollar and China's DC/EP couldn't be more different. This means that the ability to communicate between an account-based CBDC system in one country like Sweden and a token-based CBDC system like China's is by no means guaranteed, without constructing a relatively sophisticated purpose-built bridge. Imagine such bridges being built across multiple currencies, each with a different design, and the inherent challenges of such an undertaking begin to take shape. China's participation in the m-CBDC trials which will try to connect three different CBDC systems using a "private blockchain" or Distributed Ledger Technology (DLT) system sheds some light on the magnitude of the technical challenge.

That isn't to say that there is no hope for interoperability and the real promise of smooth cross-border cash transfer it offers to countries whose CBDCs participate. The Bank of International Settlements Innovation Hub recently hosted representatives from the Bank of Canada, Bank of England, Bank of Japan, Central Bank of Sweden, European Central Bank, The Federal Reserve, and the Swiss National Bank to discuss CBDC design choices, including interoperability. China was notably absent making its subsequent participation in m-CBDC a pleasant surprise. The report issued following this meeting made it clear that interoperability, while desirable for cross-border payments, faces many technical and legal hurdles. While the report raised the issue of creating standards for CBDCs to encourage interoperability, it also warned that "Different legal and regulatory frameworks present a significant obstacle to cross-border payments. Harmonizing these frameworks would be a challenge."

In legal and regulatory frameworks China's PBOC also appears to have a plan with the shock announcement in February 2021 of a joint venture (JV) company with none other than its nemesis SWIFT. The new company named "Finance Gateway Information Services Co." has the PBOC's digital currency research institute as its primary shareholder with Chinas Cross-Border Interbank

Payment System (CIPS) and the Payment and Clearing Association of China also participating. The JV "will be able to obtain necessary licenses for local network management activities and its services will be limited in scope and entirely focused on maintaining compliance with applicable regulations in China," It appears that SWIFT will assist the PBOC in licensing its CBDC cash transfer operations a task with which it is well acquainted. That the PBOC would enlist the assistance of SWIFT shows both its intent in taking its CBDC international and its deal-making prowess. SWIFT already works with the PBOC on the CIPS transfer system, so partnering with SWIFT on its CBDC is not entirely unprecedented. Given the CBDCs intent of reducing reliance on SWIFT, it can certainly be seen as ironic.

The m-CBDC project will not be alone in its search for a means of providing blockchain-based cross-border CBDC interoperability. Several leading blockchain vendors are now promoting their products as the missing link required to fulfill CBDC's promise of interoperability. More than a few are likely onto something even if the CBDCs haven't been built yet. Tightly linked trade currency pairs like euro and sterling or euro and Swedish krona will have both the similarity in regulatory frameworks and the financial incentive to build some meaningful form of interoperability—just as China is doing now with its BRI partners. It isn't just a utopian dream; it's a way to link economies and decrease the costs associated with cross-border trade—potentially big wins that will make this a popular topic as more CBDCs launch.

REDUCING DOLLAR HEGEMONY

The biggest question on everyone's mind is whether China's pursuit of a digital currency can make a dent in the dollar's hegemony. What is clear is that China isn't wasting time. It is enlisting its BRI partners to join in with them in creating both CBDCs and the network to trade them. China is also wisely enlisting the assistance of international organizations like SWIFT and the BIS to assure participants that what they are building lives up to international standards. These are smart moves that show China's good-faith effort to build a system that will be broadly attractive to users and not draw unwarranted suspicion. China's pace of development is blistering, its organizational acumen without parallel, and most importantly, its partners are eager to join. All of these factors bolster prospects that the digital RMB can help China reduce dollar dependence.

Initially, the vast majority of China's partners will not have native CBDCs. They will need to convert their currency to China's CBDC in order to gain access to its new "digital entry token." Here again, China is well organized and has a clear strategy to motivate users. As a means of enticing users, any trade partners who question whether using CBDC is worth the effort will be politely shown the advantages in both time and cost of using China's digital trade platforms. Given the no-loss nature of the transaction, why wouldn't trade partners try? It is suspiciously similar to what AliPay and WeChat Pay offered noodle shops when rolling out their digital payment systems: "Try us for free, what do you have to lose?" We know how that story ended.

The advantages of using these digital trade platforms have already been quantified within China's Greater Bay Area but are still unproven with regional trade partners. The new RCEP will give China's neighbors the first real opportunity to try these platforms. How well they are received, even if not yet using CBDC, will have a significant impact on the adoption of China's CBDC; we should follow these developments carefully. If there is any choke point in China's CBDC strategy, it is that the trade platforms must deliver real monetary benefits in order to entice users to switch.

In chapter 14, I showed that the potential market size for China's CBDC in global trade will easily exceed that of the euro. What cannot be shown definitively is whether the incentives and convenience it offers will be enough to win over users. That answer won't be known for some years to come. The launch of the CBDC into international trade will likely be in 2023, but because the transformation will be gradual, we need to look at adoption over a ten-year horizon as I did with all of my projections. There will be a tendency for some to claim failure if there isn't a long queue for users when the system is first opened for international trade. I do not believe that this expectation is realistic. I anticipate, as I think China does, a long slow build-up. The savings in using the CBDC will need to be quantified with each trade and the system will win users market by market. China's relief from dollar dependence will be slow but deliberate.

Many will see the RMB as an unworthy store of value and be unwilling to break their fixation on the paradigm of dollar-based trade. China's CBDC will not be the first digital currency to break paradigms. A few brief years ago Bitcoin enthusiasts were widely mocked by investment professionals; now Bitcoin is considered an investment worthy of institutional investors. I certainly do not predict an explosion in CBDC popularity to match Bitcoin's, but I do think that the rapid change of heart that we saw with Bitcoin may very well match that of digital RMB.

Granted, many still don't like Bitcoin, but even its detractors would be hard-pressed to claim it was unworthy of attention given its uptake by institutions. China's CBDC may accomplish a similar feat for the RMB. Many may still not like the RMB, but if its digital version is effective in reducing costs in cross-border trade it would be impossible to claim it was unworthy of further investigation. The key to this transition, and a difficult paradigm for many to break, is acknowledging that the holding times of China's CBDC in a trade transaction may be as short as hours or minutes. Using China's CBDC is less an endorsement of the RMB as a long-term store of value, and more an acknowledgment of the practicality, low cost and convenience of transacting with digital currency.

China's CBDC was never designed to supplant the dollar, and the PBOC has never made the claim it would. Instead, China is claiming first mover advantage by launching its CBDC in what it considers "a new battlefield of competition between sovereign states." One thing that is beyond debate is that the world genuinely wants cheaper, faster, and more convenient currency transfers. Grassroots adoption of cryptocurrency and the rise of fintechs promising low-cost currency transfer prove this beyond a doubt. China's CBDC will provide its users with the tangible advantages of digital currency at a time when there are simply no alternatives. Timing is certainly in China's favor, and without competition, it's hard to see how its CBDC could fail in helping to reduce dollar dependence in the short to mid-term. More insidious is the long-term revaluation of commodities and services trade into RMB that will follow, with a significant impact on dollar hegemony.

AN "OPEN AND ACCOMMODATING" FUTURE

Our shared "cashless" CBDC future will be bright. While I may have dwelled in this final chapter on what could go wrong with CBDCs, there is much more that can go right. We are all in a transitional period in our new digital world. The coronavirus showed us just how much we can accomplish using digital services and pushed forward the timetable for adopting pervasive digital lifestyles. The natural fallout of this digitization is that money will go digital to match the immediacy and speed that we are accustomed to with all of our digital services. Waiting for the transfer to go through or paying high fees is no longer acceptable.

CBDCs are a natural evolutionary step; digital societies require digital money. I've tried to show the real benefits that China realized through its experiment digitizing payment and how it changed a nation. What should be clear is that there is an interplay between digital payment and a society becoming increasingly digital. They are two, mutually dependent sides of the same digital coin. I already see references to launching a CBDC as an "arms race" or a "cure-all" for all digital ills. China may be the first to launch a CBDC, but it did so in conjunction with a push to build its digital society.

China's digital economy accounts for an astounding 36.2% of GDP, primarily driven by China's unparalleled use of Version 1.0 digital payment. China's motivation to launch its CBDC is clear; it sees its CBDC as necessary to drive even broader societal digitization. Both the US and UK, with digital economies at 6.9% and 7.7% of GDP respectively, will strive to emulate this advancement as a strategic necessity and a step toward the future. Launching a CBDC will help, but certainly won't get either country to China's 36% figure without emphasis on building a more pervasive role for digital services in society. CBDCs are only half of a two-part solution.

Over the next few years, we can watch China's experience with CBDCs as we await their arrival in our home countries. That doesn't mean that all solutions will copy China's, but most will likely have many features familiar to readers of this book. For further confirmation of how the West borrows China's fintech, readers should note that both PayPal and Google's new Plex checking accounts in the US use QR codes. The influence from China on these systems to those who have read this far is obvious, while to others, the use of QR codes will simply be an oddity or a nice new convenience. CBDCs will be the same, with some elements of what we will use in the future undoubtedly influenced by China if we know where to look.

CBDCs raise the stakes for digital payment in the West just as they do in "cashless" China. CBDCs represent a way to embed digital payment more deeply in every part of our lives and offers a vision of the future featuring both opportunity *and* fear, depending on your perspective. For those enamored with the ease of use and mobility provided by digital currencies, they are a godsend. They represent the abandonment of disease-spreading paper and coin, the reduction of black market economies, the promise of greater inclusion, and a better way to distribute the financial aid critical to so many during these difficult times. To others, they are our digital overseers perpetually monitoring, imposing government's will, and robbing us of our illusion of privacy in a world that is already highly digital. My hope is that readers will be in the first group, paying no heed to those exploiting people's fear by promoting a dystopian vision of our cashless future.

What must be acknowledged is that we owe many of our advances in digital payment to entrepreneurs like Jack and Pony Ma, the founders of Alipay and WeChat Pay, respectively, and others like them. Visionaries who start fintech companies are on a mission to merge technology and finance to make the world a better place. In China and the West, many recent advances in payments were born from fintech companies who thought they could build a better payment mousetrap, and they did. Were it not for such individuals, incumbent financial institutions would never be incentivized to change.

Similarly, CBDCs owe their existence squarely to cryptocurrencies and those who saw a future in digitizing currency. While I understand opinions on cryptocurrencies may be divided, the CBDCs we will all soon be using owe their existence to them and to those who envisioned a different kind of money. Ironically, many of those who invented cryptocurrencies look at CBDCs with disdain. Still, we have to acknowledge their contribution even if our appreciation is unwelcome.

What I hope for most of all is an "open and accommodating" cashless future for all—one where governments and the financial institutions controlling payments in your country are open to the potential benefits of digital payment, and to accommodating the inevitable, evolutionary changes in how we use money. I don't think this is asking too much; it's a process that is inexorable.

Being on the cutting edge like China may not be practical for all countries. I am in no way a proponent of the immediate adoption of CBDCs by all countries to pursue a utopian digital dream. Instead, I see this as an evolutionary process, with each country weighing the relative advantages and deciding when the timing is right. That said, in an ever-accelerating digital world, the penalties for delay can be significant. If going cashless can deliver for your country some degree of the benefits it did for China, delay will be costly.

As we wait for our cashless future to come into focus, I urge you to continue to follow China's advances in the news or even better, come to China to see it for yourself. China gives us a glimpse into the future to show us what we can expect, and, most importantly, how we can prepare for going cashless. The future is at hand, if our eyes are open and our minds are willing.

POSTLOGUE: CBDC MAJOR MILESTONES

China's CBDC hasn't yet launched, and what follows is an incomplete list of likely news items to be aware of as China and other CBDCs ready for launch. The timing of these events is impossible to predict, so their order is only roughly chronological.

2021

- China's ongoing DC/EP tests
- Integration of DC/EP into Alipay and WeChat Pay wallets
- China's state-owned enterprises announce salary or benefits paid in DC/EP

2022

- China's Winter Olympics, full launch or trial stages only?
- International testing of DC/EP within Greater Bay Area trade between Shenzhen with Macau and Hong Kong.
- Japan CBDC trials.
- A full launch of DC/EP in China, likely already widely used.
- Hong Kong announces its role as DC/EP hub for international trade.
- First international tests with a BRI country, likely also a country within the RCEP.
- Swedish central bank readies CBDC launch.

2023

- Digital euro trials.
- Singapore announces DC/EP connectivity with its banking systems.

- International trades normalized with select RCEP and BRI countries.
- Launch of DC/EP-embedded smart contracts.
- Use of selected interest rates or exchange rates within BRI.
- Announcement of limited RMB capital controls replaced by DC/EP-controlled capital.

BIBLIOGRAPHY

Accenture. "Accenture Global Payments Pulse Survey,"
September 9, 2019. https://www.accenture.com/us-en/
insights/banking/payments-pulse-survey-two-ways-win.

Access to Cash Review. *The Access to Cash Review - Final
Report*. Access to Cash Review, 2019. https://www.
accesstocash.org.uk/media/1087/final-report-final-web.pdf.

Ant Group. *Ant Group H Share IPO (Prospectus)*.
Citi, JP Morgan, Morgan Stanley, CICC, 2020.
https://www1.hkexnews.hk/listedco/listconews/
sehk/2020/1026/2020102600165.pdf.

APCO Worldwide. *China's 12th Five-Year Plan: How It
Actually Works and What's in Store for the Next Five Years*,
2010. http://www.export.gov.il/UploadFiles/03_2012/
Chinas12thFive-YearPlan.pdf.

App Annie. "The Average Smartphone User Accessed Close
to 40 Apps per Month in 2017." App Annie, February 2,
2018. https://www.appannie.com/en/insights/market-data/
apps-used-2017/.

Auer, Raphael, and Rainer Bohme. "The Technology of
Retail Central Bank Digital Currency." *BIS Quarterly
Review*, March 2020. https://www.bis.org/publ/qtrpdf/r_
qt2003j.pdf.

Azzara, Mike. "Challenges of China's B2B Payments Systems
for Customers, Suppliers & Distributors | American
Express." Accessed March 10, 2021. https://www.
americanexpress.com/us/foreign-exchange/articles/
b2b-payment-system-challenges-in-china/.

Bain. "As Retail Banks Leak Value, Here's How They Can
Stop It." Bain, November 18, 2019. https://www.

bain.com/insights/as-retail-banks-leak-value-here s-how-they-can-stop-it/.

Bank for International Settlements. "Central Bank Digital Currencies," March 2018. https://www.bis.org/cpmi/publ/d174.pdf.

———. "Central Bank Digital Currencies: Foundational Principles and Core Features." Bank for International Settlements, October 9, 2020. https://www.bis.org/publ/othp33.htm.

———. "III. Central Banks and Payments in the Digital Era." *BIS Annual Economic Report*, June 24, 2020. https://www.bis.org/publ/arpdf/ar2020e3.htm.

———. "Payment, Clearing and Settlement Systems in China," Red Book, 2012. https://www.bis.org/cpmi/publ/d105_cn.pdf.

———. "Total Credit to Households and NPISHs, Adjusted for Breaks, for China." FRED, Federal Reserve Bank of St. Louis, January 1, 2006. https://fred.stlouisfed.org/series/QCNHAM770A.

Bank of Japan. "(Research Lab) Summary of the Report of the Study Group on Legal Issues Regarding Central Bank Digital Currency : 日本銀行 Bank of Japan." Bank of Japan. Accessed March 10, 2021. https://www.boj.or.jp/en/research/wps_rev/lab/lab19e03.htm/.

BBC News. "Google Plans to Track Credit Card Spending." *BBC News*, May 26, 2017, sec. Technology. https://www.bbc.com/news/technology-40027706.

Bikes, Sonali Paul, Stefica Nicol. "Coronavirus Can Last 28 Days on Glass and Currency, Study Finds." *Reuters*, October 13, 2020. https://www.reuters.com/article/health-coronavirus-australia-study-idUSKBN26X03F.

Binance. "First Look: China's Central Bank Digital Currency." Binance Research, August 28, 2019. https://research.binance.com/en/analysis/china-cbdc.

Bindseil, Ulrich. "Tiered CBDC and the Financial System." Working Paper Series. European Central Bank, January

2020. https://www.ecb.europa.eu/pub/pdf/scpwps/ecb. wp2351-c8c18bbd60.en.pdf.

Bloomberg News. "Ant Considers Holding Company with Regulation Similar to Bank, Sources Say." Bloomberg, December 29, 2020. https://www.bloomberg.com/news/ articles/2020-12-29/ant-said-to-mull-holding-compan y-with-regulation-similar-to-bank.

———. "China Plans Caps on Ant's Lending Rates to Control Risk." Bloomberg, September 7, 2020. https:// www.bloomberg.com/news/articles/2020-09-07/ china-said-to-plan-caps-on-ant-s-lending-rates-to- control-risk.

———. "Jack Ma's $290 Billion Loan Machine Is Changing Chinese Banking." Bloomberg, July 27, 2019. https://www.bloomberg.com/news/ articles/2019-07-28/jack-ma-s-290-billion-loa n-machine-is-changing-chinese-banking.

Boar, Codruta, Henry Holden, and Amber Wadsworth. "Impending Arrival – a Sequel to the Survey on Central Bank Digital Currency." Bank for International Settlements (BIS), January 2020. https://www.bis.org/ publ/bppdf/bispap107.pdf.

Banque de France. "Book « Payments and Market Infrastructures in the Digital Era »," June 28, 2019. https://publications.banque-france. fr/en/economic-and-financial-publications/ book-payments-and-market-infrastructures-digital-era.

Brahm, Laurence. "Yuan Globalization: The World Needs a New Reserve Currency." China Daily, January 31, 2019. https://www.chinadaily.com.cn/a/201901/31/ WS5c528b4ea3106c65c34e78c0.html.

BrandZ. "BrandZ Global Top 100 Most Valuable Brands." Accessed March 10, 2021. https://www.brandz.com/ brands.

Brennan, Matthew. "Mark Zuckerberg Is on WeChat! - China Channel." Accessed March 10, 2021. https://chinachannel.co/mark-zuckerberg-wechat-facebook/.

Brown, Tanner. "How the Latest Steps by Alipay and WeChat Bring China Closer to Replacing Cash with Cellphones." MarketWatch. Accessed March 10, 2021. https://www.marketwatch.com/story/how-the-latest-steps-by-alipay-and-wechat-bring-china-closer-to-replacing-cash-with-cellphones-2019-11-06.

BSN Development Association. *Blockchain Service Network (BSN) Introduction White Paper V1.05*. BSN Development Association, 2019. https://bsnbase.io/g/main/documentation.

Bureau, E. T. "Innovation Could Help Companies Survive US-China Conflict: Tencent." *EnterpriseTalk* (blog), May 23, 2019. https://enterprisetalk.com/news/innovation-could-help-companies-survive-us-china-conflict-ceo-tencent/.

Carney, Mark. "The Promise of FinTech –Something New Under the Sun?" Speech by Mark Carney, Governor of the Bank of England presented at the Deutsche Bundesbank G20 conferenceon "Digitising finance, financial inclusion and financial literacy," Wiesbaden, January 25, 2017. https://www.bis.org/review/r170126b.pdf.

CBNEditor. "AiBank, MYBank and WeBank Apply AI and Big Data to Online Lending in China." *China Banking News* (blog), September 19, 2018. https://www.chinabankingnews.com/2018/09/19/aibank-mybank-webank-apply-ai-big-data-online-lending-china/.

———. "Ant Group's IPO Scuppered by China's Launch of New Online Micro-Loan Rules, Will Face Major Re-Valuation as a Consequence: Analysts." *China Banking News* (blog), November 5, 2020. https://www.chinabankingnews.com/2020/11/05/ant-groups-ipo-scuppered-by-china

s-launch-of-new-online-micro-loan
-rules-will-face-major-re-valuatio
n-as-a-consequence-analysts/.

———. "China's Consumer Credit Balance
Expected to Exceed 10T Yuan by 2020." *China
Banking News* (blog), January 21, 2019. https://
www.chinabankingnews.com/2019/01/21/
chinas-consumer-credit-balance-expected-t
o-exceed-10t-yuan-by-2020/.

———. "China's P2P Lending Sector Crushed out of
Existence Completely." *China Banking News* (blog),
November 30, 2020. https://www.chinabankingnews.
com/2020/11/30/chinas-p2p-lending-sector-crushed-ou
t-of-existence-completely/.

———. "Digital Retail Solutions Provider Dmall
Enters Strategic Cooperative Agreement with China
Construction Bank." *China Banking News* (blog),
November 21, 2019. https://www.chinabankingnews.
com/2019/11/21/dmall-and-china-construction-bank-ente
r-fintech-focused-strategic-cooperative-agreement/.

———. "Direct Banking the Necessary Path for Chinese
Finance: Minsheng White Paper." *China Banking News*
(blog), April 23, 2019. https://www.chinabankingnews.
com/2019/04/23/direct-banking-the-necessary-path-fo
r-chinese-finance-minsheng-white-paper/.

———. "Foreigners Misunderstand China's P2P Lending
Industry." *China Banking News* (blog), October 30,
2019. https://www.chinabankingnews.com/2019/10/30/
foreigners-misunderstand-chinas-p2p-lending-industry/.

———. "Online Banks Outperform China's Conventional
Lenders in 2018." *China Banking News* (blog), May 14,
2019. https://www.chinabankingnews.com/2019/05/14/
online-banks-outperform-chinas-conventional-lender
s-in-2018/.

———. "Online Payments Transactions Processed by Chinese
Banks Rise 37.14% YoY in 2019, Mobile Payments

up 67.57%." *China Banking News* (blog), March 19, 2020. https://www.chinabankingnews.com/2020/03/19/ chinas-online-payments-transactions-rise-3 7-14-yoy-in-2019-mobile-payments-up-67-57/.

———. "Tencent Leads Chinese Tech Giants in Online Banking." *China Banking News* (blog), February 26, 2019. https://www.chinabankingnews.com/2019/02/26/ tencent-leads-chinese-tech-giants-in-online-banking/.

———. "The Credit Reference Center of the People's Bank of China." *China Banking News* (blog). Accessed March 10, 2021. https://www.chinabankingnews.com/wiki/ the-credit-reference-center-of-the-peoples-bank-of-china/.

———. "White Paper on Chinese Direct Banking Says Smaller Lenders Are Taking the Lead." *China Banking News* (blog), January 22, 2019. https://www.chinabankingnews. com/2019/01/22/white-paper-on-chinese-direct-bankin g-says-smaller-lenders-are-taking-the-lead/.

———. "Xiong'an New Area to Trial Use of Digital Renminbi for Cross-Border Payments." *China Banking News* (blog), September 2, 2020. https://www.chinabankingnews. com/2020/09/02/xiongan-new-area-to-trial-us e-of-digital-renminbi-for-cross-border-payments/.

CEIC. "China | Bank Card: No of Issued: Credit Card | Economic Indicators." CEIC Data. Accessed March 10, 2021. https://www.ceicdata.com/en/china/ bank-card-statistics/bank-card-no-of-issued-credit-card.

———. "China | CN: P2P Network Lending: No of Platform: Private | Economic Indicators." CEIC Data. Accessed March 10, 2021. https://www.ceicdata. com/en/china/p2p-lending-number-of-platform/ cn-p2p-network-lending-no-of-platform-private.

———. "China | Cross-Border RMB Settlement: Accumulation: Trade: Goods | Economic Indicators." CEIC Data. Accessed March 10, 2021. https://www. ceicdata.com/en/china/crossborder-rmb-settlement/ crossborder-rmb-settlement-accumulation-trade-goods.

————. "China Total Deposits, 1997 – 2021 Data." CEIC Data. Accessed March 10, 2021. https://www.ceicdata. com/en/indicator/china/total-deposits.

Central Bank of The Bahamas. "The Sand Dollar Is on Schedule for Gradual National Release to The Bahamas in Mid-October 2020," September 25, 2020. https:// www.centralbankbahamas.com/news/public-notices/ the-sand-dollar-is-on-schedule-for-gradual-national-releas e-to-the-bahamas-in-mid-october-2020.

CGTN. "China's Digital Economy Reaches $5 Trillion in 2019." China Global Television Network, July 6, 2020. https://news.cgtn.com/ news/2020-07-05/Value-added-of-China-s-digita l-economy-totals-5-trillion-USD-in-2019-RSMcs86HmM/ index.html#:~:text=China's%20digital%20economy%20 registered%2035.8,and%20Communications%20 Technology%20(CAICT).

————. "China's Digital Economy Reaches 36.2% of Its GDP in 2019." China Global Television Network, November 24, 2020. https://news.cgtn.com/ news/2020-11-24/China-s-digital-economy-reaches-3 6-2-of-its-GDP-in-2019-VFBgg6wpck/index. html#:~:text=China's%20digital%20economy%20 reached%2035.8,Cyberspace%20Studies%20(CACS)%20 said.

Chamber of Digital Commerce. "People's Bank of China Patent Repository: A Roadmap to the Digital Yuan." *Chamber of Digital Commerce* (blog). Accessed March 10, 2021. https://digitalchamber.org/pboc-patent-repository/.

Cheung, Eric. "Greater Bay Area: 10 Facts to Put It in Perspective." South China Morning Post, April 1, 2019. https://www.scmp.com/native/economy/ china-economy/topics/great-powerhouse/article/3002844/ greater-bay-area-10-facts-put.

Chin, Alex W. H., Julie T. S. Chu, Mahen R. A. Perera, Kenrie P. Y. Hui, Hui-Ling Yen, Michael C. W. Chan, Malik

Peiris, and Leo L. M. Poon. "Stability of SARS-CoV-2 in Different Environmental Conditions." *The Lancet Microbe* 1, no. 1 (May 1, 2020): e10. https://doi.org/10.1016/ S2666-5247(20)30003-3.

China Internet Watch. "Nearly Half China Smartphone Users to Use Proximity Mobile Payment by 2020." China Internet Watch, June 16, 2016. https://www.chinainternetwatch.com/17823/ proximity-mobile-payment-insights-2016/.

Cox, Joseph. "Leaked Document Shows How Big Companies Buy Credit Card Data on Millions of Americans." Vice, February 19, 2020. https://www.vice.com/en/ article/jged4x/envestnet-yodlee-credit-card-bank-dat a-not-anonymous.

Dalio, Ray. "Chapter 4: The Big Cycles of the Dutch and British Empires and Their Currencies." Linkedin, May 21, 2020. https://www.linkedin.com/pulse/ big-cycles-over-last-500-years-ray-dalio.

Davoodalhosseini, Mohammad, Francisco Rivadeneyra, and Yu Zhu. "CBDC and Monetary Policy," February 25, 2020. https://doi.org/10.34989/san-2020-4.

Der Spiegel. "NSA Spies on International Bank Transactions." Der Spiegel , September 15, 2013. https://www.spiegel.de/international/ world/spiegel-exclusive-nsa-spies-on-internationa l-bank-transactions-a-922276.html.

CoinDesk. "Digital Yuan May See a Hardware Wallet," September 1, 2020. https://www.coindesk.com/ digital-yuan-hardware-wallet.

EqualOcean. "Tencent's WeBank: A Tech-Driven Bank or a Licensed Fintech?" EqualOcean, August 4, 2020. https:// equalocean.com/analysis/20200804 14410.

———. "WeBank and a Changing Chinese Banking Sector." EqualOcean, August 4, 2020. https://equalocean.com/ analysis/20200804 14411.

European Central Bank. "An ECB Digital Currency – a Flight of Fancy?," May 11, 2020. https://www.ecb.europa.eu/press/key/date/2020/html/ecb.sp200511~01209cb324.en.html.

European Commission. "Passenger Name Record (PNR)." European Commission, Migration and Home Affairs, n.d. https://ec.europa.eu/home-affairs/what-we-do/policies/police-cooperation/information-exchange/pnr_en.

Evans, Peter C., and Annabelle Gawer. "The Rise of the Platform Enterpirse, A Global Survey." The Emerging Platform Economy Series, January 2016. https://www.thecge.net/app/uploads/2016/01/PDF-WEB-Platform-Survey_01_12.pdf.

EY Global. "EY Global Fintech Adoption Index 2019." Accessed March 9, 2021. https://www.ey.com/en_us/ey-global-fintech-adoption-index.

———. "How China's Open Banking Experiment Is Unfolding," December 17, 2018. https://www.ey.com/en_gl/banking-capital-markets/how-chinas-open-banking-experiment-is-unfolding.

Fannin, Rebecca. "China's Web Challenges The West By Innovating Faster, Like 15-Second Video Apps." Forbes, July 21, 2019. https://www.forbes.com/sites/rebeccafannin/2019/07/21/chinas-web-challenges-the-west-by-innovating-faster-like-15-second-video-apps/.

Faridi, Omar. "World's Most Valuable Fintech Ant Financial Partners with China Merchants Port to Launch Blockchain Platform for Local Banking and Logistics Businesses." Crowdfund Insider, May 30, 2020. https://www.crowdfundinsider.com/2020/05/162114-worlds-most-valuable-fintech-ant-financial-partners-with-china-merchants-port-to-launch-blockchain-platform-for-local-banking-and-logistics-businesses/.

FDIC . "How America Banks: Household Use of Banking and Financial Services, 2019 FDIC Survey." Federal Deposit

Insurance Corporation (FDIC). Accessed March 10, 2021. https://www.fdic.gov/householdsurvey/.

———. "The 2017 National Survey of Unbanked and Underbanked Households." Federal Deposit Insurance Corp. (FDIC), October 2018. https://economicinclusion.gov/surveys/2017household/.

Federal Reserve. *Changes in U.S. Payments Fraud from 2012 to 2016: Evidence from the Federal ReservePayments Study.* Board of Governors of the Federal Reserve System, 2018. https://www.federalreserve.gov/publications/files/changes-in-us-payments-fraud-from-2012-to-2016-20181016.pdf.

———. "Charge-Off Rate on Consumer Loans, All Commercial Banks." FRED, Federal Reserve Bank of St. Louis. Board of Governors of the Federal Reserve System (US), February 22, 2021. https://fred.stlouisfed.org/series/CORCACBS.

———. "Speech by Governor Powell on Innovation, Technology, and the Payments System." Board of Governors of the Federal Reserve System. Accessed March 10, 2021. https://www.federalreserve.gov/newsevents/speech/powell20170303a.htm.

———. "The Fed - How Much Does It Cost to Produce Currency and Coin?" Board of Governors of the Federal Reserve System. Accessed March 10, 2021. https://www.federalreserve.gov/faqs/currency_12771.htm.

Feng, Coco. "Digital Yuan Will Not Compete with WeChat Pay or Alipay." South China Morning Post, October 26, 2020. https://www.scmp.com/tech/policy/article/3107074/chinas-digital-currency-will-not-compete-mobile-payment-apps-wechat-and.

Foroohar, Rana. "We May Be Heading towards a Post-Dollar World." Financial Times. The Financial Times. Accessed March 10, 2021. https://www.ft.com/content/68e5f028-a1a1-11ea-94c2-0526869b56b0.

Gambacorta, Leonardo, Yiping Huang, Zhenhua Li, Han Qiu, and Shu Chen. "Data vs Collateral." *Bank for International Settlements, Working Paper*, no. 881 (September 1, 2020). https://www.bis.org/publ/work881.htm.

Gingrich, Newt. "A Government Snoop That Puts the NSA To Shame." *Wall Street Journal*, July 7, 2015, sec. Opinion. https://www.wsj.com/articles/a-government -snoop-that-puts-the-nsa-to-shamea-government-snoo p-thatputs-the-nsa-to-shame-1435785463.

Goh, Sophie Yu, Brenda. "China Ups Scrutiny of Tech Giants with Draft Anti-Monopoly Rules." *Reuters*, November 10, 2020. https://www.reuters.com/article/ china-regulation-ecommerce-idUSKBN27Q0JB.

Greeley, Brendan. "The Comfort of Cash in a Time of Coronavirus." The Financial Times, July 16, 2020. https://www.ft.com/content/ b0182ea4-afc2-4d5d-a8cf-fc7407fa8a18.

Gunning, Gavin. "The Future Of Banking: Asia-Pacific Opens Up To Open Banking." S&P Global, April 11, 2019. https://www.spglobal.com/ratings/en/ research/articles/190411-the-future-of-banking-asia-pa cific-opens-up-to-open-banking-10948051.

———. "The Future Of Banking: Virtual Banks Chase the Dream in Asia-Pacific." S&P Global, July 17, 2019. https://www.spglobal.com/en/research-insights/ articles/the-future-of-banking-virtual-bank s-chase-the-dream-in-asia-pacific.

Hayes, David. "Apple Market Cap Now about 1.5x Entire US Banking Industry." S&P Global. Accessed March 10, 2021. https://www.spglobal. com/marketintelligence/en/news-insights/ latest-news-headlines/apple-market-cap-now-about- 1-5x-entire-us-banking-industry-60056007.

He, Amy. "EMarketer Apple Pay Forecast Estimates, US Mobile Proximity Payment Forecast Estimates." Insider Intelligence. Accessed March

10, 2021. https://www.emarketer.com/content/
apple-pay-dominance-drives-mobile-paymen
t-transaction-volume.

He, Amy. "EMarketer Forecast Estimates for P2P
Payments, Venmo, and Zelle." Insider Intelligence.
Accessed March 10, 2021. https://www.emarketer.
com/content/strong-growth-from-venmo-and-zell
e-drives-p2p-transaction-volume.

Helm, Burt. "Credit Card Companies Are Tracking
Shoppers like Never Before: Inside the Next Phase
of Surveillance Capitalism." Fast Company, May 12,
2020. https://www.fastcompany.com/90490923/
credit-card-companies-are-tracking-shopper
s-like-never-before-inside-the-next-phase-
of-surveillance-capitalism.

Hope, Bradley. "Provider of Personal Finance Tools Tracks
Bank Cards, Sells Data to Investors." *Wall Street
Journal*, August 7, 2015, sec. Business. https://www.wsj.
com/articles/provider-of-personal-finance-tools-track
s-bank-cards-sells-data-to-investors-1438914620.

ICBC Bank. "ICBC Group 2017 Annual Report." Industrial
and Commercial Bank of China Limited, March 27, 2018.
http://v.icbc.com.cn/userfiles/Resources/ICBC/haiwai/
ICBCLondon/download/2018/ICBC_Group_2017_
annual_report.pdf.

ICO. "What Is Personal Data?" Information
Commissioner's Office, January 1, 2021. https://ico.
org.uk/for-organisations/guide-to-data-protection/
guide-to-the-general-data-protection-regulation-gdpr/
what-is-personal-data/what-is-personal-data/.

IHL Group. "Research from IHL Group Shows
Retailers' Cash-Handling Costs Range from
4.7% to 15.3%, Depending on Retail Segment."
Businesswire, January 30, 2018. https://www.
businesswire.com/news/home/20180130005244/
en/New-Research-from-IHL-Group-Shows-

Retailers%E2%80%99-Cash-handling-Co
sts-Range-from-4.7-to-15.3-Depending-on-Retail-Segment.

IMF. "Currency Composition of Official Foreign
Exchange Reserves." IMF Data, Access to
Macroeconomic & Financial Data. International
Monetary Fund, December 23, 2020. https://data.imf.
org/?sk=E6A5F467-C14B-4AA8-9F6D-5A09EC4E62A4.

———. "Patterns in Invoicing Currency in Global Trade."
International Monetary Fund, July 17, 2020. https://
www.imf.org/en/Publications/WP/Issues/2020/07/17/
Patterns-in-Invoicing-Currency-in-Global-Trade-49574.

———. "The People's Republic of China: Financial
Sector Assessment Program; Systemic Oversight
of Financial Market Infrastructures - Technical
Note." International Monetary Fund, June 26,
2018. https://www.imf.org/en/Publications/CR/
Issues/2018/06/26/The-People-s-Republic-of-Chin
a-Financial-Sector-Assessment
-Program-Systemic-Oversight-of-46024.

IMF Blog. "Central Bank Digital Currencies: 4
Questions and Answers." IMF Blog (blog). Accessed
March 10, 2021. https://blogs.imf.org/2019/12/12/
central-bank-digital-currencies-4-questions-and-answers/.

Insights, Ledger. "China Wants to Link Central
Bank Trade Finance Blockchain with Asia,
Europe." Ledger Insights - enterprise blockchain,
September 14, 2020. https://ledgerinsights.com/
china-central-bank-trade-finance-blockchain-asia-europe/.

———. "China's Central Bank Endorses CITIC $42
Billion Trade Finance Blockchain." Ledger Insights
- enterprise blockchain, August 6, 2020. https://
ledgerinsights.com/china-central-bank-endorses-citic-4
2-billion-trade-finance-blockchain/.

———. "Transcript: US Congressman Raises Spectre of
Threat of Digital Renminbi CBDC to US Dollar.
Fed Governor Responds." Ledger Insights - enterprise

blockchain, February 13, 2020. https://www.ledgerinsights.com/digital-dollar-federal-reserve-central-bank-digital-currency-cbdc/.

iResearch. "China's Third-Party Mobile Payment Transactions Rose 22.6% in Q2 2019." Accessed March 10, 2021. http://www.iresearchchina.com/content/details7_58033.html.

———. "Revenue of China's SME B2B Platforms Hit 29.2 Bn Yuan in 2017." iReseach Global, February 1, 2018. http://www.iresearchchina.com/content/details7_40801.html.

Jeong, Gil-won, and Minjeong Kyeong. "How to Value Financial Platforms: Volume II." Mirae Asset Daewoo Co. Ltd., June 23, 2020. https://www.miraeassetdaewoo.com/bbs/download/2075820.pdf?attachmentId=2075820.

John, Alun. "China's Digital Currency Will Kick Off 'Horse Race': Central Bank Official." *Reuters*, November 6, 2019. https://www.reuters.com/article/us-china-markets-digital-currency-idUSKBN1XG0BI.

Johnston, Lauren. "COVID19 Pushes Forward Jack Ma's Plans for a World Trade Revolution." SOAS Blog, July 2, 2020. https://study.soas.ac.uk/covid19-pushes-forward-jack-mas-plans-for-a-world-trade-revolution/.

Johnston, Lauren. "What the West Gets Wrong about China's Belt and Road Initiative." Nikkei Asia, January 15, 2021. https://asia.nikkei.com/Opinion/What-the-West-gets-wrong-about-China-s-Belt-and-Road-Initiative.

Kai, Ryssdal. "IRS Is Struggling to Reach Millions of Americans Who Need Their Stimulus Checks." *Marketplace* (blog), November 9, 2020. https://www.marketplace.org/2020/11/09/irs-struggling-to-reach-millions-of-americans-who-need-their-stimulus-checks/.

Kantar. "Future Finance from Bricks to Clicks. The Impact of Neobanks So Far," 2019. https://www2.kantar.com/future-finance-neobanks-2019.

Kapronasia. "Is WeBank the World's Top Digital Bank?
- Kapronasia," November 18, 2019. https://www.
kapronasia.com/china-banking-research-category/
webank-the-world-s-top-digital-bank.html.

Kharif, Olga. "Crypto Stablecoins Find a Toehold in
Shadows of Global Trade." Bloomberg. Bloomberg,
January 23, 2020. https://www.bloomberg.com/news/
articles/2020-01-22/crypto-stablecoins-find-a-toehold-i
n-shadows-of-global-trade.

Kharpal, Arjun. "Report Finds $50 Billion of Cryptocurrency
Moved Out of China Hinting at Capital Flight against
Beijing Rules." CNBC, August 21, 2020. https://www.
cnbc.com/2020/08/21/china-users-move-50-billion-o
f-cryptocurrency-out-of-count
ry-hinting-at-capital-flight.html.

Kobielus, James. "Sorry, but Blockchain Databases
Are Just Not That Secure." InfoWorld, June 21,
2018. https://www.infoworld.com/article/3282413/
sorry-but-blockchain-databases-are-jus
t-not-that-secure.html.

KrASIA. "KrASIA | Uncovering the World's Emerging
Markets." Accessed March 10, 2021. https://kr-asia.
com/investors-in-ponzi-scheme-ezubao-finall
y-get-35-of-their-money-back.

Lau, Jack. "China's Yuan Replaces US Dollar as Most
Used Currency in Greater Bay Area." South China
Morning Post, January 16, 2021. https://www.scmp.
com/business/banking-finance/article/3117971/
chinas-yuan-replaces-us-dollar-most-used-currency-greater.

Lee, Georgina. "China's Regulator Ring-Fences Runaway
Fintech Giants to Rein in Risks." South China
Morning Post, November 11, 2020. https://www.
scmp.com/business/banking-finance/article/3109386/
fintech-firms-must-behave-banks-china-regulator-says-it.

Lee, Kai-Fu. *AI Superpowers: China, Silicon Valley, and the New
World Order.* Boston: Houghton Mifflin Harcourt, 2018.

Leng, Cheng and Engen Tham. "In China, P2P Insiders Say Regulatory Shortcomings Have Choked Industry." *Reuters*, September 6, 2019. https://www.reuters.com/article/us-china-p2p-regulation-analysis-idUSKCN1VR055.

Levitt, Hannah. "Biggest U.S. Banks Flooded With Deposits in 'Flight to Quality.'" Bloomberg, March 28, 2020. https://www.bloomberg.com/news/articles/2020-03-27/biggest-u-s-banks-flooded-with-deposits-in-flight-to-quality.

Lin, Karen Jingrong, Xiaoyan Lu, Junsheng Zhang, and Ying Zheng. "State-Owned Enterprises in China: A Review of 40 Years of Research and Practice." *China Journal of Accounting Research* 13, no. 1 (March 2020): 31–55. https://doi.org/10.1016/j.cjar.2019.12.001.

Lomas, Natasha. "Researchers Spotlight the Lie of 'Anonymous' Data." TechCrunch, July 24, 2019. https://social.techcrunch.com/2019/07/24/researchers-spotlight-the-lie-of-anonymous-data/.

Marous, Jim. "Big Tech Firms Push Further Into Banking With New 'Super Apps.'" The Financial Brand, November 14, 2019. https://thefinancialbrand.com/90275/open-banking-platform-uber-google-apple-amazon-data-trends/.

MasterCard. "Mastercard Study Shows Consumers Moving to Contactless Payments for Everyday Purchases As They Seek Cleaner, Touch-Free Options." MasterCard Social Newsroom. Accessed March 10, 2021. https://newsroom.mastercard.com/asia-pacific/press-releases/mastercard-study-shows-consumers-moving-to-contactless-payments-for-everyday-purchases-as-they-seek-cleaner-touch-free-options/.

Matsakis, Louise. "How the West Got China's Social Credit System Wrong." *Wired*, July 29, 2019. https://www.wired.com/story/china-social-credit-score-system/.

Matsangou, Elizabeth. "China's Transitioning Economy." World Finance, April 23, 2018. https://www.worldfinance. com/markets/chinas-transitioning-economy.

McKinsey. "African Retail Banking's Next Growth Frontier | McKinsey," February 28, 2018. https://www.mckinsey. com/industries/financial-services/our-insights/ african-retail-bankings-next-growth-frontier.

McMorrow, Ryan. "Ant's Huge Lending Business Powers $30bn IPO." The Financial Times, October 2, 2020. https://www.ft.com/ content/935401f8-a374-4c15-ba8a-12c600ac3443.

Mead, Derek. "The NSA Spied on Credit Cards and Bank Transactions." Vice, September 16, 2013. https://www. vice.com/en/article/ezzjxn/the-nsa-spied-on-credit-card s-and-bank-transactions.

Merchant Savvy. "50+ Global Mobile Payment Stats, Data & Trends," February 2020. https://www.merchantsavvy. co.uk/mobile-payment-stats-trends/.

Mester, Loretta J. "Payments and the Pandemic," September 23, 2020. https://www.clevelandfed. org/newsroom-and-events/speeches/ sp-20200923-payments-and-the-pandemic.

Milliken, David and Tom Wilson. "BoE's Cunliffe: Not Our Job to Protect Banks against Digital Currencies." Reuters, November 13, 2020. https://www.reuters.com/article/ us-britain-boe-cunliffe-idUKKBN27T1ZR.

Moon, Louise. "Sneakerheads Fuel Resale Market Despite China's Crackdown." South China Morning Post, November 10, 2019. https://www. scmp.com/business/money/article/3036916/ china-cracks-down-speculative-trading-limite d-edition-shoes.

Morris, Nicky. "China's Big 3 Blockchain Trade Finance Projects Hit $63 Billion in Volume." Ledger Insights - enterprise blockchain, November

29, 2019. https://www.ledgerinsights.com/
china-enterprise-blockchain-trade-finance-63-billion/.

MSCI. "MSCI Emerging MarketsIndex (USD)." MSCI,
n.d. https://www.msci.com/documents/10199/
c0db0a48-01f2-4ba9-ad01-226fd5678111.

MYbank. "MYbank Served Over 20 Million SMEs As of
2019, Further Spurring the Growth of China's Small and
Micro Businesses." Businesswire, April 27, 2020. https://
www.businesswire.com/news/home/20200427005353/
en/MYbank-Served-Over-20-Million-SME
s-as-of-2019-Further-Spurring-the
-Growth-of-China%E2%80%99s-Small-a
nd-Micro-Businesses.

Nedopil, Christoph. "Countries of the Belt and Road Initiative
(BRI) – Green Belt and Road Initiative Center," January
2021. https://green-bri.org/countries-of-the-belt-and-roa
d-initiative-bri/.

Nielsen. *2019 New Trends for Mobile Payment in Chinese
Outbound Tourism.* Nielsen Holdings PLC, n.d. https://
www.nielsen.com/wp-content/uploads/sites/3/2020/0
1/2019-new-trends-for-mobile-payment.pdf.

OECD. "OECD Observer, Volume 2005 Issue 4."
Text. Organisation for Economic Co-operation and
Development. Accessed March 10, 2021. https://www.
oecd-ilibrary.org/economics/oecd-observer/volume-2005/
issue-4_observer-v2005-4-en.

———. "OECD Observer, Volume 2005 Issue 4."
Text. Organisation for Economic Co-operation and
Development. Accessed March 10, 2021. https://www.
oecd-ilibrary.org/economics/oecd-observer/volume-2005/
issue-4_observer-v2005-4-en.

Okuda, Koji. "China's Global Yuan Push Makes
Inroads in Asia and Africa." Nikkei Asia, August
25, 2020. https://asia.nikkei.com/Business/
Finance/China-s-global-yuan-push-make
s-inroads-in-Asia-and-Africa.

Paulson, Henry M. Jr. "The Future of the Dollar," June 4,
2020. https://www.foreignaffairs.com/articles/2020-05-19/
future-dollar.

Peters, Michael A., Benjamin Green, and Haiyang (Melissa)
Yang. "Cryptocurrencies, China's Sovereign Digital
Currency (DCEP) and the US Dollar System." *Educational
Philosophy and Theory*, August 5, 2020, 1–7. https://doi.
org/10.1080/00131857.2020.1801146.

Pew Research. "Americans Fault China for Its Role
in the Spread of COVID-19." *Pew Research
Center's Global Attitudes Project* (blog), July
30, 2020. https://www.pewresearch.org/
global/2020/07/30/americans-fault-china-for-its-rol
e-in-the-spread-of-covid-19/.

Prasad, Eswar. *Has the Dollar Lost Ground As the Dominant
International Currency?* Global Economy and
Development. Brookings Institution, 2019. https://
www.brookings.edu/wp-content/uploads/2019/09/
DollarInGlobalFinance.final_.9.20.pdf.

Redman, Jamie. "Stablecoin Supply Doubles in 3
Months as Combined Market Cap Surpasses $20B."
Bitcoin News (blog), October 4, 2020. https://news.
bitcoin.com/stablecoin-supply-doubles-in-3-month
s-as-cumulative-market-cap-surpasses-20b/.

Reuters Staff. "China Funds Targeting Ant IPO Rake in
$9 Billion from Over 10 Million Investors." *Reuters*,
October 11, 2020. https://www.reuters.com/article/
ant-group-ipo-funds-idUSKBN26U0DS.

———. "China's Digital Currency Not Seeking 'full Control'
of Individuals' Details: Central Bank Official." *Reuters*,
November 12, 2019. https://www.reuters.com/article/
us-china-markets-digital-currency-idUSKBN1XM0H2.

Rio, I. T. S. "6. Ant Financial and Its Alipay." *FinTech: China
& Brazil*, December 18, 2018. https://its-fintech.pubpub.
org/pub/6/release/2.

Roser, Max. "As the World's Poorest Economies Are Stagnating Half a Billion Are Expected to Be in Extreme Poverty in 2030." Our World in Data, May 6, 2019. https://ourworldindata.org/extreme-poverty-projections.

Schaverien, Anna. "Bank of England Rebuked Over 'Missing' $67 Billion of Cash." *The New York Times*, December 4, 2020, sec. World. https://www.nytimes.com/2020/12/04/world/europe/bank-england-missing-cash.html.

Science and Technology Daily. "China's Poverty Alleviation Has Made Great Contribution to Global Poverty Reduction." PR Newswire, May 26, 2020. https://www.prnewswire.com/news-releases/chinas-poverty-alleviation-has-made-grea t-contribution-to-global-poverty-reduction-301065055.html.

Shen, Lan, and Ding Shuang. "China – Belt and Road Is Taking Shape." Global Research. OTG On the Ground. Standard Chartered Bank, November 8, 2017. https://av.sc.com/corp-en/content/docs/China-Belt-and-Road-is-taking-shape.pdf.

Shen, Sean, and XiaoDong Lee. "SM2 Digital Signature Algorithm." Internet Engineering Task Force, August 18, 2014. https://tools.ietf.org/html/draft-shen-sm2-ecdsa-02.

Shenzhen Daily. "China: Largest e-Commerce Market." Shenzhen Daily, August 17, 2020. http://www.szdaily.com/content/2020-07/17/content_23355693.htm.

Sironi, Paolo. FinTech Innovation: From Robo-Advisors to Goal Based Investing and Gamification. The Wiley Finance Series. Chichester, West Sussex, UK: Wiley, 2016.

Sveriges Riksbank. *The Riksbank's e-Krona Pilot*, 2020. https://www.riksbank.se/globalassets/media/rapporter/e-krona/2019/the-riksbanks-e-krona-pilot.pdf.

SWIFT. "Rise of the Chinese Influence Strengthens RMB Demand." SWIFT, June 5, 2019. https://www.swift.com/news-events/news/rise-of-the-chinese-influence-strengthen s-rmb-demand.

————. *RMB Internationalisation: Where We Are and What We Can Expect in 2018*. RMB Tracker. SWIFT, 2018. https://www.swift.com/swift-resource/166161/download.

Tang, Frank. "China's Central Bank Calls for Faster Digital Yuan Roll-Out." South China Morning Post, October 12, 2020. https://www.scmp.com/economy/china-economy/article/3105174/chinas-central-bank-urges-faster-digital-yuan-roll-out-other.

The Nilson Report. "Nilson Report – General Purpose Cards—U.S. 2019." Accessed March 10, 2021. https://nilsonreport.com/mention/472/1link/.

————. "Nilson Report – Global Network Card Results in 2019." Accessed March 10, 2021. https://nilsonreport.com/mention/1248/1link/.

The World Bank. "Exports of Goods and Services (% of GDP) - China | Data." Accessed March 10, 2021. https://data.worldbank.org/indicator/NE.EXP.GNFS.ZS?locations=CN.

————. "Services, Value Added (% of GDP) - China." The World Bank. Accessed March 10, 2021. https://data.worldbank.org/indicator/NV.SRV.TOTL.ZS?locations=CN.

Thomas, Yves, Guido Vogel, Werner Wunderli, Patricia Suter, Mark Witschi, Daniel Koch, Caroline Tapparel, and Laurent Kaiser. "Survival of Influenza Virus on Banknotes." *Applied and Environmental Microbiology* 74, no. 10 (May 2008): 3002–7. https://doi.org/10.1128/AEM.00076-08.

UK DCMS. "Digital Sector Worth More than £400 Million a Day to UK Economy." GOV.UK. Department for Digital Culture Media and Sport, February 5, 2020. https://www.gov.uk/government/news/digital-sector-worth-more-than-400-million-a-day-to-uk-economy.

U.S. Bureau of Economic Analysis. "Digital Economy Accounted for 6.9 Percent of GDP in 2017." Bureau of

Economic Analysis, U.S. Department of Commerce, April 4, 2019. https://www.bea.gov/news/blog/2019-04-04/digital-economy-accounted-69-percent-gdp-2017.

Victor, Mallet. "G7 Warns on 'Serious Risks' Posed by Libra and Other Digital Coins." The Financial Times, July 18, 2019. https://www.ft.com/content/a6cbf244-a926-11e9-984c-fac8325aaa04.

Walker, Martin C.W. "Do We Need Programmable Money?" *LSE Business Review* (blog), September 14, 2020. https://blogs.lse.ac.uk/businessreview/2020/09/14/do-we-need-programmable-money/.

Wang, Fern. "Tech Disruption In Retail Banking: China's Banks Are Playing Catch-Up To Big Tech." S&P Global, May 14, 2019. https://www.spglobal.com/en/research-insights/articles/tech-disruption-in-retail-banking-china-s-banks-are-playing-catch-up-to-big-tech.

Wang, Shou. "Transcript: Zhou Xiaochuan Interview - Caixin Global." Accessed March 10, 2021. https://www.caixinglobal.com/2016-02-15/transcript-zhou-xiaochuan-interview-101011865.html.

Ward, Orla, and Sabrina Rochemont. *Understanding Central Bank Digital Currencies (CBDC) - An Addendum to "A Cashless Society - Benefits, Risks and Issues (Interim Paper)."* Institute and Faculty of Actuaries, 2019. https://www.actuaries.org.uk/system/files/field/document/Understanding%20CBDCs%20Final%20-%20disc.pdf.

WeBank. "WeBank: The World's Leading Digital Bank Decoded," October 31, 2019. https://www.prnewswire.com/news-releases/webank-the-worlds-leading-digital-bank-decoded-300949025.html.

Wheatley, Jonathan. "Pandemic Fuels Global 'Debt Tsunami.'" The Financial Times, November 19, 2020. https://www.ft.com/content/18527e0c-6f02-4c70-93cb-c26c3680c8ad.

World Bank Group and People's Bank of China. *Toward Universal Financial Inclusion in China.* World Bank and People's Bank of China, 2018. https://doi. org/10.1596/29336.

———. "Toward Universal Financial Inclusion in China." BBVA Center for Financial Education and Capability, June 11, 2018. https://www.bbvaedufin.com/en/publicacion/ toward-universal-financial-inclusion-in-china/.

World Tourism Organization (UNWTO), ed. *International Tourism Highlights, 2019 Edition*. World Tourism Organization (UNWTO), 2019. https://doi. org/10.18111/9789284421152.

WTO. "Global Trade Growth Loses Momentum as Trade Tensions Persist." World Trade Organization, April 2, 2019. https://www.wto.org/english/news_e/pres19_e/ pr837_e.htm.

Xinhua News. "China's Trade with BRI Countries Booms in 2019 - Xinhua | English.News.Cn," January 14, 2020. http://www.xinhuanet.com/ english/2020-01/14/c_138704581.htm.

Xu, Jemma, and Dan Prud'homme. "China's Digital Currency Revolution and Implications for International Business Strategy." SSRN Scholarly Paper. Rochester, NY: Social Science Research Network, August 1, 2020. https://papers. ssrn.com/abstract=3672240.

Yang, Felix. "Baihang Credit Finally Receives Its License, Although the Future Remains Bleak - Kapronasia." Kapronasia, March 29, 2018. https://www. kapronasia.com/china-banking-research-category/ baihang-credit-finally-receives-its-licens e-although-the-future-remains-bleak.html.

Yao, Qian. "Experimental Study on Prototype System of Central Bank Digital Currency." *Journal of Software* 29, no. 9 (2018). http://www.jos.org.cn/1000-9825/5595.htm.

Yao, Qian. "Technical Aspects of CBDC in a Two-Tiered System." New York, NY, USA: People's Bank of China, Institute of Digital Money, 2018. https://www.itu.int/en/

ITU-T/Workshops-and-Seminars/20180718/Documents/
Yao%20Qian.pdf.

Young, Gordon. "Russell Buckley Declares That
QR Codes Are Dead and Predicts the Dawn of
Google Contact Lenses." The Drum. Accessed
March 10, 2021. https://www.thedrum.com/
news/2012/05/15/russel-buckley-declares-thatt-qr-code
s-are-dead-and-predicts-dawn-google-contact.

Yu, Howard, and Feng Yunfei. "In the Field with Ping An:
How Can an Incumbent Go beyond the Boundaries of
Its Traditional Business and Become a Tech Giant?" IMD
business school, November 2020. /research-knowledge/
articles/in-the-field-with-ping-an/.

Yu, Tao, and Shen Wei. "Funds Sharing Regulation in the
Context of the Sharing Economy: Understanding the Logic
of China's P2P Lending Regulation." *SSRN Electronic
Journal*, 2019. https://doi.org/10.2139/ssrn.3310288.

Yuan, Li. "How WeChat Founder's Obsession With
QR Codes Reshapes Chinese Internet." *Wall Street
Journal*, January 25, 2017, sec. Tech. https://www.wsj.
com/articles/how-wechat-founders-obsession-with-q
r-codes-reshapes-chinese-internet-1485364619.

Zhang, Yuzhe. "Ant Financial Braces to Be Regulated
as Financial Holding Company." Caixin
Global, June 7, 2018. https://www.caixinglobal.
com/2018-06-07/ant-financial-braces-to-be-regulate
d-as-financial-holding-company-101266609.html.

———. "In Depth: The Fight for Dominance in
China's Mobile Payment Market - Caixin Global,"
September 23, 2019. https://www.caixinglobal.
com/2019-09-23/in-depth-the-fight-for-dominanc
e-in-chinas-mobile-payment-market-101464880.html.

Zhao, Wolfie. "China's Digital Fiat Wants to
Compete With Bitcoin – But It's Not a Crypto."
CoinDesk, August 16, 2019. https://www.

coindesk.com/is-chinas-digital-fiat-a-cryptocurrenc
y-heres-what-we-know.

Zhou, Cissy. "China's New Digital Currency 'Isn't
Bitcoin and Is Not for Speculation.'" South China
Morning Post, December 22, 2019. https://
www.scmp.com/economy/china-economy/
article/3043134/chinas-new-digital-currency-isnt-bitcoi
n-and-not-speculation.

Zou, Chuanwei. "Global Stablecoins and Central Bank
Digital Currencies Blockchain Network." Wanxiang
Blockchain. Accessed March 10, 2021. https://blocking.
net/24668/popular-science-zou-chuanwei-global-stablecoin
s-and-central-bank-digital-currencies/.

中国人民银行. "央行就'金融改革与发展'答记者问_中
国政府网和新华网2017年全国两会联合现场直
播." Accessed March 10, 2021. http://www.gov.cn/
zhuanti/2017lh/live/0310b.htm.

余继超. "透视建行测试'数字人民币钱包'背后--财经--人
民网," September 7, 2020. http://finance.people.com.cn/
n1/2020/0907/c1004-31851533.html.

姚前. "区块链与央行数字货币 - 碳链价值," April 3, 2020.
https://www.ccvalue.cn/article/216773.html.

网贷之家. "Online Loan Platform Data." 网贷之家, n.d.
https://shuju.wdzj.com/problem-1.html.

———. "网贷之家." Online Loan Platform List. Accessed
March 10, 2021. https://www.wdzj.com/dangan/.

邹传伟. "对人民银行DC/EP的初步分析_观点频道_财新
网." Accessed March 10, 2021. https://opinion.caixin.
com/2019-11-01/101477903.html.

金丹. "Mobile Pay Encouraging Tourists to Spend More."
Accessed March 10, 2021. https://www.chinadaily.com.
cn/a/201901/30/WS5c50faeca3106c65c34e73a6.html

CPSIA information can be obtained
at www.ICGtesting.com
Printed in the USA
LVHW080400180621
690564LV00032B/1758/J